www.wadsworth.com

www.wadsworth.com is the World Wide Web site for
Wadsworth and is your direct source to dozens of online
resources.

At *www.wadsworth.com* you can find out about
supplements, demonstration software, and student
resources. You can also send email to many of our
authors and preview new publications and exciting new
technologies.

www.wadsworth.com
Changing the way the world learns®

Scottish Crofters

A Historical Ethnography
of a Celtic Village

SECOND EDITION

Susan Parman
California State University, Fullerton

 Case Studies in Cultural Anthropology: George Spindler, Series Editor

THOMSON
TM
WADSWORTH

Australia • Canada • Mexico • Singapore • Spain
United Kingdom • United States

THOMSON
＊
™
WADSWORTH

Anthropology Editor: *Lin Marshall*
Assistant Editor: *Nicole Root*
Editorial Assistant: *Kelly McMahon*
Marketing Manager: *Matthew Wright*
Marketing Assistant: *Tara Pierson*
Project Manager, Editorial Production:
 Rita Jaramillo
Print/Media Buyer: *Rebecca Cross*

Permissions Editor: *Stephanie Lee*
Production Service: *Sara Dovre Wudali,*
 Buuji, Inc.
Copy Editor: *Cheryl Hauser*
Cover Designer: *Rob Hugel*
Cover Image: *Susan Parman*
Compositor: *Buuji, Inc.*
Cover and Text Printer: *Webcom*

The logo for the Cultural Anthropology series is based on an ancient symbol representing the family: man, woman, and children.

Printed in Canada
1 2 3 4 5 6 7 08 07 06 05 04

For more information about our products,
contact us at:
Thomson Learning Academic Resource Center
1-800-423-0563

For permission to use material from this text
or product, submit a request online at
http://www.thomsonrights.com.

Any additional questions about permissions
can be submitted by email to
thomsonrights@thomson.com.

Library of Congress Control Number: 2004100957

ISBN 0-534-63324-2

Thomson Wadsworth
10 Davis Drive
Belmont, CA 94002-3098
USA

Asia
Thomson Learning
5 Shenton Way #01-01
UIC Building
Singapore 068808

Australia/New Zealand
Thomson Learning
102 Dodds Street
Southbank, Victoria 3006
Australia

Canada
Nelson
1120 Birchmount Road
Toronto, Ontario M1K 5G4
Canada

Europe/Middle East/Africa
Thomson Learning
High Holborn House
50/51 Bedford Row
London WC1R 4LR
United Kingdom

Latin America
Thomson Learning
Seneca, 53
Colonia Polanco
11560 Mexico D.F.
Mexico

Spain/Portugal
Paraninfo
Calle/Magallanes, 25
28015 Madrid, Spain

Dedicated to
Jacob Pandian and Gigi Pandian

In memory of
Gordon and Rowan Adams, Rody MacLeod,
Effie and Donald Matheson, Murdo and Angus Murray,
Louise Spindler, and Robert J. Storey

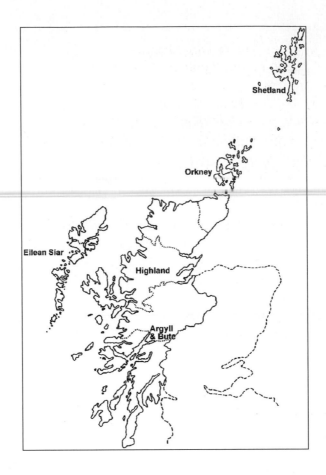

Shetland

Orkney

Eilean Siar

Highland

Argyll
& Bute

Contents

Foreword

ABOUT THE SERIES

These case studies in cultural anthropology are designed for students in beginning and intermediate courses in the social sciences, to bring them insights into the richness and complexity of human life as it is lived in different ways, in different places. The authors are men and women who have lived in the societies they write about and who are professionally trained as observers and interpreters of human behavior. Also, the authors are teachers; in their writing, the needs of the student reader remain foremost. It is our belief that when an understanding of ways of life very different from one's own is gained, abstractions and generalizations about the human condition become meaningful.

The scope and character of the series has changed constantly since we published the first case studies in 1960, in keeping with our intention to represent anthropology as it is. We are concerned with the ways in which human groups and communities are coping with the massive changes wrought in their physical and sociopolitical environments in recent decades. We are also concerned with the ways in which established cultures have solved life's problems. And we want to include representation of the various modes of communication and emphasis that are being re-formed and reformed as anthropology itself changes.

We think of this series as an instructional series, intended for use in the classroom. We, the editors, have always used case studies in our teaching, whether for beginning students or advanced graduate students. We start with case studies, whether from our own series or from elsewhere, and weave our way into theory, and then turn again to cases. For us, they are the grounding of our discipline.

ABOUT THE AUTHOR

When Susan Parman was 18, she set off on a voyage of discovery that hasn't yet ended. As an undergraduate at Antioch College planning to spend her junior year abroad at the University of Edinburgh in Scotland, she spent 9 days traveling across the Atlantic on an Italian student ship called the Aurelia and 2 months working in a charity-run organization called the Children's Village in Humbie 12 miles south of Edinburgh. Convinced that language was the route to cultural understanding (she had already enlisted the help of the children of Humbie—mostly from poorer families in Glasgow, Edinburgh, and Dundee—to help her on a dictionary project called "A Is for Auchenshoogle Tattie Bogle"), she studied Gaelic, which provoked diverse reactions among her Scottish friends and stimulated her interest in the uses of history and the multiple meanings of Celticity.

Five years after her year as an undergraduate in Edinburgh, she returned to Scotland to do 14 months of anthropological fieldwork in a crofting community called Ciall (originally "Geall"—both pseudonyms) on the west side of the island of Lewis in the Outer Hebrides. She completed her PhD at Rice University in 1972 and began teaching in California, where she is now professor and chair of the department of anthropology at California State University, Fullerton, which has constructed a new Research and Teaching Facility based on a $1 million grant from the National Science Foundation that she wrote. Linked to Scotland through multiple ties of descent and fictive kinship, friendship, and poetic sympathies, she has continued to return to Scotland and Ciall. She and her husband, the anthropologist Jacob Pandian, have a daughter who began to travel with her to Scotland when she was 9 years old (and also studied at Edinburgh during her junior year); both mother and daughter consider themselves part of the extended community of Ciall identified as "exiles."

The recipient of grants from the National Science Foundation, the National Endowment for the Humanities, the Wenner-Gren Foundation, the Social Science Research Council, the American Philosophical Society, and numerous faculty research grants from California State University, Fullerton, Susan Parman has published numerous articles on crofting, Scottish patterns of nick-naming, and medical folklore. Her interest in Scottish crofters is part of a larger framework of interest in the relationship among Europe and anthropology, the history of anthropology, and the uses of history in cultural construction. As editor of the book *Europe in the Anthropological Imagination* (1998), she reviewed the significance of Europe in anthropology. In 2000–2002 she served as president of the Society for the Anthropology of Europe.

Susan Parman's catholic interests encompass the human condition, biological as well as cultural. She has written about the evolution of the brain, a cross-cultural analysis of the uses of salt, and medical anthropology. Her book *Dream and Culture: An Anthropological Study of the Western Intellectual Tradition* (1991) was translated into Turkish *(Ruya ve Kultur)* in 2001 by Kemal Basci for the Ministry of Culture. She has done research and writing on various groups including a Mexican-American community, Japan, and the American South.

Susan Parman credits Antioch College with establishing models of innovative teaching that she has attempted to emulate throughout her teaching career. As director of the Teaching Museum at California State University, Fullerton, she promotes use of the museum not to display collections but to encourage experimentation and debate about the visual representation of ideas. As department chair, she promotes critical thinking and historical awareness in the context of four-field anthropology. Her paper "The Mushroom Method: How to Write a Paper" is widely used (see the electronic link on anthro.fullerton.edu/sparman/). Despite being increasingly inundated with administrative work, she continues to teach and prefers introductory undergraduate classes that are filled with minds yearning to begin their own voyages of discovery.

ABOUT THE NEW EDITION

For the second edition of *Scottish Crofters*, Sue Parman wanted to replace the cover photograph of a sheep fank with a photograph of a crofter reading the first edition (a decision that was considered too "postmodern"). This request reflects her awareness of the ambiguities that an anthropologist faces when studying a literate, well-educated, critical population that would prefer to write its own ethnographies, thank you. Laura Nader may advise anthropologists to "study up" (that is, to incorporate the wealthy, the high-status, and the Western in their universalistic "study of humankind"), but the fact is that anthropological studies connote marginal, non-Western worlds of exotic "differentness." Changes in the discipline that include critical histories of anthropology and the founding of subunits in the American Anthropological Association such as the Society for the Anthropology of Europe—of which Dr. Parman is a past president—herald a trend toward an anthropology committed to humanity, self-conscious of its own cultural traditions, calling attention to processes by which culture makes itself. The multiple perspectives, self-reflecting humility, and spirit of critical irony contained in the first edition of Sue Parman's thoughtful and sensitive book continues in the second. Although the book reflects the traditional categories of these case studies useful in cross-cultural comparison (economics, politics, kinship, etc.), it is also a vehicle for voices, diverse and poignant, that attempt to convey the humanistic experience of what it is like to live in a certain time, place, and culture.

What is different in the second edition? The first chapter highlights the major changes since the first edition, and the other chapters provide updates as well. The most important change to affect crofting communities is the introduction of various statutes that enable land to be "decrofted" or taken out of crofting. The economic value of land as a source of housing has opened the door to non-crofting residents who are not linked by kinship, language, or shared histories. The commodification of land and heritage is poised to bring about dramatic changes in crofting communities.

However, while crofting may be economically fragile as an agricultural enterprise, it has proven to be protean in its symbolic transformations. This new edition charts the changing use of land and the meaning of land use in the crofting counties of the Scottish Highlands and Islands. Fewer hectares may be planted in oats and potatoes, and fewer sheep browse the vast inner moorland of Lewis, but incomers from the rest of Britain put up greenhouses and plant organic crops, sell eggs, and launch photography and pottery studios, while playwrights, poets, and journalists walk the sea strand and poke fun at the tourists and anthropologists. The Crofters Commission funds new initiatives that promote communal management, a new Scottish Parliament promises support for Gaelic education, and the European Union provides development funds for diverse projects. Gaelic speakers diminish in numbers but have louder voices, and the Free Church grows in stature among evangelical Christians (promoted by various web sites) while at the same time losing ground to commercial, anti-sabbatarian forces. Gaelic preaching and psalm singing are giving way to English sermons and English hymns.

The population pyramid of crofting communities is still top heavy, but new technologies (and the new decrofting statutes) make it possible for young people to remain in the community, or at least remain more closely in touch with it. Emigres return filled with the desire to take up "traditional" crofting (keep sheep, play a role in township committees), while local residents take up new jobs in fish farms and call centers. Harris Tweed is woven on new looms and is marketed in Paris and Las Vegas as well as in the traditional venues of aristocratic grouse preserves. The Bible and the Bottle continue to fence with each other in people's lives.

Ciall is no Brigadoon marooned in time; no community ever is. Ciall, crofting communities, and Scotland itself continue to adapt to changing circumstances. Lucky is the community that has someone with the skill and sensitivity of a Sue Parman to record its passing voices.

George Spindler
Series Editor
geospinner@aol.com

Preface

My first visit to Scotland was as an undergraduate at Antioch College doing a year abroad at the University of Edinburgh, where I had the good fortune to meet two people from the Outer Hebrides: the Reverend Willie Mathieson, under whom I studied Gaelic, and Morag MacLeod of Scalpay who worked at the School of Scottish Studies. Five years later, when I wanted to study crofting communities in the Highlands and Islands, these contacts gave me legitimacy in the eyes of Robert Storey, Research Officer for the Highlands and Islands Development Board, whose function it was to filter requests for assistance. That I had studied Gaelic, and that Morag vouched for me as a reasonably sensible American, opened doors that made it possible for me to live in a community that did not normally take in outsiders.

I had learned about crofting communities during my year at Edinburgh, and my picture was of an economic system determined in part by 19th-century legislation that both hindered and protected it; agricultural and yet not agricultural; defined in part by social characteristics (the communal aspects of township requirements) and cultural features (Gaelic-speaking in many areas, but not completely; strongly evangelical in parts but with pockets of Catholicism and none of the conflict experienced by Ireland). I knew that although they were defined in terms of their relationship to the land, crofters worked at other jobs to survive economically—sometimes managing to work at home as weavers of Harris Tweed, or having to leave for long periods of time (in construction or sea-going jobs, for example).

At Rice University I studied with Edward Norbeck, Fred Gamst, and, for a year, with Leslie White, which gave me a strong commitment to cultural materialism (imagine culture as a pyramid, the base of which is how people make a living in a certain environment, which determines social structure in the middle, which determines ideological systems at the top). At the same time, I had a degree in psychology and a strong background in the humanities (especially literature, music, and philosophy), so I had a healthy respect for how individuals and idea systems shape human life.

Crofting communities seemed a good place to explore the effect of economic systems on other aspects of culture because the 19th-century legislation created common features. I would study variations in crofting adaptations—communities that supplemented crofting with Harris Tweed weaving, as compared with communities that supplemented crofting with fishing, where the men of the community were away for long periods of time. My research question was how did variations in these economic adaptations affect organization of the crofting township? Research at the Highlands and Islands Development Board suggested that Ciall would be a good place to start because, as the only rural area with Harris Tweed mills, it supported a large number of Harris Tweed weavers and mill workers. People I met through Bob Storey introduced me to the accepted leaders of Ciall, the minister, schoolmaster, and mill owner, but it was historical accident and the hospitality of one family that made it possible for me to stay in the community.

Once settled in Ciall, the questions that I wanted to ask as an anthropologist began to change. Raised in an era of "community studies," I quickly realized that it was impossible to understand a community in the traditional sense of a conservative unit resistant to change. Every decision that crofters made was determined by how they perceived the incentives and constraints imposed by agencies at the local, county, and national level (today the European Union adds an international dimension that affects decision making). The village community was a much larger entity, linked with Scots abroad throughout the world (it has been said that Scotland has 5 million people at home and 40 million abroad). Although economic systems were important, it was also important to understand how people defined their identities and options, and in particular how they created cultural realities through storytelling—through the endless whispers of gossip, and particularly through the telling of life histories and episodes of village life. At wakes and sheep fanks, over tea and whiskey, at late-night ceilidhs and communion services, I listened and wrote. The choice of Gaelic or English, the identification of certain people whose life stories were emblematic, the rocky choices and linkages among Bible and Bottle and Abroad, the relationship between withdrawal and religious absolutism, the significance of scholarship, the power of communal fellowship, and the searing power of humor were all a necessary part of the picture. Economic structure may make life possible, but meaning makes it human.

I lived in Ciall for 14 months in 1970–71 and was extraordinarily blessed in the friendships I made there and on the mainland with people whose emotional and intellectual commitment was to crofting and its cultural associations. For the past 30 years I have kept in touch by return visits and letters (now e-mail).

One of the primary functions of ethnographies is to convey what other cultures are like. Anthropological theories may change, but ethnographies remain as open doors to other worlds. As you step through the door of this book, may the wind be at your back.

ACKNOWLEDGMENTS

Monday 17th December 1990

Dear Sue,

Just a few lines to acknowledge receipt of your book *Scottish Crofters*. It was very kind of you to let us have a copy, we read it beside a blazing peat fire and found it very enjoyable. Your book is remarkably accurate in describing the way of life found here.

We both trust that you are all quite well, we are keeping well and active, it snowed last week and bitterly cold but did not last long. We realise that you will not receive this note and the calendar enclosed in time for Hogmanay but hope you receive early in the New Year. We shall be pleased to hear from you again at any time meantime

Nollaig Chridheil agus bliadhna mhath Ur, Slainte mhath,
Murdo and Angus

After the first edition of *Scottish Crofters* was published in 1990, it received several gratifying reviews, for example, one that identified the book as having made "crofting" for the first time into a useful sociological term (Svensson 1992) and another stating that the book was "important theoretically for its integration of symbolic analysis with political economy" (Ulin 1991). But most important to me have been the letters such as the one above. Over the years, I have sent complementary copies of the book to anyone from the community who requested them, and have met and corresponded with township members to discuss various issues raised in the book (the most frequent being why I used a pseudonym for the community). I have been met unfailingly with courtesy, hospitality, and thoughtful comments. These comments helped me conceptualize the difference between writing a book that constitutes a local history, and a book that attempts to speak to general issues in social science, which resulted in a decision to continue the use of a pseudonym. I am deeply grateful to all those who discussed this issue with me.

I have benefited greatly from the wisdom, insight, and hospitality of a variety of poets, politicians, philosophers, theologians, economists, social scientists, and all-around scholars (Scotland is a vibrant community in which to work), including Gordon, Jean, and Euan Adams, Susanne Barding, Roger Bland, John and Sheila Clegg, Tony Cohen, Eric Cregeen, Gordon Gair, Bruce and Christine Gardner, Patrick Guiton, Jonathan Hearn, Andrew Hinson, James and Beatrys Lockie, Seonag MacAuley, Calum and Johnina MacDonald, Calum and Margaret MacDonald, Fraser Macdonald, Norman MacDonald, Sharon Macdonald, D. J. MacKay, Annie Mackay, Maggie MacKay, Finlay and Norma MacLeod, John MacLeod, Morag MacLeod, the Matheson clan (Iain, Duncan, and Angie—long may their flags fly; Kenny and Christie Ann; Catherine Ann, Kenny, and Kathy Sue), Emily McEwan-Fujita, John McQueen, Donald Meek, Alec Murdo Morrison, John Murdo Morrison, Alastair Munro, Mary Noble, John Sheets, and Lisa Storey. I am also grateful for funding over the years from the National Science Foundation, Social Science Research Council, Wenner-Gren Foundation, the National Endowment for the Humanities, the American Council of Learned Societies, and California State University, Fullerton. I am grateful to Anhhoa Lu, computer master of the Anthropology Computer Lab, and Patrick Crispen of the Faculty Development Center at CSUF, and to my colleagues in the department of anthropology.

Special thanks to Fraser Macdonald for his excellent work monitoring the Highlands List, for organizing the seminar "Scottish Crofters Observed" at the University of Aberdeen, and for the kindness shown by members of the Arkleton Centre for Rural Development; to Peter Vasey and Neil Miller at West Register House for their assistance in sorting through the archival intricacies of agricultural statistics; to Roslyn Robertson and Ann Blackwood at Ladywell House for their help in locating population statistics; to the faculty and staff of Sabhal Mor Ostaig; to Shane Rankin of the Crofters Commission, Chris Higgins of Highlands and Islands Enterprise, Iain MacKenzie of the Harris Tweed Authority, and Andrew Hinson and Andrew Welsh of the Scottish Parliament; and for all past and present kindnesses shown by the faculty and staff of the School of Scottish Studies. Thanks also to my colleagues in the Society for the Anthropology of Europe for their efforts to reduce Eurocentric privileging in the anthropological paradigm, especially Pat Heck (who labored for 10 years to produce the SAE Bulletin) and Tony Galt (who has carried SAE communications into the electronic vastness of the 21st century). And a very special thanks to George Spindler, whose friendship, critical eye, and creative scholarship in Europe and education have contributed greatly to the completion of this project.

My deepest thanks go to the people of Geall (repseudonymized as Ciall in this edition), whose hospitality, humor, and humanity can never be adequately portrayed or repaid; to Gigi Pandian, my daughter and favorite traveling companion; and to my husband, Jacob Pandian, whose understanding, compassion, and wisdom are rare in any age or culture.

It is one of the harder duties of long-term fieldwork to live on while good friends and acquaintances die. The absence of voices such as those of Rowan and Gordon Adams, Kate Cory, Eric Cregeen, Hamish Henderson, Rody MacLeod, Effie and Donald Matheson, Murdo and Angus Murray, Louise Spindler, and Bob Storey makes the world emptier, marginally less interesting. In *Travels with a Donkey in the Cevennes,* Robert Louis Stevenson commented that "we are all travellers in what John Bunyan calls the wilderness of this world; and the best that we find in our travels is an honest friend. We travel, indeed, to find them. They are the end and reward of life. They keep us worthy of ourselves." And while social science often requires revelation of motives and underlying symbols at the expense of what Erving Goffman called the presentation of self in everyday life and what Umberto Eco might call the necessary lies of daily existence, I hope that everyone who contributed to the making of this book will find that their friendship has been honored.

1/Introduction to
the Second Edition

This book is about a Gaelic-speaking, crofting community on the island of Lewis in the Scottish Outer Hebrides, its social organization and relationship to larger British and European society. It is also about the construction of culture, especially the creation of culture in narratives that use historical references. Although the primary focus of the book is a particular village in the Scottish Outer Hebrides, and descriptions of interaction that occurred in 1970–71, I have added other contexts of meaning as well, from centuries before 1970–71 to as recently as January 2003.

Although the book is called "Scottish Crofters," it would more appropriately (but more cumbersomely) be titled "Gaelic-speaking, Free-Church, island, and specifically Lewisian crofters." Crofters also exist in Scotland who are Catholic vs. Protestant, Church of Scotland vs. Free Church, Free Presbyterian vs. Free Church, English-speaking vs. Gaelic-speaking, English-speaking-with-Norse-background vs. English-speaking-with-Lowland/BBC-background, Sasunnach (English or Lowland) vs. Highland, mainland vs. island, Inner Island vs. Outer Island, more independent vs. less independent, and so on. What all crofters have in common are the economic anomalies and opportunities provided by the crofting system, a shared sense of the connotations of Highland/Island distinctiveness, and a shared sense of historical peripheralness and privilege (the Clearances confer a sense of indebtedness, a "you-owe-me" spirit, similar to that generated by the Holocaust) that gives them special claims to Scottishness.

To be a crofter on Lewis, however, evokes two additional stigmata of Scottish distinctiveness: Gaelic-speaking and the extreme evangelical Protestantism of the Free Church. Although Scotland was never totally Gaelic-speaking, Gaelic has for various historical symbolic reasons connoted the distinctive heritage of the Highlands and therefore (courtesy of Walter Scott and Co.) of Scotland as a whole. And although there are Catholics, Mormons, Jehovah's Witnesses, Muslims, and Jews scattered throughout Scotland, the moral consciousness of Scotland is driven by the Reformation in all its

The lineal pattern of crofts (house on main road, croft land in strips encompassing higher drained land and lower boggy land) is visible in this photo in the upper right.

Susan Parman

Protestant, Presbyterian, and Calvinist incarnations; and there is no church more reformist than the evangelical, self-critical, continuously splitting (through righteous indignation over unfulfilled purity) Free Church. As one Church of Scotland minister expressed his feelings about the position of the Free Church in theological puritanism, "The Church of Scotland is always looking over its shoulder at the Free Church." The Protestants on Lewis are perceived by many to be 25 feet tall; and to Lewis many theological mendicants make their pilgrimage.

The second edition updates the analysis of crofting, explores further the links among crofting, Gaelic-speaking, the "Gaelic Renaissance" occurring in Scotland and among Scottish communities abroad, and Scottish nationalism; updates the status of crofting as a form of land tenure, especially with regard to efforts to allow crofters to buy their own land and to bring land out of crofting (the "decrofting" statutes passed by the Crofters Commission); and assesses the symbolic significance of a movement to promote crofting as an ecologically sound economic practice in the European Union and a promoter of renewable energy resources. Although, as per the mission of the case studies series, it is a structured account of life in a community, the book attempts to shed some light on Scotland and its complex history of linguistic, economic, and political processes, and to provide a brief analysis of the relationship among regional, ethnic, national, and transnational processes in the European Union today. It seeks to demonstrate that anthropology has a role to play in the study of Western (rather than non-Western) peoples and hopes to contribute to discourse on Scotland, the European Union, and anthropology's critical self-evaluation of its role as a "universal," comparative social science.

CULTURE, HISTORY, AND NARRATOLOGY

> Believing, with Max Weber, that man is an animal suspended in webs of significance he himself has spun, I take culture to be those webs, and the analysis of it to be therefore not an experimental science in search of law but an interpretive one in search of meaning.
>
> —Clifford Geertz

Anthropology is the study of humans, who are symboling animals. Symbols are organized in patterned, environmentally responsive, interconnected, changing systems called culture as the result of attempts by these symboling animals to survive and create meaning. Meaning is generated through interaction. When ethnographers interact or observe interaction, they are observing how people create and maintain meaning in various contexts. Meaning is always contextual.

As meaning-creating animals, humans do more than passively inherit culture; they must constantly create it in various contexts of interaction. In the process of maintaining identity in social interaction, humans create cultural systems. Culture changes as the conditions of social interaction change. Crofters and crofting culture are interpreted not as museum pieces, or as an example of cultural conservatism, but as a direct result of crofting communities' relationship with the rest of Scottish and European society. One of the reasons that the crofting system continues to exist, despite its various economically anomalous features, is that crofters play an important role in the national symbolism and self-identity of Scotland as the modern representatives of the Celt. (Malcolm Chapman expresses this relationship in the title of his book, *The Gaelic Vision in Scottish Culture* [1978], and in his more recent book, *The Celts* [1992].)

> It was clear from the evidence put before us during our visits to the crofting areas that the history of the past remains vivid in the minds of the people and, in some measure, conditions their attitudes to current problems.
>
> —Taylor Commission, 1954

Anthropologists have become increasingly concerned about the relationship between anthropology and history. History or historical thought is often associated with literacy and civilization, and contrasted with myth (which is associated with oral, "traditional" societies [cf. Goody 1977, Ong 1982]). History is perceived to be "factually accurate"; myth is perceived to be factually inaccurate but "metaphorically true."

The position taken in this book is that history and myth should be compared not for their factuality but for their meaning. In other words, history should be interpreted not as a recording of what "really" happened but as a cultural construction that is meaningful in the present to the people interpreting the past—a narrative mode that connects events (cf. Appadurai 1981, Boon 1982, Borofsky 1987, Cohn 1980, Herzfeld 1982, 1987, Hill 1988, Peel 1987, Price 1983, Rosaldo 1980, Sahlins 1985, Sturtevant 1968, Wolf 1982). A history, like a myth, is effective not because of the accuracy of the research but because of the relevance of the conclusions for the narrator. For example, both British and Americans agree that, factually, Americans issued a Declaration of Independence on July 4, 1776. This

Top: A black house (tigh dubh) preserved for tourism. Bottom: one being phased out of the township

day symbolizes pride, independence, and rebellion against tyranny to American children who learn this date in their history books; but to the British, including the modern-day members of the Scottish regiments that fought for King George against the unruly Americans, the date is considered merely an unfortunate incident in the glorious record of the British Empire. See MacDonald (2000:144) for an example of history as "an active, dynamic agent of contemporary social behaviour" in a current Free Church drama.

Chapter 2 describes two "histories of Europe" that arrive at two different conclusions, one tracing the origins of European civilization to the Romans, and another tracing the origins of European civilization to the Celts. The characteristics of the Celt—moody or fierce, dark or fair, poetic or militant—have changed through the centuries; and who is defined as a Celt—the aboriginal inhabitants of Europe, cattle-raiding clans, or Harris Tweed-weaving crofters— and their significance, has also changed. As Europe struggles to achieve the unification promised in 1992, national boundaries compete with regional, linguistic, occupational, and ethnic distinctiveness. Various European groups that identify themselves as Celtic—Bretons in Brittany, Galicians in Spain, the French as a whole, the Gaelic speakers of Ireland and Scotland, the Welsh, and their descendants among immigrants throughout the world—have established ties with each other during a recent period of Celtic revival. It will be interesting to see whether and how these ties are used in the European Community, especially in Scotland with its upsurge of Scottish nationalism and establishment of a Scottish Parliament, and what symbols of nationalistic identity will be used.

Many of the men who joined the regiments that fought against the American colonists were Scottish Highlanders who accepted military recruitment as a solution to the economic crises that wracked Scotland during the 18th century. The events remembered today during that tumultuous time must be understood in terms of the meaning that is attributed to them. When Scottish crofters recall the past that is responsible for making them crofters today, they talk about the Clearances that began in the late 18th century and continued into the middle of the 19th century—the forced removal of people from their homes to make way for sheep. To landlords and economic historians, the Clearances were unfortunate but necessary events in a process of agricultural improvement that was widespread throughout Europe, and have no relevance to the economic events affecting crofters today; but to crofters casting their votes for members of parliament, or in matters affecting crofting, Harris Tweed weaving, planting forests, and other issues, the Clearances serve as a powerful symbol affecting their actions in the present.[1]

To illustrate the contextual, pragmatic, shifting process of constructing meaning, I discuss changing definitions of "the Celt" in relation to changing relationships among European countries, between England and Scotland, and between the Scottish Highlands and Lowlands. I discuss the difference between the meanings attributed to crofters by Scottish Nationalists and urban romantics, and meanings created by the crofters themselves. I have called the book a historical ethnography because I concentrate on comparing and contrasting the use of events from the past to serve the needs of the present.

But there is another sense in which this book might be thought of as a historical ethnography. Narratology, a study that crosses many disciplinary boundaries, refers to the structuralist study of narrative (see, for example, the writings of Ferdinand de Saussure, Roman Jakobson, and the Russian Formalists, Claude Levi-Strauss, Tzvetan Todorov, Roland Barthes, and Jerome Bruner), the ultimate goal of which is to construct a taxonomy of narrative elements by which

---

[1]See discussion of the symbol of the Clearances in Chapter 2.

cultures (or literary genres or individuals) can be compared for how they construct knowledge of the world through storytelling. Whether focused on the narrative features of the modern novel (Virginia Woolf's multiple points of view vs. single first-person/third-person [Leaska 1970]) or how Greeks and Americans differ in how they report on a film they just saw (Chafe 1980), narratology provides a vehicle by which storytelling conventions may be systematically compared. While not strictly a narratological analysis, *Scottish Crofters* provides many examples of a style of storytelling that might be called "concretizing and personalizing the historical."

When residents of Ciall narrate stories of the past, it is as if they were there themselves, experiencing the hurts, insults, and destruction. It sometimes took me awhile to realize that the events being described occurred several centuries earlier; that the evil Factor (estate agent) who quenched fires and stole cattle is long dead, that the neighbor whose insult still rankles had insulted the narrator's great-great-grandfather. In Ciall, the actions of kings, queens, princes, landlords, highwaymen, neighbors, and kinsmen are not abstract points on a timeline but actions felt in the present, with history riding a direct line from the emotional brain of the limbic system to the cortex. When describing an event, people do not identify a person by his or her English name or even by his or her patronymics, if they are linked to the person through the mother's side of the family; they specify who the person is through their particular kinship link to him or her, and describe an event in terms of the kin group's reaction to it. This is one of the reasons that histories proliferate, because there are so many points of view. Why was the Free Church founded in Ciall? There are several versions of the story, one of which derives from the personal experience of some narrators' ancestors who were insulted by the Church of Scotland minister's wife who refused to give them hot water for their tea. Other perspectives yield other histories.

Thus, to say that this ethnography is about the contexts in which certain meanings, especially meanings that make use of historical symbols, are generated in Scotland concerning Gaelic-speaking crofters (both by them and by others) is only the beginning of a historical ethnography. A "historical ethnography" is not about the past but about the uses of the past in the present. Some cultures invest a lot of energy in imagining the future (Americans, who continuously invent themselves, take extensive license in manipulating the past as they focus on a constantly changing future) and some (such as Scottish crofters) draw heavily on the past as a resource, and are more likely to view it as factually accurate rather than metaphorically true. I suggest that a new focus in Scottish ethnography might be a closer look at cultural patterns of bringing the past into the present in narrative structure; but such a detailed analysis is beyond the scope of this book.

THE SIGNIFICANCE OF CROFTING

Every year around 1,000 idealistic city folk write to the Crofters Commission in Inverness in the hope of finding a nice wee Highland croft to shield them from the trials and tribulations of their present existence.

—*The Glasgow Herald,* October 14, 1976

A croft is a piece of land entirely surrounded by legislation.

—Attributed to a crofter

Top: The "wee Highland croft". Bottom: the busy township.

What Is a Croft?

Etymologically, the word "croft" comes from Old English and corresponds to the Dutch *kroft,* a field on high ground or downs. The croft is a strip of land (on Lewis typically 3 to 5 acres) that encompasses both well-drained and boggy land, and adjoins a main road; the croft house (owned by the crofter) sits next to the road and usually has a small garden patch behind it. Possession of a croft includes a share of the common grazing land held by a crofting township, the members of which share the responsibility of maintaining the land and fencing, organizing communal sheep roundups, and in general acting to promote the agricultural viability of the township. In recent years, nonagricultural activities have been recognized as significant aspects of crofting as well.

A croft is, with a few exceptions that will be explained, rented rather than owned by a crofter in designated crofting counties of the Highlands and Islands of Scotland—a region often romantically portrayed as full of glens, heather-covered moors, seagirt islands—the land of Sir Walter Scott, Wee Geordie, the Loch Ness monster, second sight, Bonnie Prince Charlie and Flora MacDonald, "Braveheart" and "Brigadoon," the noble crofter relishing the simple life away from the evils and turmoil of urban-industrial Scotland. The tenancy carries privileges formulated in 1886 to protect the small tenantry from arbitrary eviction and excessive rents (the horrors of "the Clearances"). After the Crofters Holdings (Scotland) Act of 1886 conferred rights to fair rent, security of tenure, and hereditary succession, the croft took on its paradoxical symbolic weightings of security (the land from which the crofter will no longer be cleared) and futility (the holdings too small to be agriculturally viable).

One way to define a croft is to say that it is a small unit of agriculturally substandard land (the amount of land used to designate a croft changes over time, from less than 50 acres to no more than 30 hectares or 74 acres), as contrasted with a farm, which is larger and agriculturally more viable. Also, a croft is associated with communal responsibilities that focus on grazing (formerly cattle, now mostly sheep), and is located in designated areas of the Highlands and Islands of Scotland. But to stop with this definition would neglect the unique flavor that permeates crofting culture—its claims, its rootedness, its communitarian promise, its baffling economic pretensions, and its connotations of ecological righteousness that now echo through the European Union (see Parman 1993).

> *Aonghas Aobronn, who has always considered himself a sophisticated city-dweller, comments in a recent e-mail, "I don't think I ever realised until now just how badly, and how deep down, I have always wanted a croft." He is moving to Ciall after years spent living on the mainland, and plans to keep cattle and sheep, grow potatoes—not because it is essential for his survival, but because it is part of his new set of responsibilities in taking on the role of crofter.*

The definition of croft and crofter appears complex and sometimes contradictory, which may be explained by two major concerns in the history of crofting legislation: the attempt by a socially conscious government to rectify the injustices of the past (and, pragmatically, to prevent the land wars and social uprisings that had occurred in Ireland, to which the situation in the Highlands and Islands was compared in the second half of the 19th century); and the attempt to preserve, revive, and invigorate declining rural communities. The first explains the creation of special status of crofter, with its protections and opportunities; the second explains the continuous efforts at reform that sometimes seem to undermine the first concern.

Because of legal changes that have enabled a crofter to buy the croft, a crofter is now defined as any authorized occupier of a croft—that is, either as owner or as tenant; and because of changes that enable crofters to take land out of crofting (decrofting), the door has opened for crofting communities to take in more and more non-crofting residents and thus change forever the culture of a kin-linked people who share memories of individual and communal marginality and mistreatment.

Scotland is about the size of the American state of South Carolina, the distance between the Outer Hebrides in northwestern Scotland and Edinburgh in the southeast being about equal to the distance between Greenville and Charleston.

Croft work: Scything hay

In the subjective map of the Scottish mind, however, the cultural distance is enormous. When I studied Gaelic as an undergraduate at the University of Edinburgh, my Lowland Scots friends referred to the Highlands, and in particular the Outer Hebrides, as if this region of northwest Scotland were a foreign country, much as Tobias George Smollett did in *The Expedition of Humphry Clinker* in 1771.[2] The cultural dichotomy of Lowland (which includes Edinburgh) and Highland (which includes the Outer Hebrides) was emblematic, reflecting how people defined Scotland, Celts, crofting, and so on.

Geographically, the Highlands are heavily eroded plateaus carved by glaciers and streams into low mountains, broad straths, narrow twisting glens, and an abundance of lochs. The region lies north of a line drawn between Dumbarton along the Firth of Clyde and Stonehaven just south of Aberdeen, and includes the counties of Sutherland, Ross-and-Cromarty, Inverness, Argyll-and-Bute, and part of the counties of Nairn, Moray, Banff, Aberdeen, Perth, Stirling, and Dumbarton. When the term "Highland" is used to refer to a way of life (as defined, for example, by speaking Gaelic and crofting), the geographically eastern Highlands that do not have Gaelic speakers are excluded, and the islands of the Inner and Outer Hebrides (but not Shetland and Orkney) are included—indeed, the islands, in particular the Outer Hebrides, are the main conservators

---

[2]The contrast between Highland and Lowland, however, emphasizes differences that are not those emphasized in 1771 (about the time that American colonists were preparing for war with Britain, and the "fiery and ferocious" Highlander was in demand as a British fighting soldier). "They are undoubtedly a very distinct species from their fellow subjects of the Lowlands, against whom they indulge an ancient spirit of animosity; and this difference is very discernible even among persons of family and education. The Lowlanders are generally cool and circumspect, the Highlanders fiery and ferocious..." (Smollett 1950: 295).

Scotland in Europe

of the Highland image, possessing the greatest number of Gaelic speakers and the largest crofting townships (but not the largest crofts, which are found on more fertile land, for example, in the Orkneys).

Crofting is administered in seven crofting regions (the former Crofting counties, meaning the previous Local Government Administrative areas of Argyll, Inverness [including Skye], Ross and Cromarty [including the Western Isles], Sutherland, Caithness, Orkney, and Shetland) by the Crofters Commission, an executive non-departmental public body (NDPB) that was first established in 1886, dismantled in 1911, and then reestablished in 1955. The seven crofting regions are now identified by five council areas (Eilean Siar, Highland, Argyll-and-Bute, Orkney, and Shetland).

The Crofters Commission is funded by the Scottish Executive Environment and Rural Affairs Department, and carries out the directives embodied in the various crofting acts that have emerged over the past 100 years. In 2001 the Crofters Commission reported 17,721 registered crofts, of which 6,087 were in the Outer Hebrides or Western Isles and 3,611 on Lewis. The crofts are occupied by about 11,500 crofting households (of which about 7,500 are considered to be headed by active crofters engaged in agricultural production), for a total crofting population of about 33,000. Thus, although crofts occupy about one-third of the agricultural holdings in Scotland (17,721 out of 49,738), both the acreage and the population they represent are small in proportion to the total acreage of agricultural holdings and population; but they loom large in the Scottish imagination (both resident and émigré).

A number of position papers, debates, statutes, and acts have affected the interpretation and functioning of crofting since 1886, beginning with the Crofters Holdings (Scotland) Act 1886 that created crofting tenure in seven designated crofting counties (Argyll, Inverness, Ross-and-Cromarty, Sutherland, Caithness, Orkney, and Shetland). The Small Landholders (Scotland) Act 1911 dissolved the special status of crofters, identifying two categories of protected

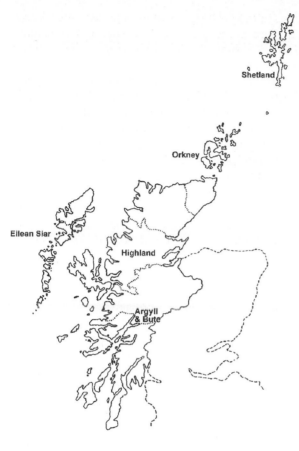

*Highlands and Islands
council areas*

tenants within Scotland as a whole, "landholder" and "statutory small tenant."
The Crofters (Scotland) Act 1955 resurrected crofters (the term now encompassing both categories of protected tenants) in the seven crofting counties, and
created the Crofters Commission. The Crofters (Scotland) Act 1961 amended
and added to the 1955 act. These acts laid the foundation for the crofting community that I studied in 1970–71: a community in which crofting status conferred security of tenure and a subtle hierarchy (crofters with land, squatters with
land on suffrage, and landless); a community with strong boundaries that prevented the incursion of outsiders and preserved a way of life that was characterized in many areas by strong ties of kinship and shared customs such as
Gaelic-speaking and religious beliefs; and an aging population whose young
people were siphoned off to the mainland or overseas by jobs, education, and the
paradoxical desire to both leave and return (giving rise to the conception of
themselves as "exiles").

The Crofting Reform (Scotland) Act 1976 attempted significant reform. It
gave crofters the legal right to buy their own croft, which gave them the opportunity to apply to have the land decrofted (taken out of crofting)—an extremely
significant step in the history of crofting. Decrofting is intended to provide flexibility in land use and enhance the community, but the overall effect has been to

stimulate a new housing market in the crofting counties. The decrofted house eventually is put up for sale; the new houses built on croft land may eventually be decrofted and sold as well. The consumable, shrinking croft: today's family farm, tomorrow's housing development.

Another effort to strengthen the community was the planning and creation during the 1990s of the University of the Highlands and Islands, a set of 13 designated learning sites established in the Highlands and Islands whose purpose was to provide jobs and provide further education for members of these communities, thus keeping young people at home. The idea that this plan suits "the crofting lifestyle" (The Crofters Commission Annual Report 1997/1998) reflects the conception of crofting as a community-based, multitasking enterprise. Although young people from crofting communities continue to leave (thus reflecting many of the same desires of college-age children the world over to taste a world outside the community), these learning centers have attracted many from outside the community. One of the most vibrant centers in UHI is Sabhal Mor Ostaig on Skye, which is a pillar of light for the preservation of Gaelic.

THE SIGNIFICANCE OF GAELIC

"If you're going to understand what it means to be a crofter, you must have the Gaelic," I was told repeatedly. According to Gillanders (1968:97), "Crofting and Gaelic Scotland are synonymous both in the English and Gaelic tongues." While not true (Shetland and Orkney, for example, are English-speaking crofting regions), the statement reflects a recurring theme: that in distinctive characteristics such as Gaelic-speaking and crofting can Scotland claim its unique identity on the European playing field of regionalism.

Scottish Gaelic is one of several "Celtic" languages (including Irish Gaelic, Welsh, Manx, Cornish, and Breton) spoken (or until recently spoken) along the "Celtic fringe" of Europe. In reviewing the evidence of the distribution of Gaelic place-names on maps, Nicolaisen (1986:135–6) makes it clear that there was never a time in Scottish history or prehistory when Gaelic was spoken as the everyday language throughout Scotland. In the 11th century Gaelic was spoken widely in Scotland, but by the 13th century English had become the culturally dominant language. The Scottish nobility and the merchants spoke English, and the commoners spoke Gaelic. Only in the Highlands did Gaelic cross class boundaries and signify the persistence of an integrated linguistic community. But by the 14th century Gaelic became socially stigmatized; it was considered a barbarous language to be destroyed as part of the national attempt to subdue the "wild Highlander." Gaelic made a significant comeback from its stigmatized status when crofters, agitating against the landlords in the 19th century, emerged as the embodiments of a traditional, Highland, Celtic way of life. They formed a political party called the Highland Land Law Reform Association (later the Highland Land League) that presented Highland issues to parliament, including the promotion of Gaelic as the language of Scotland. The relationship between crofter and Gael, between Gael and Celt, and the linkage of crofter, Gael, Celt, Highlands, Scottish nationalism, and European identity are like the tangled weft and warp of a dense tweed.

Many signs in the Highlands and Islands are now in both Gaelic and English

Both the number and percentage of Gaelic speakers has been declining in Scotland since an official census was first taken (see Table 1, "Historical Trends and Area," in the *1991 Census: Gaelic Language*), from 254,415 (6.3%) in 1891 to 65,978 (1.3%) in 1991. Nancy Dorian uses the term *Language Death* (1981) to describe the process of destruction that is occurring in a Gaelic-speaking community in East Sutherland as the regional Gaelic dialect is replaced by the regional English dialect. According to Ken MacKinnon, whose discussion of the 2001 Gaelic census figures at http://www.smo.uhi.ac.uk/gaidhlig/suil/cunntas-sluaigh-2001/ was posted on the Highlands listserv May 8, 2003, the number of Gaelic speakers in the Western Isles, age 3–15, has dropped to 1,966 (or 45.3% of the total age group) from 2,584 (or 49.3%) in 1991. The reduction between 1991 and 2001 is smaller than the reduction between 1981 and 1991, which he attributes to Gaelic-medium schooling.

Despite the decline in number of Gaelic speakers in the official census and Dorian's grim pronouncements of "language death," Gaelic has undergone a remarkable "renaissance" (Macdonald 1997) over the past 30 years. Added to the long-term efforts of organizations such as *Comunn na Gaidhlig,* the Highland Council, Highlands and Islands Enterprise, the old Highlands and Islands Development Board, and Celtic and Scottish Studies at the University of Edinburgh (a recent merging of the Department of Celtic and the School of Scottish Studies) are the notable efforts of Sabhal Mor Ostaig and the support of Gaelic playgroups (*croileag*) begun by the Highlands and Islands Development Board's funding of *Comhairle nan Sgoilean Araich* (Gaelic Playgroup Association) in 1982. In addition, the lightning-speed communication

EILEAN SIAR (BY CIVIL PARISH)*

| | Percent Gaelic speakers[1] | |
	1891	2001
Barra	93.8	77.1
Barvas	95.7	80.9
Harris	95.4	78.0
Lochs	94.1	70.7
North Uist	93.8	76.2
South Uist	95.0	75.0
Stornoway	86.8	62.7
Uig	96.2	77.3

*Gaelic: 1891–2001

[1] I calculated these figures by subtracting the number of people identified as having "no knowledge of Gaelic" from the total population for each parish, as listed in the 2001 Census, Table UV12 "Knowledge of Gaelic" at www.SCROL.gov.uk. Thus "Percent Gaelic speakers" includes any variation on speaking Gaelic, from "Understands spoken Gaelic" to "Speaks, reads, writes Gaelic" to "Writes, can't speak or read," and so on, resulting in a figure for "Gaelic-speaking" that is generous.

available now on the Internet supports Gaelic web pages, listservs, and discussion groups, which contribute to an increasing sense of the presence if not the proliferation of fluent Gaelic speakers. William Gillies (1987:38) warns of the dangers of festivalizing Gaelic rather than using it, and credits the regional reorganization of the mid-1970s that produced the Western Isles Council (*Comhairle nan Eilean Siar*) as having provided new hope for Gaelic-speaking. In 1975 it adopted a policy of bilingualism in the schools; middle-school children in Ciall today have the option of taking a Gaelic-language track, whereas their parents and grandparents were punished for speaking it on the playground. The availability of Gaelic-track education has generated certain ironies; one student in Ciall told me that he no longer enjoyed speaking Gaelic because it was now the language of the schoolroom rather than the playground.

In Ciall today, Gaelic is taught in P1–P6, French in P6 and P7; Gaelic playgroups attempt to build Gaelic-speaking from the ground up, as occurred in Wales; Sabhal Mor Ostaig is a Gaelic-medium College of Further Education founded in 1983 dedicated to teaching everything from statistics to export marketing, in addition to Gaelic arts, literature, and history, and the poet Sorley MacLean was a cofounder, trustee, and first writer in residence; the University of the Highlands and Islands supports a community-based approach to population retention that recognizes the significance of Gaelic. (See Thomson's 1980 "assessment and prognosis" of Gaelic in Scotland; and Sharon Macdonald [1997:57–59] for a comprehensive review of pro-Gaelic developments between 1950 and 1990.)

It would be reasonable to say that more people now are influenced by and conscious of Gaelic than 30 years ago, although the actual number of fluent

Gaelic speakers has declined. How may this paradox be explained? Are we witnessing a pseudo-Celtomania parallel to the popularity of MacPherson's Ossian in the 18th and 19th centuries or Sir Walter Scott's celtification of Scottish identity after the pacification of the Jacobite clans? Is the Gaelic renaissance being fueled by a sense of regionalism in the European Union (and by European economic and linguistic support for "Disadvantaged Areas" and "Lesser-Used Languages"), or by a sense of Scottish nationalism in the ongoing effort to shrug off the yoke of English domination and internal colonialism? To what extent are the North Sea oil revenues, general increase in Scottish prosperity, and the return of a Scottish Parliament linked with this renaissance? Perhaps even more important is the issue of how and why people report their linguistic abilities in contexts that shift from opprobrium to pride (see Macdonald 1997 and MacKinnon 1978 for an interpretation of the 9.8% increase in Gaelic speakers in 1971—the first increase since 1891—due apparently to increased willingness among Lowland bilinguals to report their Gaelic-speaking abilities rather than to the entry of new Gaelic speakers into the pool).

Macdonald (1997) addresses the ambivalence that Gaelic speakers feel about the increased artificiality of promoting Gaelic as a marker of identity. It is more likely that Scots abroad and in the cities, and the "white settlers" moving into rural communities, identify Gaelic as a means of distinguishing their uniqueness from English speakers and English (as opposed to Scottish) culture, whereas Gaelic speakers in primarily Gaelic-speaking environments speak it because it feels right and natural. "The jokes are better in Gaelic," as one Ciall resident expressed it, "and the church services more frightening. 'Death' is just death, but *bas* reminds me of my doom." When English starts feeling natural (my Gaelic lessons from children were usually a mixture of Gaelic and English, with no distinctions made between them), language changes, no matter what feelings of politicized, moral linguistic duty to preserve heritage obtain. In Ciall, bureaucratic forms from the Crofters Commission or the Department of Agriculture are not easy to fill out, but rendering them into Gaelic would not make sense except to the more militant Gaelophiles. Tax forms and grant applications are as natural in English as jokes are in Gaelic. The "renaissance" may change this by expanding the arenas within which Gaelic is practiced; and to many of the more insistent Gaelophiles (those that refuse to let their children participate in English conversations, for example), this period of artificiality (like minority quotas in university admissions) is necessary to usher in a renewed sense of the naturalness of speaking Gaelic. But for many, Gaelic remains the language of home and community, and English is the language of "out," "away," "getting on," and the majority culture.

Promoters of Gaelic are caught between a rock and a hard place. Accused of being part of a "Gaelic Mafia" if they become too aggressive, they run the equal risk of being identified as "dreamy Celts" if they glorify the language without providing concrete solutions to its revival. Establishing Celtic Studies departments, providing classes for Gaelic learners (including tapes and Internet instruction for people living abroad), and supporting other Gaelic song and poetry festivals, are in themselves insufficient. A language comes alive only in the context of community interaction—in the playground, the workplace, the sheep fank, the wake.[3] A mother in Ciall worries that her child, who is just graduating from the Gaelic playgroup and going on to middle school, may fall behind if the child is placed in the Gaelic track—not because the track is Gaelic, but because only one Gaelic-speaking teacher is available to teach all the subjects, whereas the English track has many more teachers. On the other hand, another mother observes that English-speaking parents take pride in placing their children in the Gaelic playgroups ("It's very posh to speak the language of Scotland"), and that many of these mothers are picking up the language from their children.

The Western Isles Council has built an office building in Ciall that currently stands empty. If it is used to house telephone attendants who interact only with callers and not with each other, the effort is wasted as a means to promote Gaelic in the workplace. A woman in her 40s observes that when she was in school, all the children spoke Gaelic on the playground; now they tend to speak English on the playground, and while they might understand their Gaelic-speaking parents, they respond in English. When developing programs for teaching Gaelic, planners scratch their heads over which Gaelic to use—the dialectic variation is so great. It would be worth studying whether the increase in Gaelic on TV has generated a "BBC Gaelic" that is working to standardize dialects, just as BBC/London English worked to standardize the speaking of English; and which dialect is used to standardize Gaelic educational instruction, especially in rules of spelling and grammar. While such choices are sure to infuriate some segments of the Gaelic-speaking community, they are a natural and inevitable part of linguistic change; survival of Gaelic does not ensure survival of all forms of Gaelic.

One institution that has contributed enormously to the conservation of Gaelic is Scottish churches, especially the Free Church and the Church of Scotland. Although associated with a more stilted, formalized version of Gaelic (Bible Gaelic vs. fireside Gaelic[4]), the Gaelic spoken in sermons has nevertheless contributed to the linguistic webs of meaning and symbolic reference in Gaelic speakers' minds. In Ciall in 1970–71, all services (two on Sunday, a prayer meeting on Wednesday, and services twice a day for the week of Communion) were in Gaelic, except for the rare occasion when an English speaker was present. Today, because of the influx of English speakers, only one service on Sunday is in Gaelic, and even that is eroded by the frequent arrangement of crèches, when children are present during the first part of the service and the language used is English. Notably absent during English services is the distinctive Gaelic psalm singing (see Chapters 7 and 8). See Meek (2001) for a discussion of the effect of church schisms on language continuity.

If there were a scale of conservation of Gaelic, the churches would exist at one end and at the other would be placed the efforts by various educators to encourage a looser, more creative approach to the maintenance of Gaelic in a

---

[3]Smout (1969:32) argues that it was the introduction of Flemish, Norman, Anglic, and Scandinavian tradesmen and merchants into the burghs established by David I in the 12th century that led to the decline of Celtic languages in the lowlands; Gaelic was no longer the vehicle of economic transactions in everyday life.

[4]"G idhlig a' Bhiobaill" vs. "G idhlig taobh an teine" (Cheape 1997:307).

changing world. An example of the latter is the production in 2002 of *Leabhar Mor* (The Great Book of Gaelic), a celebration of 1,500 years of Gaelic poetry and art from Ireland and Scotland edited by Malcolm Maclean and Theo Dorgan. Educational materials based on the book are intended to encourage pride and more creative expressions in contemporary forms of Gaelic, as well as changing attitudes toward the Irish/Gaelic connection across the Catholic/ Protestant divide.

WHAT IS A HIGHLANDER
IF NOT A GAELIC-SPEAKING CROFTER?

The "Highland" way of life has other connotations besides Gaelic-speaking and crofting, for example, preferring an easygoing rural life to the fast-paced indus- triousness of Lowland life (e.g., Blake 1919:3, 41); presenting a quiet courtesy but cannily subversive resistance to the dominant interests of landlords or gov- ernment organizations; thriftiness; independence; a "poor but proud manner;" hospitality and honesty; wearing the kilt, sporran (belt purse), dirk (small knife), and other distinctive items of dress; possessing a strong sense of loyalty to fam- ily and clan; having the ability to play or at least to enjoy the skirling, cacopho- nous bagpipe (which, for awhile after the Jacobite rebellions of the 18th century, was banned as an instrument of war); taking great pleasure in music and poetry; possessing second sight; and so on.

Most of these indicators of ethnicity are embraced by émigrés, or by Scotsman, Lowland and Highland alike, who have left their native land (I even met someone from the northern part of England who, when he attended Cambridge, found himself treated as such an outsider that he began to study Gaelic, saying that as long as he was being treated as a foreigner he might as well acquire the identity of one). In the current arena of international discourse on the Internet, discussions of identity draw on local, national, and international partic- ipants (as, for example, the very interesting discussions on the Highlands listserv moderated by Fraser Macdonald at http://www.jiscmail.ac.uk, and the current discussion on what constitutes "Highland culture" in preparation for the Scottish Year of Highland Culture 2006 at http://www.think-net.org—a list that includes, according to one discussant, "Highland Games, curling, golf, tartan and the kilt, bagpipes, Highland dancing, pipe bands, heather, castles, hills and lochs, whisky, haggis, salmon and venison, and Gaelic in all its forms" in addition to the writ- ings of Sorley MacLean, Neil Gunn, Robert Burns, Robert Louis Stevenson, Walter Scott, James Barrie, and the distinctively hideous McGonagall).

The Highlanders themselves vary in their uses of these cultural constructs. Some of them have become self-conscious spokespeople for Highland ethnicity as poets, playwrights, and politicians. Others are frequently embarrassed by the attention called to their cultural distinctiveness, covet the possessions portrayed in mail-order catalogs and disdain homemade products, downgrade their own language and customs, and poke sly fun at the earnest Sasunnachs (Englishmen, Lowlanders, townies—the term derives from "Saxon," which has as its implicit contrast the concept "Celt") who wear the kilt and win the gold medals at Gaelic song contests. In recent years, the term "white settler," with all of its colonial connotations, has become a significant means of distinguishing Highland natives from Lowland and English incomers (see Jedrej and Nuttall 1996). Kohn (2002) reminds us that communities have always had an influx of incomers, and that what distinguishes an incomer from an outsider is not "blood" but social action.

WHAT IS A SCOT IF NOT A HIGHLANDER/CELT/ GAELIC-SPEAKING SCOTTISH CROFTER?

Chapter 2 explores changing conceptions of identity in Scottish history, in particular the significance of "the Celt" (and who serves as the vehicle of Celtic identity) in representations of Scotland. But as Nadel-Klein (1997:90) points out, it is important to remember that Scotland is a much more complex entity than "the West and the rest." On the one hand she argues that east-coast fishing communities constitute the Lowland analogue to the crofter (1997:96): comparably exotic, linguistically distinctive, struggling with issues of authenticity and identity. On a more general level, she argues that an "anthropology of Scotland" requires a critical exploration of all discussions of Scottishness at local, regional, and national levels. In an article titled "Too Much on the Highlands? A Plea for Change," R. H. Campbell (1994) argues that the study of Scottish rural history has neglected the relations of landowners and tenants in the Lowlands.

Representations of identity are always strategic and situational rather than essentialist. An American college president with Scottish and black ancestry identifies himself as black in his home political arena and as Scottish while touring Scotland. At a Smithsonian Folklife Festival occurring in 2003, Scotland was one of three identities being celebrated (along with the Republic of Mali and Appalachia), and was represented by Harris Tweed weavers from the Outer Hebrides. Scots abroad are more likely to discuss Culloden than Harlaw or Flodden. To me the important question is not "why aren't we listening equally to all the voices of Scotland," but "why are certain symbols given greater play than others, and in what contexts and for what reasons?" People living in local communities carry on with their lives, sometimes ignoring and sometimes interacting with the discourse occurring among statesmen, writers, and EU think tanks. It is this interaction and differences in uses that interests me—following symbols, listening to stories, noting ironies and discrepancies. When Prince Charles visits Stornoway, he wears a kilt rather than a knitted jersey, trousers, and tweed cap. While crofters at home are struggling to translate the land-use requirements of grant-application forms so that they can qualify for grants, statesmen in Brussels are representing them as role models for an ecologically sound land-management plan for the EU.

Who knows what Scotland will become in the heady days of devolution, and what role Scottish crofters/Gaelic-speakers/Highlanders (or Doric-speaking inhabitants of the Moray Firth, or Shetlanders, or residents of the Borders, Edinburgh, and Glasgow) will play in constructions of Scottishness in the 21st century? Perhaps Nadel-Klein's article will constitute a rallying point for those grown weary of Highland representations; perhaps many will concur with a young woman from Edinburgh for whom the Scotland portrayed in Lewis Grassic Gibbon's *Sunset Song* is "her song." In the meantime, a 5-foot cardboard representation of a kilted piper stands guard outside official Scottish tourism offices as the official symbol of Scotland.

ETHNOGRAPHERS AND ETHNOGRAPHIES

I came to Ciall because it had two mills involved in the production of Harris Tweed, and most Ciall crofters were also weavers or worked in the mills. My research was concerned with the effect that different economic strategies had on the social organization of crofting townships.

Through a series of contacts, I was introduced, as an anthropologist, to the three persons in Ciall considered most likely to be able to help me find a place to live: the minister, the schoolmaster, and the owner of one of the local Harris Tweed mills. But I was finding that my label as anthropologist was having decidedly negative effects on my attempts to gain help. "So, you've come to study the primitive natives of Ciall?" was the sardonic comment of the minister. The schoolmaster asked if I had run out of South Sea islanders to study. The mill owner was less direct, but murmured a jest about my coming out to study the rustic *siarachs* (a Gaelic term meaning "western ones," used by the "townies" of Stornoway to refer to people from the west side of the island where most of the rural villages are concentrated; the term connotes lack of urban sophistication).

It was my first lesson in a very important aspect of doing fieldwork: I was not going to be able to "observe culture" as if it were an object; my very presence turned me into a participant in a continuing process of interpretation, much like a fly caught in Geertz's "webs of significance." My own presence and actions would become part of the processes that formed the basis for description in an ethnography. (About 8 months into fieldwork, I had a long dream about an anthropologist who plans and executes an explosion, setting off earthquakes, volcanic eruptions, and general havoc; it was a dramatic psychological realization that I was far from invisible, that I occupied interactional space.)

The town of Stornoway, 18 miles away on the eastern side of the island, had many bed-and-breakfast homes and several hotels, but the tourist association, which had established an office there some 10 years before I arrived, had found it extremely difficult to make arrangements with rural households. Only one woman in Ciall took "outsiders"—an elderly widow who had lived in Canada for years before retiring to her original island home, and who was away on vacation when I arrived in the village.

The schoolmaster informed me, regretfully, that he was unable to help me find a place to stay because the widow was away. I discovered, from the minister whom I visited shortly afterward, that all three of them had gone to the same woman; and I suspected that they would all give me the same answer. I was standing with the minister on the single-lane, tar-macadam road that overlooked the village and its natural harbor of white sand and stone. It was a beautiful sun-filled evening in August, cold from the wind that moved in swift gusts, and I could see thin sheets of rain moving across the sea and the intervening hills. The sea turned black, then gray-green, then molten silver, and I felt displaced and lonely. I noticed a nearby sign, a square board neatly lettered with the word Chirrapungi that had been planted in the boggy peat.

Stornoway festival, 1970

"Chirrapungi," a name borrowed from a place in India known as the wettest spot on earth, is given to a boggy football field.

"Chirrapungi—that's not Gaelic, is it?" I asked.

The minister burst out laughing—at my expense, I suspected—and looked at me over the tops of his glasses. "It is not. It is a place in India—the wettest spot on earth."

It was several months before I understood the complex message of his humor—the combination of self-deprecation (the boggy homeland) and ambivalent pride in the Highlander's far-flung travel experiences, and the subtle jibe at the naive anthropologist. To a population that contributes a disproportionately high percentage of its young people to the highly selective and competitive British university system, that esteems books and honors positions of learning, anthropology could only be interpreted as an intrusive insult, one more piece of evidence of their social marginality at the fringes of the English-speaking, urban-industrial mainland.

When I finally found a place to stay, it was not because I was an anthropologist, and not because the public leaders had used their influence, but because of accident and human courtesy. A young family offered me temporary and finally permanent residence. The house was large, the siblings scattered to various cities on the mainland. The absent living and the absent dead continue as a vital part of crofting communities—population figures that do not show up in the statistics of census reports.

I lived in the village for 14 months, evolving from "anthropologist" to "an American student studying the economics of crofting." I stopped doing formal interviews and asked direct questions only of those whom I had gotten to know well; otherwise, I participated and observed. I learned that the public leaders were relatively ineffective compared with the network of leaders who kept a low profile and mobilized public opinion. I scribbled phrases in small notebooks that I carried in my pocket, and as soon as possible tried to recreate the context in which such discussions occurred. I typed the notes up on half-sheets of paper (with carbons that I periodically mailed back to the States; today I use a laptop and mail home discs), heading each page with the name of the person or persons I talked to, the context of the discussion, and the date. I separated out portions of the conversations and typed them again on new half-sheets headed with categories that emerged inductively (e.g., "mill history," "diet," "nicknames"). I was initially suspected of being a spy for the Crofters Commission and various other government organizations, I was criticized for being nosy (one of my early nicknames, friendlier than some of the others, was "Why"), and my meeting with all types of people, from grandmothers to bachelors, from the *curamach* (converted) churchgoers to the dedicated drinkers, put me in an ambiguous category—a person of uncertain status. Over the year as I faded into the woodwork, my identity evolved from that of an anthropologist and spy to variations on my name (Sue Palmer, Paxman, Pelman, or usually just plain Sue) who was assumed to be distantly related to the family. I was given a series of nicknames that reflected attempts to make sense of my presence and identity, such as "the Mexican" because I came from New Mexico, "Yank," "Pest," "Tramp," "Lady," and "Why."

My theoretical orientation when I first did fieldwork was influenced by neo-evolutionists such as Marvin Harris, Leslie White, and Julian Steward (my original conception was to study the impact of different types of economic supplements to crofting on the social structure of crofting townships—weaving vs. fishing, for example); by Fredrik Barth's novel approach to culture reflected in works such as *Ethnic Groups and Boundaries;* by network analysis; and by the idiosyncratic study of social boundary systems by Yehudi Cohen. I came to

Tools of fieldwork: A typewriter (or laptop) and notebooks

anthropology with a background in the sciences and the humanities (neurophysiology and literature), with a strong commitment to both scientific and humanistic methods. When interviewed by the Foreign Area Fellowship committee about what methods I would use, I showed them the household/crofting survey form that I planned to use and then said, "After that, I'll play it by ear."

During the 1980s, anthropological debate was dominated by a critique of ethnographic writings (e.g., Clifford 1983 and 1988, Clifford and Marcus 1986, Marcus and Cushman 1982, Marcus and Fischer 1986) that identified ethnographies as subjective texts, and the only honest (if not good) ethnographies as reflexive. Despite the significance of the insights generated by these publications, it must be said that many anthropologists under their influence spent more time tying themselves up in navel-gazing, solipsistic knots than in trying to record, however limited their vision, the lifeways of others. As Smith points out (1990:369), "The subjects of ethnographies, it should never be forgotten, are always more interesting than their authors."

It is customary in anthropology today, under such headings as narrative, critical, interpretive, and reflexive anthropology, to think of the ethnography as a fictional genre. The ethnographer is like a novelist who, from a position of relative power and with peculiarities of background that structure his or her interpretive framework, observes, interprets, and creates a reality that tells the reader more about the author than about what is being described.

The danger of this argument is that it implies that there is no reality except what is in the anthropologist's head. The usefulness of this argument is that it sensitizes us to the fact that anthropological fieldwork is more than objective observation by a "participant observer." Observer and observed have a social, political, and economic relationship that influences how they behave toward and interpret each other. It is important for students to be aware of this relationship when they read ethnographies, and in particular to realize that (1) the ethnography reflects a power relationship, with the ethnographer on top, and (2) the ethnography is an edited, artificially fixed version of what was and continues to be an ongoing, changing creation of meaning. The trick is to create an ethnography of the present rather than "the ethnographic present" of some idealized, artificial, frozen moment (see Fabian 1983 and Sanjek 1990 and 1991).

What I have attempted to do is to tell the stories of Ciall in an organized framework of meaning; to capture contextualized speech events; to explore the relationship between action and significance while staying as close to the raw data of experience as possible.[5]

The term "Celtic" in the subtitle is intended to be ironic—that is, the romanticism implicit in the use of the term by 20th-century lovers-of-things-Celtic is undercut by the reality portrayed by this ethnography. The term is intended to convey the contradictions and contrasts among the many levels of meaning (crofters exist in part because of their meaning to non-crofters, but their own meanings are often quite different) and thus promote a sense of detachment among readers that I believe is necessary to anthropological enquiry. Today the term "Celtic" is used primarily by linguists, historians, novelists, and organizers of festivals; and although the children of crofting households may join Celtic departments at Scottish and Canadian universities, few would consider the term to refer to a cultural identity, and no Western Isles crofter would think to identity him or herself (or anyone else) as a Celt. A more correct subtitle of this book would be "A Historical Ethnography of a Village of the Gaidhealtachd in the Western Isles," but such a subtitle would suggest that issues of Gaelic nationalism are central to the book's thesis, which is not the case. The terms "Celtic" and "Gael" are treated as aspects of contextual identity along with many other elements.

The use of pseudonyms in anthropological research is common. Although they are sometimes criticized as pretentious and artfully coy, and as part of the maintenance of the power relationship ("I can make you invisible") between the anthropologist and those who have been anthropologized, pseudonyms play an important role in the maintenance of privacy. Anthropologists work hard to fulfill their obligations to multiple audiences that include the funding world, the scholarly world, and the community, but they usually give primary place to the people among whom they have worked, to whom they owe the greatest debt of friendship and loyalty. Because the purpose of social science is to describe and explain the functioning of society (which means describing how rules are actually developed and applied—a process that is often messy and frequently unsavory—rather than present an ideal picture), anonymity is sometimes necessary to protect the placeholders of these mechanisms of social order and disorder (as, for example, when writing ethnographies that focus on piracy, prostitution, or drug dealing). But even when the social environment is benign,

---

[5]My dislike of many postmodernist writings is that they smack of intellectual arrogance. In my opinion, ethnographies are humble things. Like Stevenson's donkey, they plod along, covering many miles and wonders external to the self.

anonymity remains a form of courtesy. If I am presumptuous enough to interpret you, the least I can do is give you the option to say to the strangers who read the book that it was not you but someone else.

On the other hand, the use of pseudonyms can be enormously frustrating to the community itself, for whom the ethnography is interpreted as or expected to be a form of local history. When I asked people in the community if they would prefer that the second edition of the book use real names rather than pseudonyms, many of them said yes, with comments such as, "Everyone knows the identity of the village anyway," and "You can't get the flavor of the people without using their real nicknames and stories."

On the other hand, some members of the community argued persuasively to retain the privacy conferred by the use of pseudonyms. "If you say the name, people will react with their old antagonisms, their knowing the place and what it means to them rather than what you're trying to say." The cultural pattern of keeping a low profile discussed in Chapter 5 is alive and well in the 21st century, working its contradictory way through the public media of newsletters, the Internet, and increased visibility on radio and television. Over the last 10 years, newsletters produced by local historical societies (*Comann Eachdraidh*) have proliferated through the Western Isles (in part due to the efforts of the Western Isles Council to promote local projects) and have provided a framework for rendering local gossip into the formal patterns of legitimate history. But the old rules still exist. In 2003, while showing photographs taken in 1970–71 to a family involved in the production of the local newsletter, I was struck by the ease with which a photograph of a man who had once been much admired for his scholarship was eliminated because his death was tainted. Only some histories are acceptable, and the white-hot fires of local gossip rather than the cooler heat of analysis are the arenas within which history is negotiated.

It was the intense hunger for local details demonstrated in pouring over the 1970–71 photographs that persuaded me to maintain the use of pseudonyms. By doing so I am on the one hand adhering to the community rule of the functionality of secrets: by veiling events with the polite pretension of an alternative interpretation, peace is more likely to be maintained (in this sense, communities are inveterate practitioners of pragmatic postmodernism in their efforts to maintain the viability of alternative interpretations and thereby keep their options open).

On the other hand, by using pseudonyms I am also upholding a social science commitment to the abstract over the concrete. If I describe the famous incident of a local man who saved the lives of his men during a war-time disaster and was awarded an MBE by the Crown, I want to be able to use this incident to describe abstract patterns of class (crofters and charwomen are awarded the MBE, Oxford dons receive the OBE) or life cycle (the movement from Bottle to Bible), rather than subject the story to arguments about whether it was the man's maternal or paternal uncle who taught him the sailing skills that enabled him to save the crew. The difference between local histories and ethnographies is the difference between the value of the concrete and the value of the abstract. In local histories, the concrete details are ends in themselves. In social science, the ethnography provides the concrete details from which the abstract laws of culture in ethnology are generated.

On the other hand, the use of pseudonyms raises issues of reliability and validity, important concepts in social science. If the concrete details are wrong, then the abstractions are wrong. The choice of pseudonyms presents a Scylla and Charybdis choice: the danger of being mired in the concrete vs. the danger of having one's (possibly wrong) interpretations uncorrectable. The "scientific" anthropologists would say that interpretation must be faithful to the facts, whereas the "postmodernists" would say it is all interpretation anyway. I belong to both traditions. As a scientific humanist, I try to walk gracefully as well as firmly in the world of negotiated meanings.

Thus, the landscape on which I write is both factual and poetic. The choice of pseudonyms draws heavily on inner landscapes. The pseudonym Geall used in the first edition is a Gaelic word with multiple meanings. Similar in appearance to both Gael (Gaelic-speaker/Highlander) and Gall (Lowlander, foreigner), it can mean, depending on the context, a bet or wager, great fondness, mortgage, and promise, pledge or vow. I chose the name to make explicit my sense of being somewhere in between Gael and Gall in writing the book, as well as to convey the elements of risk, fondness, and promise that accompanied the writing—a complex mishmash of sentiment.

Over the years, my inner landscape has grown a little more orderly, which has prompted me to change the pseudonym of the community. The name change, from Geall to Ciall, draws on the ability of the Gaelic word *ciall* to convey both love and wisdom, as expressed, for example, in the poetry of Sorley MacLean (see, for example, "A Chiall's a Ghraidh" in MacLean 1999: 22–23). Scotland is a place I have loved for almost 40 years, and from it I have gained some small wisdom.

The community, of course, is not changed by the name. It changes, of course, and this book attempts to document some of these changes. Like two friendly strangers we grow old, complexly, together. This book is a gift of reason, a product of love.

A NOTE ON NAMES

Gaelic speakers use English names as well as Gaelic patronymics and nicknames (Parman 1976). A child is officially baptized with a first and last name, such as "John MacDonald." His Christian name is usually derived from his grandparents, or from a deceased aunt or uncle; parents "take turns" recognizing their side of the family. The surname is that of the father. This name, which is recorded in the parish register, is often referred to as the "English name," and is used in school, in applying for crofter subsidies, in the minutes of the Village Hall meetings, in registering with the Weavers Union—in other words, in all contexts associated with record-keeping, bureaucratic, English-speaking urban society.

In addition, individuals have what are often referred to as their "Gaelic names," the patronymics and nicknames with which individuals are labeled in the informal arena of community interaction. Both a son and a daughter are identified patronymically (for example, Inis Mhurchaidh Inis Iain, "Angus [the son] of Murdo [the son] of Angus [the son] of John"; Catriona Inis Iain, "Katherine [the daughter] of Angus [the son] of John"); or, if they were raised in the home of their maternal grandfather, as when a woman bears an illegitimate child, by the mother's father. The important thing is to be able to identify someone, which is done by which household a child is raised in, or by some significant event, physical feature, mispronounced word, or other personalizing identifier, as well as by kinship connections. Patronymics and nicknames are vitally important in identifying individuals in a context in which there are so few surnames (in Ciall, there were only 22 surnames among 169 heads of household, and 10 of these surnames accounted for 86 percent of the households); they are also a source of humor and a record of historical interaction. Nicknames record a person's place of origin (e.g., Mor Scalpay from the island of Scalpay, Domhnuill Bhrue from the neighboring village of Brue), the occupations of a person or his ancestors (e.g., Inis Gobha descended from the village blacksmith, Cailean the Post who delivers the mail), distinctive physical characteristics (e.g., Murdag Gobi with a large nose), and embarrassing moments (e.g., Peter Squeak who mispronounced the English word "picturesque"). Some nicknames are nonsense words; and like a Rorschach, they invite historical inventions that meet the needs of the present.

SUMMARY OF CHANGES

A number of changes have occurred in Ciall between 1970 and 2003. A two-lane road has replaced the single-track lane between the village and the town of Stornoway, and more people have cars to drive over it. They speed through the community, stopping less often to offer lifts. The bus service is excellent, with three trips a day back and forth from Stornoway at £1.25; the bus driver no longer stops at his mother's house for dinner while the passengers wait, but personal modifications continue to be made (as for example when the bus driver, following his job description, let a partially blind man off at the end of the road; and when he found that the man had gone the wrong way, vowed to always leave people who needed extra attention at their own door). The community has a sewage system, and water from the taps comes out clear rather than peat-brown.

As services improve, the community is at the same time more vibrant and more lonely. Almost every house has a phone and at least one television (at a cost of £110 per year in tax, in addition to payments for special channels and programs), which has on the one hand cut down on the visiting, and on the other has provided new opportunities for humor.[7] Television divides even the members of a household, as a wife listens to "Coronation Street" in the kitchen, her husband to sheep trial news in the parlor, and their daughter to "So You Want to Be a Millionaire" upstairs. The hills now sprout cellular phone masts. One of the most startling changes is the streetlights (no more fumbling for torches in the pitch-black dark, as long as you stay on the road). In the past, during the visiting that goes on through the long New Year's Eve, you guided your steps between the lighted houses. The small lights on the dark moor were beacons of hospitality. Now the orange spotlights only exacerbate the loneliness of the dark.

---

[7]When television first came to the island in the 1960s, the church was opposed to it. An elder said to someone, "I hear you've got the television," to which the man replied, "Yes, and it's got a knob on it that says on and off, which is more than I can say for you."

Interpretations of "junk" : From recyclable resources to eyesore

Another startling change is the disappearance of the "junk" (old cars, tractors, harvesters, other machinery) that has served the community as a source of recyclable parts. The Western Isles Council has placed "skips" (large dumpsters) all over the island and has purchased a mobile car crusher to clean up the countryside.

Fraser Macdonald (2003) is in the process of photographing this old equipment before it disappears. The identification of certain aspects of history to retain and others to reject continues. Ancient stone brochs, old houses, and old machinery do not register as items of historical significance; all are subject to easy destruction.

The village has a new school, which has computers, Gaelic-medium classes, and a swimming pool that is open to community use. The old school is being converted to a community center.

The sense of the exile persists at many levels: the "exiles" who live on the mainland or abroad, who return at New Year and during the summer for short, intense visits and are nostalgic in between; the jack-Gaels isolated from the language by a generation or two, who dream of the Gaidhealtachd with that peculiar intensity of the exile and the refugee; the "exiles" from paradise, those for whom the catechism still resonates as they meditate on lost perfection, the glorious union of mind and heart embodied in a supernatural being (Christ, the only perfect man), compared with whom they are imperfect and doomed; the depressed critical intellect, the overactive conscience, the Presbyterian Scot in his agony.

The commercialism of international business penetrates here as elsewhere. Bathrooms are filled with aromatherapy candles and soaps, electric-heated showers have replaced the water heated at the back of the fireplace, and touch-lights illuminate the dark. A few people travel to places where they don't have relatives, just for the sake of travel. Children choose careers based on what they see on television and draw on a wealth of outside experience to name their children; words like "wow" and "brilliant" punctuate Gaelic speech. Policies promulgated by the Western Isles Council on bilingualism and tourism result in bilingual signs for streets, banks, and communities, and self-conscious signs combining English and Gaelic that direct tourists to local sights. "Welcome to (Gaelic version of village name)." A sign, "To the Shore," directs tourists to the beach where picnic tables have been set up. Posts mark the walking trails that local people have walked, un-self-consciously, for generations. An entire black-house street has been resurrected in Carloway that, when you come over the hill and see it leading down to the shore, has all the appearance of a reappearing Brigadoon; the houses have been modified to serve as meeting places and bed and breakfast services for tourists.

Harris Tweed continues to be woven, but the number of weavers in Ciall is diminishing as the weavers switch from single-width to double-width looms (but certain areas of the island, such as Ness, have switched to the new looms and increased in number). The sight of single-width tweeds sitting on fence posts to be picked up by the tweed van is gone; for the heavier double-width tweeds, a forklift comes to the door.

Sheep remain the primary focus of crofting activity, but the island-wide fanks have declined, replaced by fencing of allotments near the township. Most hay is imported from the mainland in plastic-wrapped bundles. The amount of work done on the croft appears to be inversely proportional to the number of vehicles (tractors, vans, four-wheel-drive vehicles) now available to do the work. Whereas one tractor might have done the work of two townships to bring in the hay in 1970, many households now have tractors that they use to move the imported hay, feeding units, and sheep from one part of their crofting land to another.

New businesses have emerged: fish farms and wind farms, the harvest of air and water. Many of the businesses on the island are owned by foreigners—by Germans and especially by Norwegians. The new "farms" are much more capital-intensive than the old farms; it takes at least 5 years of intensive investment before returns can be seen. The fish farms are not cottage industries but major industrial investments, with all the pollution, expense, thievery, and dangers of

Susan Parman

Susan Parman

From haystacks to hay bundles

a fluctuating market threatening the value of the investment. Although grants are available, local investors find it difficult to enter the market.

Fewer fishing boats leave from Stornoway harbor, and their catch is shellfish for the mainland rather than herring delivered by fish van, to be salted and hung over the Aga stove in local communities. Contrary to Lord Leverhulme's dream of Lewis and Harris serving as the center of a vast fishing fleet in the North Atlantic, the major locus of fishing in Scotland is in the north east; and it is this region that will be most affected by the recent decision of the European

Fish farm on west side of Lewis

Commission's Council of Fisheries to reduce haddock quota from 104,000 to 51,000 tonnes to protect stock.

Few people now cut peat, although there is still some pride of peat ("The incomers buy tons of coal, whereas we're more economical"; "I almost called off the wedding when I saw how poor the quality of his village's peat banks were"). Instead, coal, electric heating, and central heating with oil have replaced peat fires. The beautiful Aga stoves with their economical burning of peat or coal, the centers of warmth in the kitchen, are disappearing, replaced by electric stoves. The use of oil makes it difficult to tell if people are in and about and prepared for visitors, as fewer chimneys smoke.

Funerals still go on. Wakes are held, and the men still "take the lift" in sharing the burden of carrying the coffin to the hearse or graveyard. Where depression once resulted in people "going for the treatment" to Craig Dunain, the mental hospital near Inverness, it is now handled by "local community treatment." Old people whose siblings or spouses have died, or whose children have left, continue to receive support from neighbors and community services, but many are now choosing to live in retirement homes in Stornoway.

Some of the same sources of conflict exist. Poachers still thumb their noses at the laird (but the peat lunch is no longer the stage on which to display your impudence by serving salmon, because even families that cut the peat go home for lunch in their vehicles), and the Parish of Lochs, because of its rich fishing resources and history of poaching, is still identified (by other parishes) as the most likely to produce stories in the Stornoway *Gazette* about conflicts with the police. But as more cars come and go on the ferries, and as the world changes, the stories of scandal and shame include a new element: the taking of drugs (everything from Ecstasy to heroin), and in a few cases, actual dealing.

At the same time, two actions continue to be defined as the greatest evils: thievery and adultery. To steal from someone who would have given to you is to rob the relationship of obligation. To commit adultery is to threaten the web of kinship. Sex has the potential to create chaos out of kinship. (See Chapters 5 and 6.)

The bachelors, "boys" until they marry, still prowl the night highways, traveling between dances, finding privacy in their cars and behind the diminishing peat stacks. Musical talent continues to spring up in local bands (while at the same time, the bands listen to and borrow from the tangled, inventive multinational musical trends that create, for example, the Leningrad Cowboys—a Finnish band popular in the Baltic that mocks both the Americans and the Russians—and Scotland's own Battlefield Band that plays jazz and polkas with bagpipes). The new year remains a time of visiting, renewing friendships and rehashing feuds, and taking steps to make new alliances. It is also a time for people vulnerable to criticism or attack to keep a low profile; amity can turn on a dime, feelings just below the skin lash out. It is a time when declarations of marriage are made as well as the beginning of slights and missteps, irrational explosions that can reverberate down the generations.

Although there is some sense that times have changed ("People expect to have more time for themselves"), the communitarian spirit of mutual aid remains strong, as it does generally throughout Scotland. You do what you can to help your neighbors, despite the occasional feud and dispute. And the fire of hospitality burns bright, along with the rich humor from which new nicknames and anecdotes, new histories, are generated.

2/History and the Celt

My grandfather used to say the Big Vision made the Indian, but the white man invented him.

—William Least Heat Moon, *Blue Highways*

What turned this isolated medley of different peoples into a nation both Scottish and European, proud of its nationality almost to the point of obsession yet contributing to and drawing from the mainstream of European civilisation, and why when the inhabitants had once ceased to think of themselves in terms of Pict, Scot, Gallovidian, Angle, Briton and Norseman did they form themselves anew into the hardly less formidable divisions of Highlands and Lowlands which had not been envisaged before?

—T. C. Smout, *A History of the Scottish People 1560–1830* (1969:23)

History is always a cultural act. In other words, from an anthropological view, a group's conceptions of the past are part of the cultural patterning of human behavior. Why are certain aspects of the past remembered? How and why is the past interpreted in certain ways? When did "the Celt" begin to be seen as a significant category, and by whom and why? The Celt, like the American Indian referred to by William Least Heat Moon, has been remembered, forgotten, reinvented, interpreted, and reinterpreted by various groups of people—writers such as John Cleland (the 18th-century author of the highly successful pornography, *Fanny Hill,* who was obsessed with the idea that Ancient Celtic was the root of all European languages) and those Scottish Nationalists who define Scottish nationality with reference to Celtic characteristics, crofters (who by and large ignore the definition of themselves as Celts, except in certain contexts), or anthropologists (whose uses of the concept of the Celt is highly variable).

By writing this book I am also reinventing and reinterpreting the Celt, establishing certain linkages between past, present, and future. One of my motives for doing so is, quite explicitly, to make a cultural contribution to a people I admire and respect—not to idealize them or place them at the center of the universe (as the originators of European culture or universal language, for example) but to provide a series of examples of the many ways in which a people have defined themselves and been defined by others. I am reflecting my own culture in assuming that such knowledge is good, that it creates greater opportunity for discussion and self-examination, and that it shifts crofters from the status of victims to the status of self-conscious, active participators in the creation of their own culture.

WHAT IS A CELT?

The word "Celt" (selt, kelt) used today was invented by the classical civilizations of Greece and Rome, and has been continuously reinvented, reinterpreted, and re-signified by various European groups. The Greeks used the term "Keltoi," and the Romans "Celtae," to refer to a variety of peoples living in Europe north of the Alps.

The word "Celt" has been given numerous etymologies. Skeat's *Etymological Dictionary* translates it as "warriors," related to Icelandic *hildr* (war), Lithuanian *kalti* (to strike), and Latin *per-cellere* (to strike through, beat down). James Logan (1833), noting the similarity of the word *gealta* (Gaelic for whitened, from *geal,* white) to Celtae, suggests that the Greeks applied the term to denote "the milky whiteness of the skin."

Anthropologists frequently encounter the problem of how to name the people that they study (for example, they eschew the term "Eskimo," which is a Cree term meaning "eaters of raw meat," and prefer the native term "Inuit," meaning "the people"). Is the term "Celt" an indigenous term meaning, like Inuit, "we the people"? Or is it a descriptive term given to them by strangers? Chadwick (1970:51) assumes that "Their essential homogeneity can be seen from the name Keltoi . . . by which they were known to the Greeks from the fifth century." But can we use the existence of a name to assume the existence of a homogeneous people? What exactly does the name signify? Perhaps the term referred not to a particular unified people but was a description of all peoples of Europe who appeared to the incoming Greeks to be white, as opposed to Ethiopian.

The term "Celt" may have been derived from a Greek descriptive term for the barbarian hordes ("warriors") they encountered, or "Gaul" may have been the term used by the Romans (either their own or borrowed) to describe fair-haired, light-eyed peoples of northern Europe as opposed to darker-skinned populations of North Africa; or it may have been an aboriginal term that the Celts used to refer to themselves, like Inuit (note that Caesar refers to "a people who call themselves Celts"). The classical references to the names support several interpretations and demonstrate that historical interpretations may be put to symbolic purpose to argue for ethnicity or origins.

Much recent knowledge of Celtic prehistory is a byproduct of separatist, nationalistic movements in modern times. In Scotland, the wealth from the extraction of oil from North Sea beds has added fuel to the embers of Scottish nationalism that have been smoldering since the union of the crowns, and this renewed political goal is nurtured by scholarly evidence of ethnic distinctiveness. But the separatist movement is only one dimension of the long-term evolution of Scottish identity in which the symbol of the Celt, in various ways and with various characteristics emphasized at different times, has played a significant defining role. The following examples illustrate changes in the symbolic uses of Celtic identity.

WHAT IS EUROPE?

> Europe, in the most early ages, was inhabited by one race of men, whose antiquity is enveloped in inscrutable darkness. . . . Europe and Celtica were . . . synonymous: the sole inhabitants, from the Pillars of Hercules to Archangel, and from the banks of the Euxine to the German Ocean, being Celts. . . .
>
> —James Logan, *The Scotish* [sic] *Gael* (1833)

When did Europe become distinctively European? With the Greeks? With the Romans? With the Celts?

From the way that every academic discipline legitimizes itself by tracing its origins to the Greeks (the first ethnographer-historian was Herodotus, the first mathematician was Pythagoras, the first chemist was Democritus, the first evolutionist was Thales, etc.), you might assume that the Greeks are the currently preferred originators of European culture. (The Romans come in a close second.) It is interesting that of all the case studies in cultural anthropology concerned with European societies, Ernestine Friedl's book on Greece (*Vasilika*) is in continuous high demand, probably because, as Michael Herzfeld suggests and then explores (1987), "Ancient Greece is the idealized spiritual and intellectual ancestor of Europe."

Current preoccupation with the Greeks stems from the Renaissance, when humanist scholars challenged medieval genealogies (which excluded the Greeks and Romans from an ancestral relationship to a Christian Europe because they were pagans) and recreated the Greeks as honorable ancestors.

With the Celtic revival beginning in the 18th century, some scholars began to argue that the Celts, not the Greeks and Romans, deserved credit for making Europe distinctive. Contrasting points of view are represented by Piggott (who considers the Celt to be irrelevant to understanding the reality of European tradition) and Chadwick (who says that the Celt is the fundamental creator of European tradition).

Piggott (1965) emphasizes Western Europe's cultural linkage with Greco-Roman civilization. He is not concerned with the unique contribution of the Celts but with the contrast between barbarian Europe and classical, civilized Europe. Piggott argues that between barbarian Europe and civilized Rome existed a "moral barrier," an incompatibility of cultures; the Romans were innovative, logical, and law-abiding whereas the Celts (along with other barbarians) were conservative, emotional, nomadic, and likely to settle arguments by continuous feuding rather than by rational law. Although he recognizes that prehistoric, nonliterate peoples contributed to European origins (cf. Piggott 1965:257–260), he gives the greatest credit for origins to Roman civilization, saying that its achievement was "immensely superior to anything brought about by the barbarians."

Piggott portrays the modern Celt as a backwater drag on the progressive thrust of European civilization, a remnant of the early barbarian strain that contributed to but was not the principal shaper of European identity. He draws a parallel between Tacitus's description of "lazy barbarians" and an 18th-century description of Scottish Highlanders to make the point that "the Early Iron Age had perhaps its longest survival" in Scotland (1965:229). The social context in which he can imbue modern Highlanders with the connotations of "lazy barbarians," however, is a modern one: the socioeconomic conditions that have produced the crofter. (The crofter is decidedly not lazy, but this stereotype is perpetuated in jokes and stories and stems from the anomalous features of the crofting situation.)

Nora Chadwick, on the other hand, suggests that the Celts provided the foundation of a distinctive European civilization. Her book, *The Celts,* was published in 1970, two years before her death; it put the cap on a lifetime of research on the Celts. Instead of looking at the modern British Celt as Piggott does (as a drag on progressive civilization, as an archaic remnant of pre-European culture), Chadwick interprets present Gaelic speakers as precious relics of the past, original European culture. Chadwick says (1970:8) that the British Celts "have left us the most complete picture of their [ancient Celtic] civilization, having enjoyed freedom from foreign, especially Roman, conquest longer than their continental neighbors—and in parts escaped it altogether—and thus preserved their own culture in a purer form." Celts are represented as an energetic, inventive people who introduced the use of iron to northern Europe, as well as "Europe's first major industrial revolution, its first common market, its first international court of arbitration" (Severy 1977:588). These "barbarians" gave soap to the Greeks and Romans, emancipated their women, and championed abstract art.

WHO ARE THE FRENCH AND THE ENGLISH?

The symbol of the Celt has been used not only as a symbol of European tradition but to assist in identifying specific nations. Piggott (1967) traces the French use of the Gaul to define French identity; and in one chapter of a fascinating book called *The Aryan Myth: A History of Racist and Nationalist Ideas in Europe* (1974), Poliakov discusses the controversy in France between what were eventually perceived to be "two races" of France, the Franks (Germanic) and Gauls (Celtic)—the latter defined, in the 19th century, as having larger respiratory organs, rounder heads, and smaller intestines. (In a paper called "Celtic Ethnic Kinship and the Problem of Being English," Maryon McDonald [1986] describes how members of the Breton movement in Brittany manage to define themselves as more Celtic than the French [who have linked themselves with the Celtic Gauls]—by linking themselves not with the Gauls but with the Britons of the British Isles.)

The English, on the other hand, have linked themselves with German rather than French identity. When Tacitus's *Germania* was widely read throughout Europe during the 16th century, many countries linked their origins to the Germans (as did, in this pre-Revolutionary time, the French). It was suggested that the English were a pure, not a mixed, nation, because the various invading groups—Danes, Normans, Angles, Saxons—were all German. The English ("Germans") were contrasted with Celts; the English believed that Germanic values and sentiments made Europe great. David Hume, a Scotsman, supported these views in his 18th-century *History of England,* in which he described Celts as incapable of enjoying the freedom available to them after the Romans left Britain, in contrast with the Germans who manifested the sentiments (such as liberty, honor, equality, and valor), which made them superior to "the rest of mankind" and the source of European greatness.

According to Poliakov (1974), the French Revolution helped to persuade the English that they were Germanic, and a wave of pro-German, anti-Celtic sentiment swept England and Lowland Scotland in the first half of the 19th century—indeed, until the unification of Germany in 1871 when the German Empire claimed the word Teutonic[1] for themselves and denied racial purity to other groups.

At the same time, countermovements stressed the Celtic origins of Britain. McDonald (1986:335), quoting Piggott, credits a Welshman named Lhuyd for translating into English the writings of a Breton scholar (a Benedictine monk from Brittany named Dom Pezron) who had traced the "cradle" of France to the Gauls using biblical authority. Various works by British authors begin to appear that linked not only the ancient Britons but contemporary British populations to the Gaul-Celt. From the 18th century on, "Celtic Druids" (perceived to be the religious leaders of the British Iron Age) took over Paleolithic and Bronze Age monuments and were linked with various nationalist movements.

WHO ARE THE SCOTS?

West Register House in Charlotte Square, Edinburgh, has an exhibit intended to illustrate the history of Scotland. Case 1, "The Making of the Kingdom," includes a picture of Scota, the daughter of Pharaoh, arriving on the shores of Scotland—as represented by John Fordun (c. 1320–c. 1384), thought to have been a priest in Aberdeen who gathered material for an early history of Scotland called *Scotichronicon.* It was important during the Middle Ages to establish a link with the geography of the Bible.

The term "Scotland" was established by the 12th or 13th century. Despite Fordun's picturesque rendition of Scota, the name Scotland actually means the land of the Scotti—Latin for the Irish. The Scotti were a tribe from Ireland that settled in the region now known as Argyll. The kingdom of Scotland emerged in the 11th century from the amalgamation of four tribal groups (Scots, Britons, Picts, and Angles).

By the 18th century, a link had been forged between the ancient Celts and contemporary British populations in Wales, Scotland, Cornwall, and the Isle of Man,

---

[1]The term "Teutonic" has its own complicated history. The 1910 *Encyclopaedia Britannica* says the Teutonic peoples were that branch of the Celts located in northwestern Europe, especially Scandinavia, in contrast with the Alpine Celts located in central Europe. However, Nora Chadwick says that the word "Teutones" is a "cognate with a Celtic common noun *tuath* [people] . . . and our evidence on the whole suggests that the Teutons or Germans were a division of the Celtic peoples" (Chadwick 1970:53).

as illustrated by James Logan's (1833) statement that "The Scots' Highlanders are the unmixed descendants of the Celts, who were the aboriginal inhabitants of Europe, and the first known colonists of Britain." To many Scotsmen (if not to David Hume), Scotland as a whole was Celtic in identity, an idea expressed in modern writings today. For example, Moffat (1984:29), described as "a deliberately ambitious course for Scottish schools," states that "While the peoples who had populated Scotland before had brought many new ideas, the Celts, more than any, laid the foundation on which would be built the Scottish nationality. Even today Celtic blood flows abundantly in the veins of the Scottish people."

The linkage of the Scot with the Celt, done primarily by educated Scots, was fueled by the publication of Macpherson's Ossianic poems beginning in 1760. Chapman (1978) traces the emergence of a dialectic between Celt and Anglo-Saxon in Britain that has continued to the present day, and that plays an important role in understanding the conception of the crofter as the 20th-century embodiment of the Celt.

Celtic Christianity and the "Learned Scots"

Distributed along a ragged coastline and separated from the Lowlands by rough terrain, the Highland colony of Scots retained their close connection with Ireland by sea, a connection that persisted under the Vikings, and under the Celtic-Norse Lords of the Isles. During the sixth century, Ireland sent Christian missionaries to convert the Picts. The Angles of southern Britain were pagans and described as "intractable men, and of a hard and barbarous disposition" (Bede in Anderson 1908:15). To be "barbarian" at this time was to be non-Christian. Latin was the civilized tongue, and the Scots were "deeply learned" (cf. Bede in Anderson 1908:49).

Political Unification (9th–11th centuries): Scots as Barbarians

The change from "learned" to "barbarian" occurred as the many small squabbling groups in southern and northern Britain formed shifting alignments. In A.D. 843 the Scots united with the Picts, and fought the Norsemen who had established settlements along the western and northern coasts of the mainland and occupied the Hebrides, Orkney, and Shetland. In A.D. 924, still fighting the Vikings, the Scots formed an alliance with the English (later used as the basis for English claims to sovereignty over Scotland), but eventually allied themselves with the Norsemen against England. With malicious enthusiasm, the English chronicler Symeon of Durham describes a battle between English and Scots in which "old men and women were some beheaded by swords, others stuck with spears like pigs destined for food. . . . the Scots, crueller than beasts, delighted in this cruelty as in the sight of games" [Anderson 1908:92]). During the 11th century, Malcolm II gained the rich lands of the Lothians in what is now Lowland Scotland from the kingdom of Northumbria.

Under Malcolm II's grandson, Scots, Picts, Angles, and British were united in the kingdom that by the 12th or 13th centuries was known as Scotland. The Hebrides were recovered from the Norse by the 13th century, Orkney and Shetland by the 15th century.

Anglicization of Town and Court: The Uncouth Scot

When William the Conqueror came ashore from France at Hastings on September 29, 1066, the king of the Scots, Malcolm Canmore, fought on the side of the English and gave shelter to a fugitive named Edgar the Etheling, whose sister, Margaret, he married. From the point of view of the malicious Symeon, this noble, religious, Saxon princess reformed the barbarous ("a man to wit of the greatest ferocity and with a bestial disposition" [Anderson 1908:102]) Scottish king ("And by her zeal and industry the king himself laid aside his barbarity of manners, and became more honourable and more refined" [Anderson 1908:93]).

Under the influence of "St. Margaret," the Celtic kingdom that Malcolm governed became anglicized. Celtic-speaking courts became English speaking and centered in the Lowland south. English clergy instructed the previously "learned Scots" in the error of their ways. Margaret bore six sons, none of whom bore her husband's name; four were named after Saxon kings of England. English merchants and priests settled in Scotland, and lands and offices were granted to Saxon nobles. The rule of the Celtic mormaors or earls ceased in the 12th century as settlers were brought in to break the power of the Celts. Feudalism contributed to anglicization, as did the introduction of English trade and the provision of charters for Scottish burghs (an English concept).

Only in the Highlands was feudalism unable to displace the clan system. Gradually a distinction emerged between urban (the civilized English) and rural (the rustic, uncouth Celt requiring civilization). The Norse-dominated isles remained separate.

By the middle of the 13th century, England had emerged as a powerful nation from the fusion of Normans and Anglo-Saxons, marking the beginning of Scotland's decline into a weaker partner of the dominant south. When, at the very end of the 13th century Scotland was weakened by a problem of succession to the throne, Edward I of England declared himself feudal overlord of Scotland and, with the support of the Anglo-Norman barons of the Lowlands, invaded. The resulting devastation created widespread famine, ruined agriculture, and greatly weakened centralized authority. Scottish chieftains could defy the crown with impunity; barons were miniature kings. The southern, fertile lands were ravaged, which prevented the emergence of towns and a municipal spirit, which in turn supported the feudal aristocracy and the power of local lairds.

Crown versus Laird: The Feuding Celt

In the political alignments of these times, Highlanders did not always support Scottish nationalism. In fact, many of them were fighting not the English but the Scottish crown. Because of the weakness of the crown and the ravages of war, poverty was widespread and many Highlanders raided with impunity. In the 15th and even as late as the 17th century, Aberdeen and Inverness paid ransom to protect themselves from fire, rape, and thieving; Edinburgh replaced Perth as the capital of Scotland because of the latter's dangerous proximity to the Highlands (in the late 14th century it had about 16,000 people). In the land of the "learned Scots," the first university was founded at St. Andrews at the beginning of the

15th century, and not a single Scottish baron could sign his own name (cf. Buckle 1970:36–54).

In the Highlands, the clans feuded with the intensity of any society lacking in centralized authority. The house of Argyll, the senior branch of the clan Campbell, played a prominent role in Highland history (cf. Cregeen 1968), changing sides in response to the times. It sided with Robert Bruce against Edward I, supported the Crown throughout the 14th and 15th centuries, and then supported Protestantism against the Crown in the 16th.

In 1345, MacDonald had assumed the role of "Lord of the Isles," heir of a Celto-Norse kingship. He held court, granted charters, and negotiated treaties with foreign powers (Cregeen 1968:156). In the 15th century this independent kingdom constituted a third of the area of Scotland and was a major threat to the Crown. Between 1475 and 1607 members of the house of Argyll rose to prominence by destroying the power of the MacDonald clan, which controlled the Hebrides and much of the coast of the western Highlands. The "barbarity" of the Highlands was in large part a result of the chaos that ensued from this destruction of the authority of the Lords of the Isles.

With the aid of the house of Argyll, the Anglo-Lowland dominance of the Crown extended to the islands through various forms of legislation. James VI of Scotland, now James I of Scotland and England, sent a special commissioner to the clan chiefs of the Hebrides. Meeting on the island of Iona, one of the Inner Hebridean islands in Argyllshire, these chiefs agreed to the "Statutes of Icolmkill" in 1609. The chiefs confessed to their "great misery, barbarity, and poverty," which the statutes were designed to correct. The statutes required the establishment of inns, the elimination of traveling bards who with harp and song kept alive the clan traditions, and specified that every Highlander who had at least 60 head of cattle must send his eldest son or daughter to school in the Lowlands to learn English. The latter statute's purpose: that the *"Irishe language which is one of the chief and principall causis of the continewance of barbaritie and incivilitie amongis the inhabitants of the Isles and Ileylandis may be abolisheit and removeit."*

The Romantic Celt

Politically, socially, and economically, the Celtic Highlander was drawn into the sphere of Anglo-Lowland dominance. Long before Bonnie Prince Charlie and the Battle of Culloden, clan life was disintegrating. The clan had been a fighting force composed of the head of the clan, his close kinsmen (the *daoine uaisle* or gentry, the chieftains whose responsibility was to organize clan fighting), and commoners. The *daoine uaisle* was supported by gifts of land from the clan head.

In the 17th century, this prescribed right to land became instead a long lease or "tack." Some clan land was let directly to small tenants who had no lease and paid rent in kind, money, and service. As early as 1710, the second Duke of Argyll offered tacks of farms in open auction to the highest bidders (Cregeen 1968:169). In 1726, on forfeiture of the estate of the late Earl of Seaforth, the inhabitants of Ciall gave evidence that they possessed their town for the sum of "two hundred and twenty-four pounds sixteen shillings Scots money thirty eight bolls one firlote meal twelve stones butter and twelve mutton."

Long after it had been destroyed at home, the clan was transported overseas by displaced clansmen who served as well-integrated fighting units in the American War of Independence. The clan concept was "transported" in another sense as well—it was reinvented as part of a romantic conception of the "Highland tradition," which gained prominence among British intellectuals in the 18th and 19th centuries. With the rise of the house of Argyll as a stabilizing influence in the Highlands, the symbolic defeat of the clans at Culloden, the decline of Gaelic, and the severing of the bonds that linked Highland Scotland with Ireland, the Highlands no longer constituted a threat to an anglicized Britain but represented a core of Scottish autochthony that vitalized and distinguished Scottish, British, and even European identity. Chapman (1978) describes the process by which the Celt became spiritualized and feminized; the much-criticized Trevor-Roper (1983) describes the invention of various aspects of Highland tradition (see Chapter 4 for a discussion of tweed and kilts); Ray (2001), quoting Ezra Pound ("What thou lov'st well is thy true heritage"), analyzes the replacement of history by heritage among the descendants of Scottish immigrants to the Americas, and Hunter (1994) provides details of their settlement and, quoting McPhee, the "atavistic vibration" with which they remember the past, as through a diasporic veil.

The Crofting Celt

While the intelligentsia of Britain were romanticizing the Celt, economic and social changes were occurring that contributed to the symbolic merger of crofter and Celt.

Devine (1988) has suggested that Scottish crofting society emerged as a distinctive social and economic system by the 1840s. While land was being consolidated in the Lowlands and the eastern and southern Highlands to form large farms in the late 18th and early 19th centuries (a process occurring throughout Europe), the land along the west coast of mainland Scotland north of Fort William, and in the Inner and Outer Hebrides, was, from a landlord's point of view, more suited to animal husbandry. From the point of view of the local population, however, the cultivation of oats, barley, and, from the mid-18th century, potatoes, was at least as important as their livestock. Cultivation was done communally in the sense that narrow strips of arable land, scattered between uncultivated mountain and heath on which cattle and sheep were grazed, were held in run-rig (from the Gaelic *Roinn-nuth,* "division run"); that is, several families were joint tenants on a farm, and took turns working the arable strips. On the south side of Ciall Bay beside the sea strand is a cluster of ruins called *sean bhaile* (the old village). Talked about as an ancient remnant of the days when arable land was a scarce commodity and fishing was vital to village economy, it reflects the settlement pattern typical of run-rig.

Although the western Highlands and Islands are usually portrayed as rain-leached, acidic grazing lands more suitable to animal husbandry than to cultivation, and pre-Culloden Highland clans are usually portrayed as a seminomadic pastoral people whose wealth and status was measured in cattle, by the second half of the 18th century and the beginning of the 19th century, the rapid population growth resulted in farming strategies that emphasized arable land rather

The remains of the old village (sean bhaile), *most recently used as fish-drying sheds*

than livestock production. According to Dodgshon (1993:680–681), "Far from sharing the same perception of resources, the interests of landlord and tenant conflicted even before the clearances, the one concerned with the primacy of stock and the other with the primacy of crop."

The agricultural revolution sweeping Britain took several forms. On the one hand, many small tenants were swept off the land to make way for extensive sheep farms. The "cleared" population emigrated to the colonies or poured into the industrial Lowland towns. On the other hand, the fragmented land holdings of run-rig began to be "lotted" into the individual, compact holdings called crofts; these were organized in crofting townships as landlords sought to distribute land to a growing population, many of whom constituted families "cleared" from the sheep farms. Some people in Ciall are still considered "Uigeachs," descended from families cleared from the parish of Uig (see Moisley 1961).

According to Dodgshon (1993:682), Benbecula was reorganized from run-rig joint farms into crofting townships between 1799 and 1829; Ciall was reorganized in the mid-19th century; also see Gray's 1952 article on the abolition of run-rig, Moisley's 1961 monograph on the parish of Uig, and Moisley's 1962 discussion of crofting in the Highlands and Islands. The clustered villages or hamlets (*clachans*) were broken up and houses were isolated on compact strips of individually held land in linear, single-street villages. The street ran along high ground, connecting the houses; and from the street ran a long strip of land, the croft, that included well-drained upland as well as marshy lowland. The new arrangement gave everyone a fair share of good and bad land but reduced the flexibility of the run-rig system in which the "rigs" were reallocated according to need and ability. It also reduced the need for communal management of the land. Although crofting townships still require communal action regarding the undivided hill grazing land held in common, the trend toward individualistic use of land, reflected in apportionment requests today, began with the transition from run-rig (in the words of Richards [1973:63] "a labor-intensive, communal economy") to crofting ("a land-intensive, individualistic framework"). It may be argued that the Crofters Commission is functioning today as the communal conscience of the crofting system, trying to make judgments about what is good for the community as a whole as once the landlords did on the joint farms via their factors, grounds officers, and township constables. And as land is purchased and decrofted, the need for this communal element will dissipate.

The transition from run-rig township to crofting township did not necessarily affect the amount of arable land, but it did have consequences for the social organization of the villages. Gray (1952:55), describing the emergence of crofting townships on Mull, notes a pattern of "over-rigid systematization, of a simple standard imposed crudely on the delicate shadings of the living community. As the new and arbitrary system appears many of the old distinctions and ranks were ironed out."

In an effort to accommodate a larger number of tenants, crofting townships were laid out over empty moors and previously consolidated landholdings. Separate smallholdings (crofts) were occupied by single tenants who all paid about the same rent. As Gray notes, the result of this reorganization and reallocation of land was to level "the inequalities of the old farm," resulting in "the disappearance of the upper stratum of the peasantry" (1952:55). Although new methods of assigning status have emerged (in particular, one's standing in the Church), and although new methods of consolidating arable land continued to occur through both legal and semi-legal means (e.g., through formal and informal subletting of crofts), the crofting community has emerged as aggressively egalitarian, in part because the crofting system ensured that an unbridgeable gap existed between the crofter (with less than five acres of arable land and grazing rights to the equivalent of less than five cattle) and the farmer with hundreds of acres.

The crofting system eliminated the opportunity for middle-range farmers to emerge, and laid the groundwork for the growth of a rural proletariat (a term I prefer to the OED's "peasant tenant," a term implying primary involvement in subsistence-based agricultural production; see Kearney's [1996] critique of the concept of peasantry). Crofters were expected to survive not primarily as agriculturalists but as laborers—as fishermen, whiskey distillers, gatherers of kelp,[2] and cannon fodder for the British army. This trend accelerated as the demand for wool increased; as more sheep farmers from the south offered high rent for grazing land, lairds of the west Highlands and Islands moved their tenants to coastal

---

[2]Emigration was initially encouraged by Scottish landlords who were trying to introduce agricultural reforms during the early 18th century. However, emigration was strongly discouraged during the second half of the 18th century, up until the 1820s, because of the appearance of a strong market for kelp (seaweed), or rather, an alkaline extract of kelp, which was used in a variety of manufactured goods such as soap and glass. Men, women, and children living in coastal communities gathered and burned the seaweed in rough open kilns, earning £3–4 per ton for themselves and £18–20 per ton for their landlords. According to some historians, landlords could earn as much as £10,000–20,000 per year from the kelp-burning labor of their tenants, a fact that tempered their agricultural reforms and made them more receptive to densely crowded townships. The Passenger Vessels Act of 1803 was introduced to prevent crofters from emigrating because of their vital importance as wage-laborers to the landlords (Keating and Bleiman 1979:23).

areas where alternative sources of economic activity, such as kelping, existed. During the summer months between the 1850s and the 1880s, almost all able-bodied men and women of Lewis participated in an annual migration to the east coast of Scotland and England, the young men hiring on east coast fishing boats, and the young women following the boats to gut, pack, and kipper the fish, particularly herring. In other words, crofters were becoming incorporated as rural laborers into a variety of nonagricultural industries, vulnerable to numerous displacements of which the Clearances were only one.

In the 19th century, the economic base of proletariat crofting society was devastated by a series of disasters. All the sources of monetary income on which rents were based were undercut—the market for kelp was destroyed, fishing declined, government restrictions on the production of whiskey were enforced, the various wars of the 18th and early 19th centuries came to an end and the soldiers no longer sent money home but returned themselves, expecting land. The main source of food on the croft—the potato—was destroyed by blight, and cattle were sold or taken away to pay the rent. With the collapse of the markets for crofter labor that provided landlords with rent, even more land was leased to commercial sheep farmers (on Lewis, the decline of the Seaforth's fortunes at the beginning of the 19th century resulted in the formation of three sheep farms, Coll, Gress, and Aignish in the Stornoway district; by 1883 crofters had lost 160,000 acres to sheep and deer).

Competition for scarce land among a rising population between the mid 18th to the mid-19th century drove the price of rents higher. The records show a rapid turnover of tenants. The distrust felt by these smallholders in the face of such monumental insecurity made it difficult for Highland landlords to introduce changes—which in turn promoted the stereotype of the "lazy crofter."

Tales of extreme poverty, broken communities, the horrors of famine accompanying the potato blight, and mass emigration reached the ears of a Lowland society, which already had a romantic stereotype of the spiritualized Celt fading quietly into the Celtic Twilight, and had forged a link between Celt, Highlander, and national identity. At this time, Scottish politics were dominated by a progressive Liberal philosophy that encouraged an active social policy. After 1850, central and local government displaced private charity and various common-interest associations in efforts to improve health, supply fresh water, control intemperance, and aid the poor (cf. Day 1918). The political example of Irish unrest over "the fundamental ethics of landownership and its obligations" (Orr 1982:60) was probably influential as well. A series of government commissions reported on the plight of crofters in the Highlands and Islands, culminating in the Napier Commission Report of 1884, which was followed soon after by the Crofters Holdings (Scotland) Act of 1886.

The emergence of the term "crofter" during the period preceding the 1886 act is evident in census reports. In the 1841 Census for the parish of Barvas on the Isle of Lewis, the term "small tenant" is most frequently used to identify the head of household; the terms "crofter" or "cottar" do not appear. In 1851, the term "tenant" is the most common referent; "crofter" appears eight times, and "cottar" twice. In 1861, the term "tenant" is the most common referent, the term "crofter" does not appear, and the term "cottar" or "cotter" appears 12 times. In the 1871 Census, the term "crofter" appears more often, and by 1881 the term is everywhere as "crofter," "crofter wool weaver," "crofter's wife," "crofter's son," and "crofter's daughter."

One of the main purposes of the Crofters Holdings (Scotland) Act of 1886 was to provide smallholders with that "bit of land" to which Celts were thought to be fanatically attached. "No people in the world have so great a value for land," wrote Mackinlay in 1878. "The islander is wedded to his land," wrote Murray (1966:188). Crofter and Celt were welded during the unrest that spread throughout the Highlands. In the 1870s, several hundred crofters on Lewis marched to the castle in Stornoway and demanded the return of their common grazing, which had been converted to deer parks and sheep farms. The government, aware of the fomenting rebellion, appointed the Crofters Commission to collect evidence and make recommendations. Ciall crofters gave evidence that families had been forced on them from neighboring communities. The best grazing land for cattle had been given to a tacksman. Twenty-four families had been cleared from neighboring townships, five of them coming to Ciall, the rest being "sent to America and to other places after they had but recently erected new buildings. Their fires were quenched. Had you seen it, you could scarcely bear the sight. Their houses were broken down and their fires were quenched" (Napier 1884:962).

The Napier Commission defined the crofter as "a small tenant of land . . . who finds in the cultivation of his holding a material portion of his occupation, earnings and sustenance. . . ." In other words, the 1886 act defined the croft as an agricultural unit of land, even though it was recognized that the size of most crofts was insufficient for effective agricultural activity. William Mackay, chamberlain on the Lewis estates, reported to the Napier Commission in 1883 that he considered the soil improvements made by Sir James Matheson during 1849–1852 to have been a mistake. "I don't think it is possible to have an arable farm in Lewis that will pay" (Napier 1884:959). A crofter in Ciall gave evidence that his croft "never kept me for three months of the year" (Napier 1884:968). Because of the congestion on Lewis (which reached its peak population in 1911), even small farms were divided; and when, in 1911, the "fair rent" was changed from £30 maximum to £50 maximum in the rest of the crofting areas, it was kept at the lower rate on Lewis. The commission recommended a return to a form of agricultural organization much like the old joint farm. The 1886 act ignored this as well as the suggestion that crofts rented at less than £6 per year be consolidated. To do so would have raised the specter of the infamous Clearances.

By the time the Napier Commission was collecting its evidence and the 1886 act was being passed, the original Clearances were at an end (Highland sheep farming had experienced a severe depression in the 1870s), but the concept of the Clearances continued as a symbol of injustice in the relationship between crofter and landlord.

Ever since the 1886 act was passed, landlords have been essentially powerless to make any decisions affecting the use of crofting land. Crofters are assured of fair rent (usually only a few pounds a year), security of tenure, and hereditary succession. The affairs of crofters are monitored by a variety of government agencies, including the Crofters Commission, the Land Court, and the Highlands and Islands Development Board. Intending to rectify past injustices, the Crofters Act has contributed to a situation in which a population is maintained as a cultural reservoir whose identity is closely linked with agricultural activity in a region that cannot sustain it.[3]

The 1886 act may be interpreted in the larger context of Scottish nationalism (cf. Keating and Bleiman 1979:25), as a form of symbolic retribution against the landlords who supported English imperialism, a fusion of Celt, Scottish independence, and the drift toward Labor vs. Tory in the political climate. It gave the crofter security of tenure, fair rent, and hereditary succession, but problems remained that stemmed not from the relationship between individual crofter and landlord but from climatic conditions, unproductive soil, and the smallness of holdings in heavily populated areas. The symbolic significance of the croft as land to which the local people have an inalienable right remains an important ingredient in the politics of crofting; and so numerous are the agencies, commissions, laws, and regulations that have developed to define, protect, and perpetuate crofting that one of the most popular definitions of a croft in recent times is that it is "a piece of land entirely surrounded by legislation."

In 1911 crofters were removed from special status and merged with smallholders all over Britain; but they were resurrected in 1955 with the passing of a new Crofters Act after the Taylor Report of 1954 argued that crofting communities should be maintained because they "embody a free and independent way of life which in a civilisation predominantly urban and industrial in character is worth preserving for its own intrinsic quality." A geographer at the University of Glasgow who was studying crofting in 1970 told me, "It's neither subsistence nor commercial farming; it's a way of life."

In 1976, an act was passed that gave the crofter the right to become owner of his or her land. Appearing to fulfill the ultimate intention of the 1886 act, the 1976 act created consternation, resistance, and new cries invoking the Clearances. Commented one crofter from Lewis, in an article in *The Glasgow Herald* written soon after the 1976 act was passed, "Owner-occupation will mean the land being overrun with people not interested in the traditional crofting way of life."

Throughout all these historic events, actions, and interpretations, the symbol of the Clearances has been paramount.

The Symbol of the Clearances

Of all historical symbols in use today in the Highlands and Islands, the one that is invoked most frequently in relation to a wide variety of actions on the part of the government and the landlords is the Clearances. Books, poems, and tapes about the Clearances continue to be popular. (For example, J. M. Bumstead, *The People's Clearance: Highland Emigration to British North American 1770–1815* [1982]; Eric Richards, *A History of the Highland Clearances: Agrarian Transformation and the Evictions 1746–1886* [1982]; John Prebble's *The Highland Clearances* was first published in 1963 but continues to be reprinted and is available on cassette tape; Alexander Mackenzie's *The History of the Highland*

---

[3]Cameron (1996) provides a carefully reasoned analysis of the "interplay of politics and ideology" in the history of land policies between 1880 and 1925 that contribute to the ambiguities and contradictions affecting crofting policy today.

Clearances, first published in 1883, was reissued with an introduction by John
Prebble in 1979, and reprinted in 1986. See Ewen Cameron [1996] for an excellent review of this literature.) The Clearances represent a multitude of interconnected symbols (or what might be called a significant symbol that organizes
thoughts, feelings, and actions) in which distrust of authority, in all forms and
manifestations, is prominent. The Forestry Commission is criticized for planting
trees, as if trees were sheep displacing the crofter.

Newspaper articles and rumors about rate increases, rising freight charges,
and strikes are all tagged by the same banner—"See there, now, they'll have this
island cleared yet," "Labour, Tories, HIDB, government officials, they're all on
the side of the landlords, it's the Clearances all over again." This distrust of
authority may help to explain some of the ambivalence with which the crofter
views the prospects of becoming his or her own laird.

When meetings were held on Lewis during the early 1970s to discuss the
owner-occupancy scheme, about 100 people attended the meeting in Stornoway,
and about half that number in the rural townships. The representative of the
Crofters Commission assured me that there was 100 percent support except from
the Factor (who would be put out of a job); but the crofters had a different report.
One man said that the crofter wouldn't be protected, that his croft would be sold
to the highest bidder. Most crofters would prefer workable croft land to lie idle
and even deteriorate rather than submit to what they perceive to be the dangerous use of power by authorities.

The Crofters Act of 1886, from the crofter's point of view, has the symbolic
significance of the Magna Carta, and stories are told about that period as if it
happened yesterday. "Donald Munro was the Chamberlain of the Lews, the
Sheriff's Officer, Procurator Fiscal—whatever other names you want to give
him, he was a tyrant. He would arrest boys for throwing stones; he caused the
riots of Aignish and Berneray. His constable in Ciall was Tormod Iain Shaidear,
from Dalmore. When the 1886 act was passed, all these people lost their absolute
power. The man in Bragar hanged himself; the Saidear went mad." The 1976 act
sets up a new symbolic connection between crofter and laird, effectively turning
the crofter into a laird and bringing home the responsibility of whether to remain
or to leave.

Crofting in the 21st Century

Agnes Rennie, Crofters Commissioner for the Western Isles, notes in the
Crofters Commission Report for 2001–2002 that "Over the past year, the public
response across Britain to the crisis in agriculture has indicated that the con-
sumer does not want more intensive farming. This points to a great opportunity
for crofting areas where extensive production is the norm and clean produce is
the natural outcome." She also notes that "Our development strategy must centre on the traditional ability of crofting communities to embrace change."

Many residents of crofting townships who practice extensive rather than
intensive farming, who sell chickens and eggs and organically grown vegetables,
are not crofters but incomers who buy decrofted houses. They sell their own
houses in the south and move north because property is available at a fraction of
the cost of southern properties, the air is fresh, and the neighborhoods are safer

for their children. They are Welsh, English, and Lowland; sometimes they are linked by kinship but often still thought of as outsiders.

Decrofting was originally thought of as an effective way of separating house from land and encouraging aging crofters to give the land to younger, more active crofters. And while the statistics would seem to support this trend, one example from Ciall will suffice to indicate that things are not always what they seem. One crofter in his 70s decrofted his house site and gave his croft to his son. But the son commutes to work in Stornoway, and the father continues to work the croft (which today consists in caring for a few sheep kept close to the house); to the son, the advantage of becoming a crofter is proximity to his parents and the opportunity to apply for crofter house grants.

The conception that a crofter will assign or will his croft to a member of his family (any exceptions must be approved by the Crofters Commission) is being affected by the economic value of the land for housing. Many under-the-table agreements are being reached whereby a croft assignation is "sold" to someone who is not a member of the family but who wants the land because of the value it holds for access to grants to build a house (for example, by paying the crofter £7,000, the non-family member gets access to a house for which £12,000 in grants is available, thus coming out £5,000 ahead). The Crofters Commission is now dealing with arguments from relatives who want the commission to deny such assignations, and to give the land to them—not because they're willing to pay competitive prices but to "maintain the tradition." Does the commission act on the basis of the croft being an economic unit, or to preserve a way of life? One of the few things now slowing down the changes associated with the conception of a croft as providing access to cheap housing is that many of the houses now for sale in the crofting areas do not come with land and therefore do not fit the conception of an urban buyer's life in the country. But eventually the economic value of land as a source of housing will change the cultural profile of crofting forever as land, housing, heritage, and beauty become commodified.

Symbolizing an ancient way of life, the crofter stands as a Celtic island, surrounded by protective legislation, embroiled in the active process of creating meaning out of an image of romantic extinction. This Celtic island is slowly being eroded, as much by tides of linguistic change as by the small, subtle earthquakes of land reform that will both remove protective legislation and provide opportunity. Through croft ownership and decrofting, crofters will eventually set sail on their own recognizance out into the stormy Atlantic—latter-day Brendans in quest of their own Brasil.

3/The Crofting Township

THE WESTERN ISLES, ISLE OF LEWIS, AND CIALL

The Outer Hebrides, sometimes called "The Long Island" and now designated as a separate council area called the Western Isles (in Gaelic, Eilean Siar), is a chain of islands between 15–40 miles west of the Isle of Skye and the Northwest Highlands that resembles the skeleton of an enormous whale. Between the Butt of Lewis in the North and Barra Head in the south lie 716,000 acres of disintegrating Lewisian gneiss, more than 200 islands scattered over 136 miles. Most of the islands are small uninhabited chunks that are of little interest to anyone but seals, otters, and birds. The inhabited chunks increase in size from south to north: they include Mingulay, Vatersay, Barra, South Uist, Benbecula, North Uist, and then, after skipping over the neck bone of Berneray, the whale's head, "Lewis and Harris" (or "Lewis-with-Harris"), often thought of as two islands because Harris, joined to Lewis by a narrow strip of land, is mostly mountain whereas Lewis is relatively flat, open moor studded with marsh.[1] The climate is temperately cool and wet, and the gales carry salt spray far enough inland to sour the land, kill what few trees have been planted, and rip off roofs. The light is luminous and ever-changing.

Ciall lies on the west side of Lewis, the northern part of the island of Lewis and Harris, at the most northerly end of Eilean Siar.

Between 47°50′ and 58°30′ north latitude, Lewis is as far north as Newfoundland and farther north than Mongolia. Bathed by the North Atlantic Drift, or Gulf Stream, it rarely sees snow, but shivers in cool, windy wetness between a fairly narrow range of temperature—from an average of 55°F in summer to 44°F in winter. The wind is a relentless presence on the treeless northern

[1]In a charming history of Lewis and Harris, James Shaw Grant (1998:2) likens the difference between Lewis and Harris to "the difference between two neighbourly malts. Marginal, and almost indefinable, but very real to the connoisseur." This difference goes back at least 300 years, when Blaeu, the Dutch cartographer, noted that "Lewis and Harray of the number of the Westerne Yles which two, although they joyne by a necke of land, ar accounted dyvers Ylands." (Quoted by Grant 1998:1.)

In a communal effort scheduled by the township grazing committee, men go out to the moor to gather the sheep for dipping, pilling, marking, and shearing.

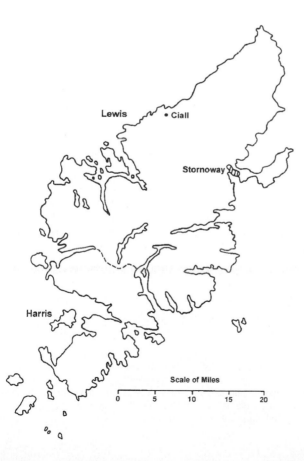

Lewis and Harris

Flying over the islands

islands, often reaching gale force; winds of 60 mph and more are common. Rain, which comes in heavy downpours or light mist, averages 55 to 65 inches a year. The water may be held in colloidal suspension with decomposed organic matter in the compact, spongy material called peat, or pour as rivers and streams off the island's shelf of nonporous Archaean gneiss into the sea. Of Lewis' total area of 437,200 acres, inland water comprises 24,863 acres (according to Murray [1966:171], the name Lewis derives from the Gaelic *leogach,* meaning marshy).[2]

Lewis has a large town (Stornoway, with around 5,000 people), an airport built in 1939, a harbor to which fishing boats and passenger ferries come, and a castle (to which 19th-century crofters once brought an annual "gift" of chickens; it was converted to a technical college and is now part of the emerging University of the Highlands and Islands). Stornoway is linked by a circular, asphalt road (now double-width, over which cars and lorries travel at much higher speeds than when the road was single-width with turnouts) and has daily bus services to small villages scattered around the island's perimeter. The location of these villages by the sea reflects the historical association of crofting with fishing, although today most villagers fish for sport and use the money they earn from weaving to buy fish from the local fish van (or, more often in 2003, from the petrol station in Barvas and the Coop in Stornoway); and many no longer buy fish at all. The central core of the island—heather-cloaked, bog-soaked, and layered with an estimated 85 tons of peat—is uninhabited, except for a diminishing number of sheep who use it as a vast, unfenced communal grazing land.

[2]Other derivations of the name include Leodhas, from the MacLeods who dominated the Outer Hebrides, a Norse term meaning "Song Houses," and various Gaelic and/or Norse words for "light," "Liot's dwelling," "wharf," and "a place abounding in pools."

Island ferries: the Loch Seaforth at Mallaig in 1970 (top) and Caledonian MacBrayne at Ullapool in 2003 (bottom)

Except when responding to some external challenge, such as increased shipping charges, the islanders do not perceive themselves as having anything in common. They have a number of stereotypes about each other. To other islanders, Lewismen appear brash, aggressive, extremist; Harrismen are retiring, gentle; or they are darker-skinned; or their Gaelic has more English in it. South Uistmen think of Barramen as boastful. North Uistmen look on South Uist as a drunken lot. Many Harrismen and Lewismen have been around the world, but have never traveled to other parts of the Hebrides. Even neighboring villages look on each other with suspicion ("In ——, every house has someone in Craig Dunain [the mental hospital near Inverness]"; "Never give a lift to someone from ——, they're dangerous"; "People from —— will eat anything, including the

Formerly a technical college, the Lews Castle in Stornoway is now part of the University of the Highlands and Islands.

The vast inner moorland, where once cattle were kept during the summer in a form of transhumance on the shielings, is now used to graze sheep.

heads of chickens"; "In —— they don't believe in live-and-let-live; they feud and carry on the feuds, not like here where everyone makes up their quarrels quickly"; "The people of —— are bitter; they think we're backward because we're so friendly"). One man was teased for going "all the way to the next village" to find a wife. The people of Ciall have different accents from people of

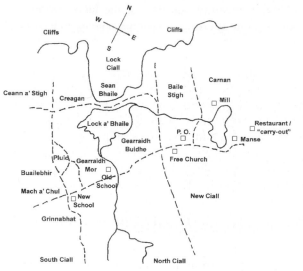

The village of Ciall

the neighboring village; and although they attend the same church, they sit on opposite sides and have a history of feuding over boundaries.

Ciall lies on three undulating hills that, except for an enclosed bay with its accessible shoreline lined with white shell sand, form cliffs that are treacherous to sheep and midnight suitors ("He left her house at dawn and went off in the direction of the cliffs; they never found his body"). The pounded, sea-washed stones ("sea eggs") are covered with brown-green, rubbery seaweed, and glistening periwinkles that when cooked yield a crunchy bit of muscle about the size of an eraser head and an aftertaste of grit and iodine.

Ciall is on the west side of the island in the parish of Barvas, one of four administrative areas in Lewis. It lies about 18 miles away from Stornoway on a circular road that provides bus service several times a day. The largest of the rural parishes, Barvas contained 3,663 persons in 1971, of whom 86.2 percent identified themselves as Gaelic speakers. In 1981 these numbers had declined to 3,598 persons, but a higher percentage of them were listed as Gaelic speakers (92.1 percent); and in 1991, the population of Barvas declined to 3,024, with 84.4 percent identifying themselves as Gaelic speakers.[3] The people of Stornoway refer to someone from the western side of the island as a *siarach* (west-sider), a term that connotes rusticity.[4]

Most of Ciall lies between the main road and the sea, except for a street that turns in toward the moor. This street is called New Ciall because it was created

---

[3]Table 1: Historical Trends and Areas, Western Isles Civil Parishes (1991 Census: Gaelic Language).

[4]Battles over images of rusticity seesaw back and forth between east and west, north and south, as in the old saw about why Highlanders are called "Teuchtars." In the Aberdeen version of the joke, the invading Romans, Vikings, and English were killed and eaten by the Aberdonians, all except the Highlanders who were *"ower teuch tae eat"* [too tough to eat]. What to the English was a signifier of mispronunciation was to the Highlander a form of recognition of his status as tutor or teacher, a civilized man among the barbarians.

in the mid-19th century—relatively recently—as part of the land reform that transformed joint farms and run-rig into crofting townships. The main territorial unit of interaction within the village is the neighborhood, which consists of streets or parts of streets. Each neighborhood evolves its own distinctive names—"Church Street" for the section of the main road that is near the church, *Carnan* (from *carn,* a heap of stones), *Gearaidh Buidhe* (variously translated as yellow shieling, fertile garden, place where yellow flowers grow, and land from which peat has been skinned), *Baile Stigh* (the town in by the sea), and a variety of teasing nicknames of the variety applied in abundance to individuals, such as calling a fertile region "Egypt," a wet place Chirrapungi, or a few boggy crofts *muinntir fluich a Charnan,* the wet people of Carnan. There are grandiose names that poke fun at pretentiousness (The Royal Road), and names that are given multiple interpretations, depending on who is doing the interpreting.

The intersection of New Ciall and the Baile Stigh at the main road is called the Gate, and is a regular meeting place. A small general store was once located there, and it was once the site of the blacksmith's shop and the home of the last constable (the person who regulated township activities) of Ciall. The school-master once lived in a house that adjoined the school (the old school is now empty, the new school is a wonder of glass and computers, and the schoolmas-ter lives elsewhere), and the minister of the Free Church lives in a manse located between Ciall and the neighboring village.

In 1970–71, Ciall contained 169 households, of which 110 were headed by crofters, or persons recognized as legal tenants of a croft. Of the remaining households, 16 occupied council houses, or houses built and maintained by the county, 11 built homes on the crofts of relatives, and 32 built homes on the com-mon grazing. Non-crofters participate equally in the agricultural activities of the township, even serving as clerks of the grazing committee. Many of the persons who spoke to me so persuasively about the importance of learning Gaelic to understand the crofter were not, technically, crofters but squatters who built their homes on the common grazing land with the permission of their neighbors, and participated fully in the ideology of crofting.

A census done by the primary grades of Ciall school in 1970 listed 571 peo-ple, 19 babies, 54 cows, no horses, 141 dogs, 165 cats, 95 televisions, 39 tele-phones, 109 looms, and 89 cars. It found 162 inhabited "white houses", 13 uninhabited white houses, 1 inhabited "black house," and 33 uninhabited black houses.

Televisions, telephones, cars, and "white houses" are symbols of progress and development, and the hills are dotted with cell phone "masts" or towers. "The light" (electricity) came to Ciall on October 31, 1951; before then, Tilley lamps, invented in Canada, were used, as were seal-oil lamps, candles, and rush lights using oil extracted from the fish called *saithe* (cf. Macalister 1910). Television was brought to Ciall in the 1960s (favorite programs in 1970–71 included English detective shows, American Westerns, the soap opera "Dallas," and sports events broadcast from abroad; today a household is likely to have more than one television set, with choices—from sports events to Gaelic pro-grams to game shows—affected by age and gender). Water was piped in from a local loch in the 1950s, but the water was brown from peat, and many people preferred to fetch water from the springs, which flow from the ground. These

The old school (top) and the new school (bottom)

springs are marked with stones but difficult to spot on the uneven ground; whether they are still in use is indicated by how well they are cleaned of growth. In 2003, the water runs clear through the pipes and is heated, not in storage basins behind the fireplace but by electricity.

The old *tigh dubh* (black house), with its thick walls of stone packed with loose earth and its roof of turf and straw weighted with stones attached to heather ropes, has been replaced by the *tigh geal* (white house), the standard house of concrete block and plaster found throughout Britain that can be erected according to "Crofter Housing Type Plans" put out by the Department of Agriculture with the aid of grants and loans. Although not really "black" or "white," the contrasting types of houses symbolize old and new, dirty and clean (the traditional *tigh dubh* had a central fire that deposited soot liberally throughout the house,

Susan Parman

Susan Parman

The new school has computer labs (top), and a pool used by everyone in the township (bottom).

and cattle were housed under the same roof), old-fashioned and progressive. Most homes are aggregates of old and new: an attachment is built onto the black house; a more modern kitchen and bathroom is added to that, and eventually the older section is torn down or used only as a barn, storage area, chicken coop, or weaving shed. Today several black houses and black-house villages are tourist attractions on the island.

The last black house (top) to be occupied in 1970 (demolished and removed in 2003); and a house (bottom) built according to "Crofting Housing Plan." The front door is seldom used in crofting communities because people enter through the back door directly into the kitchen.

CROFTING

Although assumed by most Scotsmen—crofter and non-crofter alike—to be the "traditional" pattern of land use, crofting is of recent origin (see Chapters 1 and 2).

The land incorporated by crofting townships includes several types of terrain. In Ciall, the township land, including common grazing, extends over almost 10,000 acres, and goes from sea level to about 800 feet. The harbor area consists of *machair,* sand with a high lime content that provides light, well-drained soil. There is very little machair on Lewis (the best is in Ness), as compared with the Uists, and thus the arable land consists in the *gearaidh,* the rough land from which peat has been skinned. Beyond this is the *monadh* (mountain), a source of peat and grazing land. The sheep once spent most of the year on this

Before (top) and after (bottom) spreading sand on "skinned" peat land

vast inner grazing land; but as keeping sheep declines, most of them are brought
onto the croft or onto apportionments carved out of the common grazing that are
fenced in close to the croft. Seaweed was once used to fertilize the arable land
and to supplement the diet; today the sheep are brought in from the moor to eat
it, and crofters apply for government grants to buy sand that they spread, either
as a collective unit or individually, over moorland to improve the grazing.

Ciall has 144 crofts (or shares) in the township. Each crofter has a "souming," or right to graze a certain number of animals on communally held grazing
land. For example, a typical souming would be one cow (or five sheep), one 2-
year-old heifer (or three sheep), and one horse (or two cows or ten sheep). The
sheep used are mostly Mainland Blackface, which are larger than the Lewis
Blackface, mature more quickly, and have better wool. The Livestock Division

Labor-intensive "lazybeds" are still evident, and sometimes still in use.

in the Department of Agriculture provide "AI" (artificial insemination) for cattle, ensuring good production of beef cattle. The more isolated townships in the Outer Hebrides have a township bull.

The potato was introduced to Lewis from Ireland in 1743, and cultivated widely by the end of the century in addition to oats and barley. Most cultivation was done on lazybeds, raised beds of earth fertilized with seaweed or manure. Today some high land around the house is used for potatoes and cabbage, but most of the croft is planted with grass and oats to be used as winter feed for cattle or for sheep kept on the croft.

A detailed survey of crofting conducted in 1960 (Caird, unpublished data) showed that Ciall had 345 acres of arable land and 501 acres of outrun. One hundred and twenty acres were planted with oats, and 39 with potatoes; 107

households had gardens (in which they grew such items as carrots, parsley, cabbage, beet-root, turnips, and onions), and many had chickens. Ninety-eight acres were sown with grass for hay, and 42 acres were sown with grass that was used as pasture land; over 500 acres were left alone, the naturally grown grass used for hay or pasture.

Both townships exceeded their sheep souming (the allowable number of sheep on the common grazing), but had less than their cow souming. Only five people classified themselves as full-time crofters; 111 considered themselves part-time crofters regularly employed elsewhere.

Although 110 of the 169 households were headed by crofters, Ciall actually had 144 crofts, which meant that 34, or almost a quarter, were vacant; that is, the holders lived elsewhere. One of these crofts was used by its absent tenant for holidays, and the other, on which a trailer was placed, was rented to tourists during the summer. All of the other vacant crofts were cultivated or used for grazing by crofters or non-crofters in the village who by formal or informal subletting have gained use of the land. A little over half the crofts were worked as individual units; 44 percent of the crofts were worked as combined units, 24 men working two crofts apiece, and five men working three crofts apiece.

Of the five households that had the use of three crofts each, one consisted of a bachelor who used the crofts to graze a large number of sheep. A second household was composed of two brothers who stayed at home to take care of their aging parents. After the last parent died, one of the brothers married. These men kept cattle and sheep, and both wove Harris Tweed.

A third household was headed by a married man who sold most of his livestock to "concentrate on the weaving." "My father was a crofter only. He was wounded in the war. He got a pension and sold a cow or a few sheep each year. But I didn't like to leave the loom for the time it took to look after the sheep."

A fourth household consisted of three unmarried siblings in their 40s and 50s who sold their cattle and kept only sheep for their own consumption. They cultivated a small amount of oats and hay to feed the sheep during the winter. The brother who was largely responsible for the livestock became a full-time weaver, and his brother worked in the mill. Their sister, who used to work in hotels on the mainland, kept house for them. Described as a "self-contained family," they had a tractor and a deep freeze and took care of their peat and harvesting by themselves. One of their crofts became too waterlogged even for grazing, and they have transferred tenancy to the son of a local crofter, who wanted it not for agriculture but as a prerequisite for a housing grant from the Department of Agriculture.

The fifth household was composed of a retired couple and their son and his wife and family. They had no cattle, and used the crofts for grazing sheep.

The following chart shows the changes in land use that occurred from 1891 through 1994, the latest year for which agricultural statistics were available in January 2003.

Perhaps one of the greatest changes is the reduction in the number of cattle, especially milk cattle. In the early economic history of the Highlands, cattle were much more important than sheep; and when the Clearances began, sheep connoted all the evils of landlordism. Irish folk tales are full of stories concerning cattle, and English chroniclers lamented the lawlessness of the Highland *"ban-*

CHANGES IN LAND USE (1891–1994); PARISH OF BARVAS,
ISLE OF LEWIS; AGRICULTURAL CENSUS, PARISH SUMMARIES[1];
WEST REGISTER HOUSE, EDINBURGH

Year	Potatoes (acres)	Barley (acres)	Oats (acres)	Milk Cows	Beef Cattle	Sheep (in thousand)
1891	1,105	1,172	556	1,771	—	1,7.7
1901	1,281.5	1,227.75	735.5	1,947	—	20.28
1911	1,146	959	1,107	1,951	—	19.5
1921	1,126	1149	1,039	1,932	—	16.9
1931	1,043	823	2,045	1,846	—	21.3
1941	679	401	2,451	1,544	50	22.7
1951	576	94	2,327	1,295	47	41
1961	413	14	1,432	960	1273	37
1971	138.5	1.25	452.75	243	756	34.98
1981	89	.5	83.25	22	74	20.83
1991	36.75	7.5	16.5	1	115	20.17
1992	33.5	2.5	12.5	1	98	19.22
1993	28.5	—	12.5	—	82	19.28
1994	20.25	—	10.5	—	80	18.9

[1]Various changes affect comparison of agricultural statistics since information first began to be collected in 1866. Information collected in the first series (1866–1911) was given voluntarily. Agricultural Acts of 1925 and 1947 made census returns statutory and compulsory. The parish is the lowest unit of consolidation of information. Ciall is located in the parish of Barvas, which after 1933 was identified by the number 753. In 1970 the basis of calculating minimum holdings was altered from one acre to holdings with a labor requirement of 26 standard man days or more per annum; in 1973, it was changed to 40 or more standard man days per year. In 1976, metric measurements replaced acres with hectares (2.471054 acres = 1 hectare); I have converted hectares to acres in the chart. The numerical categories in the agricultural census used to indicate numbers (of acres/hectares, of milk and beef cattle, and of sheep in thousands) are as follows: potatoes (24, 25, 26), barley (16, 18), oats (20), milk cows (100, 102, 104, 106, 111, 115), beef cattle (101, 103, 105, 107, 112, 116), and sheep (145). In 1993, the number of holdings was added; thus it is possible now to know not only the total acreage and livestock numbers but also the total number of holdings responsible for these figures (for example, in 1993, 13 holdings in the parish of Barvas were responsible for cultivating five acres of oats, whereas in 1994, only 9 holdings cultivated a total of 4.2 acres of oats).

ditti" who raided ceaselessly for cattle. The "drove roads of Scotland" were second only to military roads in their significance in establishing routes of communication in Scotland. Many Lewismen remember market days when cattle were herded into Stornoway from all parts of the island, when children were taken from school to help with the drive, and shopkeepers put up extra stalls for the occasion. Until as recently as the 1960s, a form of transhumance was practiced on Lewis. Cattle were taken away from the arable land to the central moorlands for several months during the summer. Those who stayed with them—usually the young people who looked forward to the opportunity to get out from under the watchful eye of their elders—lived in small stone huts called shielings (*airidh*), as small as 7 feet by 5. Built like the old *tigh dubh,* they had double stone walls filled with clay and a rounded thatched roof. The arrangement of the shielings duplicated neighborhoods within the village.

Since women were responsible for milking, the mothers, aunts, and grandmothers of the young people came out in the evening to milk and carry the milk back to the village. But during the day the young people kept lazy, carefree watch over the cattle—fishing for trout, gathering small blackberries, hunting the nests

Susan Parman

Catherine Ann Macleod

Nostalgia and freedom at shieling and shore

of grouse, walking to visit friends on other shielings. The boys swam in the lochs, and sometimes the girls stole their clothes. From the tops of the hills many children learned for the first time about other parts of the island. If anyone got lost in snow or fog, they followed the cows home; the cattle knew their own shielings, and crowded close during the night, sometimes sticking their heads inside.

No one ever slept alone. Girls crowded in together between the narrow walls, and boys kept to separate shielings but sometimes came in groups to court the girls or make ghostly noises. No one ventured out on the moor alone at night. Although some light was always in the sky at these northerly latitudes, the moor was eerie with the sound of birds and the lowing of the cattle. Crowded in together in the small shieling with the cattle moving outside, the young people sang songs and told stories, some of them about the *each uisge* or water horse that lurked in nearby wells to capture laggards that walked alone across that eerie landscape.

On the weekends, the older boys and girls in their late teens and early 20s came out in their best clothes and chased the younger children home. It was a time of courtship and unrestrained talk, out from under the watchful eyes of the village elders and gossips. "Also, if you were out on the shieling, you didn't need to go to church."

The agricultural statistics for Barvas show the large numbers of cattle that were kept until the 1950s. During World War II, agricultural advisors introduced cattle bred more for beef than for milk, and subsidies were introduced to encourage the production of beef cattle.

After World War II, a government act provided free milk for schoolchildren, which was brought in a van from a farm near Stornoway. Ciall villagers first started buying milk from the school milk van. Weavers were earning more money, in part because of a strike during wartime, and did not need to keep milk cows. The cows were a lot of work (everyone had to keep several cattle to make certain they had at least one with milk), and as the tweed was more profitable, it was easier to buy milk instead. As the cattle became fewer, the market for bottled milk expanded. A dairy was started on the west side of the island in the mid-1960s, and in 1970–71 carried milk from Uig to Ness, but today milk is shipped from the mainland. When the townships started reseeding schemes, the need to go to the shielings for an "early bite" stopped. A few continued to go out of habit and for health reasons. ("The air is different there, more health-giving. On the hills there's no smoke fumes, just heather. The air is heavy by the sea.") When, in the early 1960s, one couple in their 70s went out to their shieling, no one else was there. "We stayed for several days, it was a nice rest, and then we came back. My wife looked back at the dark empty hills and said, 'If I'd have known how dark it was on the shieling, I never would have gone out there.'"

The shielings that remain in use on Lewis today are huts of tin, wood, and concrete that are built within easy walking distance from the highway. They are holiday homes, used as weekend or summer retreats for harried urban dwellers. On the west side the shielings are in ruin, but remain in songs and nostalgic memories.

In 1970–71, the number of sheep kept by crofters exceeded the allowable number, whereas the number of cattle was declining. As a result, crofting land deteriorated. One of the most significant contributions of cattle was not their milk (a cow might be 4 or 5 years old before she calved and had any milk at all because people didn't have the rich feed that they can purchase today) but their dung, which helped to fertilize the croft. A major source of conflict in townships in 1970–71 concerned access to the reseedings among those who had cattle and those who had only sheep. As recently as the Napier Commission collection of evidence in 1883, the terms "tacksmen" and "shepherd" were synonymous, reflecting the association that crofters still made between sheep and the Clearances; but in 1970–71 sheep were a relatively trouble-free complement to the loom. Today, the cattle have almost all disappeared (only 80 left in the parish of Barvas in 1994), and the number of sheep have dropped by about half.

Between 1920 and 1929, 1,344 new crofts and 1,179 enlargements were created, but between 1940 and 1954, only 22 new holdings and 18 enlargements

Holiday homes close to Stornoway are called "shielings."

Sheep are kept on the croft rather than on the moor.

were made (Taylor 1954:15). In 1947, the Department of Agriculture listed 23,209 holdings in the seven crofting counties. Of these, only 6,009 were full-time agricultural units; 17,200 were part time. This part-time use of the croft is sometimes blamed on the protection afforded by the 1886 and subsequent acts, which enabled tenants to be absent from their crofts, to be employed elsewhere and return only for holidays until they were ready to retire on the croft; but the part-time agricultural use of the croft has a long history. When alternative sources of income become available, agricultural use of marginal land decreases. The continued investment in crofts today reflects in part the unreliability of the major alternative sources of income—in particular, Harris Tweed (see Chapter 4).

The number of sheep, which require less attention than cattle, increased after the late 1920s when Harris Tweed weaving commenced in earnest. Around the same time, a change in cultivation occurred. Instead of an emphasis on barley and potatoes (used largely for human consumption), more oats were grown (used largely for feeding livestock).

As crofters shifted from cattle to sheep, and from communal township activities to individual use of land, the organization of the township changed. Originally, the township was required to act as an integrated unit in conducting agricultural activities. The township was unfenced; cattle and sheep had to be kept away from arable land during the growing season, and sheep had to be brought off the vast inner moor in coordinated drives. Crofters were limited to a certain number of livestock (the souming), and the township constable reinforced this number. Today soumings are largely ignored, and the township clerk is responsible for seeing that rules are followed.

AN EXAMPLE

A man nicknamed the Craiceann Caorach (Sheepskin) receives most of his income from weaving Harris Tweed, but enjoys croft work. He has a croft and participates in a township reseeding. He married in his 40s, to a woman in her 30s, and he and his wife have no children. In 1970 he planted one-eighth of an acre in potatoes, which returned about "22 hundredweights," or enough potatoes for his family for the year ("But you never know—sometimes they're all soggy"); seven-eighths of an acre were planted with oats, and 1.5 acres with grass and hay; 2 acres were used for rough grazing.

The Craiceann keeps cattle and receives subsidies for the calves he produces each year, but he is especially interested in learning new techniques of good husbandry that enable him to raise a small flock of sheep, for which he usually receives prizes at the annual cattle show. He is teased by other crofters for "overfeeding," and for keeping his sheep on the croft and the township reseeding rather than out on the moor. "His sheep get homesick when they get out of sight of the croft," is a typical jibe that he takes with casual goodwill. He is a kindhearted man who refuses to kill his own sheep for home consumption, and tells horror stories of the suffering of sheep on the moor. ("The eagles rip out the eyes of young lambs. One year it was especially bad, and there were snowstorms in March and the men went out late to the moor after the ewes had already started lambing. There were all the men and their dogs coming in from all sides of the island, and they kept finding bodies. There was one poor lamb that was blind, and it couldn't see the dogs and went leaping about in all directions, until it came bleating to its human masters and died right their at their feet.")

In 1970 he sold three sheep to the slaughterhouse in Stornoway, and three lambs locally. He received subsidies from the government and awards from the cattle show and sold fleece to the Wool Marketing Board. He made a modest profit of about twice what he invested, but because the amount was so small (less than a £100), he refers to the croft as his "hobby." In 1970 he earned about £800 from weaving Harris Tweed, just under the amount that would have required him to pay income tax.

The Craiceann was one of the few people willing to discuss the number and type of sheep that he kept. Most crofters minimize their holdings (an average flock is 45–50 sheep, but a crofter typically reports only the number of breeding ewes), emphasize their losses, and are pessimistic about their gains. Even actions that are done with principles of good husbandry in mind are interpreted as acts of conceal-ment and secrecy, unless, as in the Craiceann's case, someone is actively explicit about their possessions and intentions—in which case they are mercilessly teased. "Domhnuill Angan moves his sheep between Ciall and his father's croft in the next village so no one will know exactly how many he has. Asking someone about their sheep is like asking somehow how many tweeds they have—there's automatic secrecy." (For a discussion of the function of such behavior, see Chapter 5.)

Since 1912 crofters have been able to apply for the exclusive personal use of part of the common grazing, and over the years there has been a steady trend toward replacement of communal township activities with individual manage-ment of land. In 1956 crofters were invited to apply for grants to reclaim the moorland with reseeding. Ten years later, 20,000 acres had been reclaimed, 10,000 on Lewis alone. The amendments to the 1955 act, in 1961, provided for individual crofters and small groups of crofters within the township to improve portions of the common grazings.

The fencing of individual land and purchase of personal farming machinery are everyday occurrences in the life of the normal capitalist farmer in the West; but in crofting areas, these practices reveal a strain between communal and indi-vidual tendencies. A crofter, by definition, has township duties. If a man asks for an apportionment, he is in effect lessening the amount of land available to the entire township. The requests for apportionments are perceived with ambiva-lence by other members of the township. A request for an apportionment is per-ceived as being forward, as violating the fundamental rule of township interaction regarding the maintenance of a low profile. Such behavior is the sub-ject of extensive gossip. Despite these negative sanctions, individuation of land use continues. In the 1960s, this individuation took the form of increasing requests for apportionments (from 32 in 1962 to 64 in 1969) and decreasing requests for township schemes (from 38 in 1962 to 2 in 1969).

The 1976 act gave crofters the legal right to buy their own croft, which put the crofter in the position of being able to apply to have the land decrofted (taken out of crofting), and the 1993 act further defined the circumstances under which land could be removed from crofting legislation. The following table (top, p. 67) reviews the last few years of statistics on number of crofts and number of owner-occupied crofts.

Even active crofters in Ciall are reluctant to become owner-occupiers, and this reluctance is reflected in lower rates of owner-occupancy on Lewis as com-pared with the crofting regions as a whole (4–6% vs. 18–20%). In the first 10 years after the 1976 act, the lowest number of applications for ownership came from the Western Isles (6 out of 427 applications, as per records of the Land Court contained in West Register House).

As the Crofters Commission makes efforts to remove inactive crofters (either by encouraging subletting or supporting the decrofting of house sites), the pat-tern of applications to the Crofters Commission (see table, p. 67 bottom) has emerged, which reflects the importance of the croft as a source of housing and the policy of current crofting legislation to preserve population.

PROPORTION OF OWNER-OCCUPIED CROFTS (TOTAL AND ON LEWIS)
1994–2001 (CROFTERS COMMISSION REPORTS)

	1994	1995	1996	1997	1998	1999	2000	2001
Crofts (Total)	17,670	17,671	17,685	17,690	17,710	17,711	17,725	17,711
Owner-Occupied (Total)	3,095	3,172	3,250	3,280	3,346	3,430	3,458	3,523
Percent Owner-Occupied	18	18	18	19	19	19	20	20
Crofts (Lewis)	3,610	3,613	3,615	3,615	3,615	3,611	3,612	3,611
Owner-Occupied (Lewis)	16	18	21	21	23	18	20	21
Percent Owner-Occupied	4	5	6	6	6	5	6	6

SUBLETTING, APPORTIONMENT, AND DECROFTING APPLICATIONS
FOR LEWIS, 1992–2002 (STATISTICS PROVIDED BY CROFTERS COMMISSION)

	Subletting	Apportionment	Decrofting		
			Croft house site/garden	Part	Whole
1992	12	44	33	4	2
1993	21	14	45	7	2
1994	10	47	57	1	1
1995	19	25	35	5	0
1996	45	22	41	18	0
1997	18	18	53	37	0
1998	24	15	47	24	1
1999	72	19	49	32	0
2000	35	18	54	24	0
2001	28	9	39	22	0
2002	33	9	53	22	1

THE YEARLY CYCLE

As indicated by the chart, "Changes in Land Use (1891–1994)," agricultural use
of land in the parish of Barvas has declined over the past 100 years. The following paragraphs describe crofting practices in 1970–71. Since 1970–71 the
acreage planted in potatoes has fallen from 138.5 to 20.25 acres, cultivation of
barley has disappeared, oats have declined from 452.75 acres to 10.5 (the beautiful stalks of golden sheaves cut with a scythe and braced upright to dry), milk
cows are gone and few beef cattle remain; and although the sheep remain (their
numbers were at their highest in 1951 through 1971), efforts are made to keep
them close to the township.

The year's croft work begins in the middle of March with ploughing and
manuring. The peaty loam requires fertilizers and lime to neutralize the acidic
soil. These were previously supplied by shell sand, cow dung, and seaweed from

Susan Parman

"Tying the corn" (oats); no matter what Johnson said in his dictionary,[5] these oats are for winter feed for animals.

the shore, and are now supplied by artificial fertilizers and shell sand shipped in from some distance away with the help of subsidies (applied for by the township clerk). The land is marshy and requires extensive drainage, once done by building up high, narrow beds of earth (called "lazybeds"), which were cultivated with a spade. Because of deterioration in croft use, much croft land has become unusable. The best grass is cut for hay, usually with a tractor that may be borrowed or rented from a relative or neighbor.

Oats are harvested in September by hand: with the help of relatives, the oats are cut with a scythe and stacked to dry. Cultivation is done primarily with tractor-drawn ploughs, spades, hoes, and rakes. In 1970 there were 5 tractors in Ciall, and the tractor was the most popular item on a hypothetical "wish list" that I asked many crofters to give me (one of the most creative wishes was for a helicopter to use to bring in the peats). Some crofters did a lot of work removing stones and flattening the old lazybeds so that a tractor could be used. Many have found it not worth the trouble, and have concentrated on weaving Harris Tweed.

Early potatoes, ready by July, are planted in March. The main crop of potatoes, which are ready by October, are planted in April, as are oats. The potatoes are weeded and hoed during the summer. Cutting peat begins in June or when the weather is relatively dry, and the process of cutting and drying continues until August, when the peats are brought home.

Many crofters plant their land and breed their cattle to meet the requirements for subsidies. Most crofters that have cattle want to be able to milk them, but subsidies are given only for beef; thus rather than getting the best milkers, such

[5]In his 18th-century *Dictionary of the English Language,* Samuel Johnson defined oats as "A grain, which in England is generally given to horses, but in Scotland supports the people."

Planting potatoes

as a Jersey or Ayreshire, they try to get a cross between a good milker and a beefy breed such as a Shorthorn or Blackpoll that will fulfill the requirements of the subsidy but still provide milk. In planting and fertilizing the croft, crofters will follow carefully the requirements of a subsidy, for example, to plough one-quarter of the land to qualify for a cropping grant. Subsidies are seen as useful but periodic. "A steady wage is better, like the loom." If, however, the subsidies are abolished, according to some crofters, "that will mean the end of crofting." The loss of the loom would be "the Clearances."

Most of the sheep are kept out on the moor during the winter, but some villagers with extra crofts or apportionments are able to keep them off the moor. When sheep are kept on the moor, they must be brought in at various times of the year in large communal sheep drives (fanks). Everyone knows roughly when to expect the call for a fank, but the specific day depends on how good the weather is, whether the mills have just sent out a large number of tweeds that they want woven immediately, the schedule of the Communions, and so on. Decisions begin to crystallize among groups of crofters (see Chapter 5), and the word goes out through the dense web of contacts that crisscross the island that the fank will be held on a certain day. People watch the roads for unusual traffic; they scan the horizon for signs of men and their dogs crossing the hills, and the word spreads. More figures appear on the far peat banks, flanked by the dancing, black-and-white figures of the border collies. The air is filled with the sound of men whistling to the dogs, and commands in both English and Gaelic ("Way to me!"—meaning circle widely around the sheep to the right, "By to me," meaning to circle to the left, *"Fuirich!"*—Wait). In gray-green Harris Tweed jackets, yellow slickers, navy blue duffel coats, or hand-knit sweaters made from the leftover bobbin threads of the tweeds, they cross the springy heather and the *maran,* the rubbery star-splayed moor grass, in long, steady strides that eat up

Susan Parman

Susan Parman

Dipping (top) and shearing (bottom) the sheep

the miles. They shout teasing insults at each other for slipping in the hidden sink holes, and take elaborate internal notes on who was on the moor and who was not, and how they handled their dogs. The sheep are driven back to large pens at the edge of the moor not far from the road. The men cluster at the fence, rolling cigarettes and discussing the characteristics of the moor, how many dead sheep they had seen, whether the eagle was back, how many weeds choked the old fresh springs; they learn of new events in other parts of the island, voice their pessimistic predictions of the fate of the tweeds, crofting, subsidies, and whatever else has immediate significance in their lives.

The ewes are brought in during April when they are ready to lamb, and cared for with special feed. The lambs are born from mid-April to mid-May and marked (ears are notched, the wool is painted, the horn is branded with the number of the croft), and the males are castrated.

After the lambs are born, ewes and lambs are put out on the moor for grazing, but brought back in June and July for shearing. Ewes are separated from their lambs in August; the ewes are put out on the moor, and the lambs are brought home for dipping to protect them against ticks, lice, and maggots. Many crofters give them pills that protect them from braxy and blackleg, worms and liver fluke; others consider this a waste of money. In October, all sheep are taken off the moor and brought to the inner grazing between the crofts and the sea to eat the seaweed; some villagers give them calcium, a mineral that is lacking in the grazing on the moor. On a dry day the sheep are dipped, marked with dyes to identify them, and given pills to protect them from disease. In November the ewes are put to the ram.

The lifespan of a sheep is about 9 years, but many are lost on the treacherous moor. I have never walked out on the moor without finding a sodden heap of fleece, the face and lower legs the only visible bones—well-dressed bones in the incipient makings of Harris Tweed. If the weather is bad, the loss of lambs may be heavy; they may be frozen in cold weather, drowned in heavy rains, blinded by birds, or be unable to get an "early bite" because the grass is late in growing. If the grass is low, they may eat it so close to the ground that they pick up worms.

Sheep require communal township labor if they are kept out on the moor, and many crofters complain that only a few are following the old code of ethics. On one occasion, a fank was held and only two people showed up; one of them was 67 years old. Working from early morning with their dogs, the two herded the sheep to the pens, only to find the road lined with cars of those who had come to identify their own sheep. As more people apply for apportionments and manage to keep their sheep off the moor, they undermine the economic basis of the communal organization of the crofting township.

THE FUTURE OF CROFTING

Some members of the Crofters Commission consider the communal aspects of township organization archaic, and favor individualizing agricultural use of the land. The conflict between these two trends help to explain many of the "anomalies" of crofting society today.

Many crofters refer to their agricultural activities as their "hobby," distancing themselves from the obligation, associated with the ideology of crofting, that they must make a living from these activities. They, perhaps more than the Crofters Commission, *An Communn Gaidhleach,* and other associations committed to the crofting concept, are painfully aware of the fact that most of the agricultural output of the Highlands comes from farms rather than crofts. Most islanders themselves do not envisage an agricultural future for their children. On January 1, 1970, the Western Isles Crofters' Union Council Meeting included in its minutes a decision to inform the Deputy Director of Education at the Balmacara Agricultural School that "there was little demand for agricultural education in Lewis since few parents wished their sons to go in for this because of the resulting very limited opportunities for jobs." Whatever agricultural knowledge they acquired would be considered "incidental to instruction in another trade."

On the other hand, the conception of crofting as an agricultural activity remains, not because of the economics of crofting but because of its meanings. The croft is a symbol of identity, a reflection of membership in a community, and a place of residence for the infirm and aged, especially for the aged female. The meaning of crofting is sustained through various means of community interaction; historical references play a significant role, and external definitions by exiles, tourists, and romantic writers contribute to its continuing evolution. (See discussion of changes in crofting in Chapter 1.)

Who owns the land? Can participation in a community be translated into monetary value?[6] The whole question of "ownership" is subject to the demands of community interaction. Although individuation has occurred, the crofting community remains intact; its boundaries are maintained by a self-definition that is born out of contrastive interaction with the Other—lairds, government agencies, the exiles. Historical events are powerful symbols that continue to be used as new options and relationships develop.

THE EXILES: EMIGRATION AND AN AGING POPULATION

From the lone shieling of the misty island
Mountains divide us, and the waste of seas—
Yet still the blood is strong, the heart is Highland,
And we in dreams behold the Hebrides!

—Canadian Boat Song[7]

[6]According to a member of Highlands and Islands Enterprise in 2003, "The crofter of the future will not be an older man who keeps sheep, or a younger man who will eventually grow into that older man. We're going to see a different kind of crofter, often an outsider who will not speak Gaelic but will have a distinctive culture of crofting. A crofter is a tenant who has control of the value of the land. Once crofters realize their power, they will have a great future. The major value of land is in housing and environmental projects like wind farms and horticulture. The current population is afraid of change, but incomers will be different. They will transform the landscape." What evidence is there for this point of view? According to a report prepared for the Crofters Commission titled "The Acquisition of Crofting Data: A Baseline Study" (2001), the average age range of the population aged 16 and over in crofting areas was 45–49; the average age of a tenant crofter was 48, and the average age of an owner-occupier crofter was 53. Fifty-seven percent were estimated to be employed full time. On Lewis, the average age range of the population aged 16 and over was 45–49; the average age of a tenant crofter was 50 and the average age of an owner-occupier crofter was 52. Fifty-eight percent were estimated to be employed full time. Crofting as pluralistic employment conducted by older men continues to be the norm.

[7]This famous poem, which has for over a 150 years evoked the intense sense of longing for home among Scots abroad, is usually attributed to John Galt (1779–1839), who opened up land for immigrants in Canada. The poem, titled "Canadian Boat Song (from the Gaelic)," was published anonymously in *Blackwood's Edinburgh Magazine* in 1829. In a cleverly argued treatise based on analysis of metrics, G. H. Needler (1941) suggests that the poem was not a boat song, was never originally in Gaelic, and was probably written by a Scottish friend of John Galt, David MacBeth Moir, who had never been to Canada. I am indebted to Gordon Adams for having called my attention to Needler's book.

Scottish and American flags welcome the return of the exiles.

Places held fondly in the heart are often best beheld from a distance. Hilda MacLeod, a Detroit schoolteacher whose father had emigrated from Ciall to the United States in the 1930s, married the daughter of a German immigrant, and after her death retired to Ciall, sat in the kitchen of her father's house smoking one cigarette after another. It was midsummer and the horizon of moorland hills was still visible through the window, although it was after midnight. "When I'm away from here I remember the light—it's sort of opalescent, isn't it?—and I can hardly wait to come back for a visit; but when I'm here I freeze, and I feel that everyone's looking at me all the time, and I suddenly look around and wonder where all the young people are."

The population of crofting townships is distinguished by a disproportionately large number of aged people, a pattern that is mirrored throughout Scotland as a whole (in 2001, the population of Scotland was 5,062,011, a decline of about 2 percent over the past 20 years, with the greatest decline occurring in the age groups 0–14 and 15–29, and increases occurring in the older age groups). An age-sex "population pyramid" of the Highlands is not so much a pyramid as a top-heavy hourglass, and Ciall is no exception.

In the 1961 national census, Ciall was listed as having a population of 598; in 1981, 564. In 1970, I counted 515 persons resident in the village (see the pyramid above), and 83 who although not living in Ciall considered themselves to be a significant part of the community—17 young people were attending school in Stornoway, and 66 people between the ages of 25 and 54 were working away from the village but were not yet unmarried, contributed to the income of their relatives in the village, and returned periodically to weave or work in the mill, care for aged parents, and visit for awhile until they became restless and set off again. Their roots are in the village, and when they are absent they are nevertheless present in the electrical storm of the village gossip system. To many villagers, the concept of "holiday" has no meaning other than the time when these "exiles" return.

Ciall 1971: Population According to Age and Sex

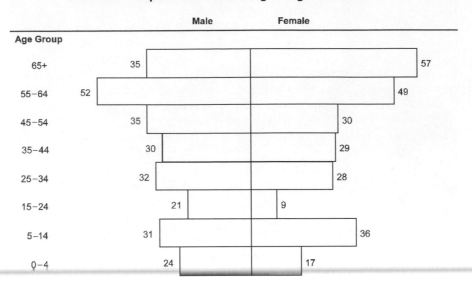

Parish of Barvas 1991: Population According to Age and Sex

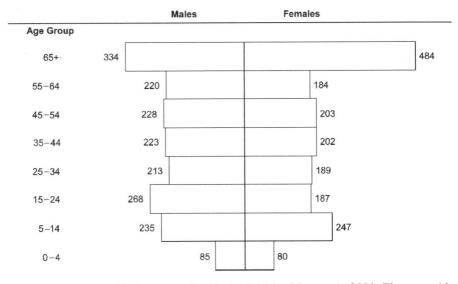

Ciall's population in 1971 compared with the Parish of Barvas in 2001. The pyramid is still top heavy (aging, with few children), but more young people (15–24) are staying home.

In 1841 the population of the Highlands and Islands as a whole reached its peak and began to decline. Lewis was unique in that its population continued to increase throughout the 19th century. In 1911 the population of Lewis peaked at 29,603. After that it declined steadily, reaching 20,622 in 1969 (about 70 percent of its 1911 peak). The 1981 census reported a slightly higher population of 20,726, but by 2001 it had decreased to 18,489.

The decline in population has two causes. The first is due to deaths exceeding births. Between 1961 and 1969, deaths exceeded births in rural Lewis by 178. One young man, about 30 years old, estimated that he had gone to at least 50 funerals in his lifetime; death plays a prominent role in Highland life. The dominant cause of population decline, however, is emigration.

Emigration is a sensitive index of social and economic health, and is highest among young wage-earners. Between 1951 and 1966, the proportion of the population in Lewis between the ages of 15 and 44 dropped from 36 percent to 32 percent, whereas the proportion of people aged 65 and over increased from 15 percent to 17 percent. Although the number of households in rural Lewis did not decline, the number of persons per household dropped from 3.7 in 1951 to 3.2 in 1966. According to some estimates, 60 percent of the young between the ages of 15 and 24 leave rural Lewis. They take their memories with them, and in music, writing, and conversation when they return, contribute to the idealization of place and ethnicity. In many of these representations, the current decline in young people is simply another version of—what else?—the Clearances.

> Seonag Thormoid was born in 1917. When she was 16 years old she left the island to work in hotels on the mainland, just as her mother had done before World War I. "You were raised with the idea that you would go away. I've prepared my children for the same thing. Any work that exists here is temporary. You can't depend on it."
>
> Seonag went to Glasgow with three other girls from Ciall and stayed with her aunt until she found a job. The wages were extremely low—about £2 a month—and wealthy families typically had five or six servants. "You were treated like scum. You worked in the kitchen fixing roast beef and fine puddings for them, and then sat down to a dinner of salt herring and potatoes. Those fine houses are gone now, broken down into smaller flats, and it does my heart good to see that when I'm in Glasgow."
>
> She moved from one job to another, and finally, when she was 37 years old, married her fiance who had returned from the war. They were both from Ciall, and had pursued a sporadic courtship whenever they happened to be home on leave. He had joined the Naval Reserve before the war. "There was always a sign up in the Stornoway Labor Exchange for men to join the Naval Reserve, because the islanders were such good seamen. They were fisherman or had been in the Merchant Service." He had spent 5 years in the navy during the war and was glad to leave the sea for the croft. He was the second son and fourth child in the family, and got the croft because he had stayed home to take care of his parents. His elder brother, who had emigrated to the United States, returned during the Depression and built a house on the common grazing. Another brother married into a croft in a neighboring village, and a fourth brother settled in Glasgow. A sister married an islander who became a policeman in Glasgow.
>
> Seonag and her husband had four children. The eldest entered the Merchant Service, and the second son became a teacher. A daughter studied domestic science in Aberdeen, and the youngest, Anna, attended the Nicolson Institute, the secondary school in Stornoway "Leave the island?" she replies, when asked about her eventual plans. "Of course. I've always had the idea that I was going away."

4/Harris Tweed

Crofters constitute a rural proletariat reliant on a variety of part-time, temporary, and seasonal activities to enable them to remain on the croft. Collecting kelp and fishing, seasonal work in the hotels, transport and construction jobs, knitwear and teddy bears have at various times provided income to crofting communities. On Lewis, and particularly in Ciall, Harris Tweed has played a major role in the economic history of the region.

FISHING

In the Old Statistical Account written in 1796, Sir John Sinclair compared Lewis to a gold-laced hat: around the vast inner moor, whose loch-covered, peat-spongy acres were suitable only for grazing, was a thin rim of gold, which represented the land that could be cultivated. The crofting townships on Lewis today constitute the jewels along the rim. The vast inner moorland belongs to the sheep, eagle, and grouse, while humans live at the edge of the sea, using its sand, seaweed, and seafood. Fresh and salted fish is still a regular part of the diet. Sand, spread on acidic peat land, neutralizes the soil and improves crop yields. The seaweed was once gathered and burned in kelp manufacture, and in some cases eaten, spread on the land, or used for medicinal purposes; the sheep eat it when they are brought into the shore once a year, and receive nutrients not found on the moor. The sea is a central theme in songs and stories, and has left its linguistic mark—one goes "in" the road when traveling toward the sea, and "out" the road when traveling toward the moor.

Before the Harris Tweed industry developed, fishing was the major supplement to crofting. Not only did local fishing boats sail from the Ciall harbor, but during the summer young men and women left the island to work for herring fishermen from the east coast. The young men worked on board, and the young women would "follow the fishing" as gutters and packers on land. Twenty pounds were good wages for a season. While the young people were away, the remaining members of the family lived on credit from the local shops. The men

Susan Parman

Fish and mutton, in this picture salted and hung up to dry with the laundry, are eaten with potatoes as an important part of the diet.

came back from the fishing in time to bring in the oats, barley, and potatoes, and the money they earned paid the rent for the croft and the loans from the shops. They usually brought enough rolls of wallpaper to cover the stone-walled or wood-lined *tigh dubh* for another year.

For young women who "followed the fishing," the opportunity to leave the island was an exciting adventure. There were two fishing seasons, a summer season in the north of Scotland and a winter season in England. A curer hired the young women by giving them earnest or pledge money (*earleas*) before the start of the season. Neighborhood girls went together, bringing bedding and cookware in large chests (*kist*). Three girls worked together in a crew, two gutting the herring and one packing them with salt in barrels. At night the boys would come in off the boats for dances. "You were so tired from being up since early morning, but you were always able to dance." Many women married men they met at the fishing and did not return home. The men were more likely to return, and if they married non-islanders, brought them home to the croft.

Before World War I, Ciall had nine sail-driven fishing boats. From five to seven men had shares in a boat. Sailing out during the night, they fished for ling, cod, skate, and halibut, baiting their lines with eel. The fish were salted and dried in curing houses, the ruins of which dot the harbor strand today. "Then the English came with their steam trawlers. They ruined the fishing here and then went west

*Once preoccupied with herring, fishing boats in Stornoway (top) now are used for
shellfish, which is being processed in a plant located along the harbor (bottom).*

to Iceland and the Faroes. In Iceland they get fined for poaching, but here the
trawlers often ignore the 3-mile limit." The inroads made by the steam trawlers,
the absence of young men during the war, plus the rise of the Harris Tweed industry, made it difficult for the fishing to come back after the war. By the late 1920s,
the market for cured herring had declined, and mainland railroad connections and
roads had improved; major fishing activity shifted to the mainland.

In some parts of Lewis, such as Ness, seagoing activities still rival weaving
in importance. And in the Outer Hebrides in general, fishing and sea-related
activities contribute significantly to the economy. By 2003, however, island

fishing had shifted to shellfish and fish farms, and Scotland in general was feeling the impact of the European Commission's decision to reduce haddock quota
from 104,000 to 51,000 tons to protect stock. Salted fish was no longer common
fare; I had to make a special trip to purchase a bucket of salted mackerel from a
petrol station that had ordered it from the mainland.

In 1971, the four 12-foot boats in Ciall were each shared by four or five men.
During the summer many men used fixed nets along the rivers, and "ottar boards"
on the lochs (pieces of wood with hooks attached that are floated out onto the
loch). They fished illegally for salmon. Fishing did not have the central significance that it once did; it was an amusement, a way of tweaking one's nose at
authority (the salmon are the property of the laird), a hobby, but not a necessity.
But its significance lingers in nicknames, in everyday speech, and in the general
cognitive map with which islanders place themselves in the world. This was made
especially clear to me about three-quarters of the way through my stay in Ciall.

It was the end of June, about 10:00 at night, and the sky was filled with the
quiet gold of northern summer light. I had spent the day cutting peat with
Caillean Uisdean and his family, and we lingered tiredly over a last cup of tea
before bed. Caillean was a crofter-weaver in his 50s; his wife Maggie Saidear
and their five teenage sons and daughters had absorbed me into their close-knit
family, doing most of the talking whenever I visited, whereas Caillean was a
quiet, reserved presence. I brought out my notebook—they were one of the few
families of whom I asked explicit questions—and was sketching the peat bank
region where we had worked that day, asking about its history, who cut peat with
whom, squabbles over peat boundaries, and so on.

Following a discussion about maps (which started because one of the children asked why it was still light this late in the evening), I asked Caillean if he
would mind drawing me a map of Ciall.

He sketched a view of the Ciall shoreline as if he were several miles out at
sea, at the bottom of the paper, looking up toward the shore that stretched from
east to west across the center of the paper. The shore was drawn in great detail;
the details became less distinct as he went from the shore toward the moor. Gone
were the conventions of north-south, east-west used in maps drawn from the perspective of someone in an airplane or satellite looking up toward the north pole
and down to the south; it was as if I were looking at Ciall from the perspective
of a fisherman. And in that context I, a mountain-dwelling landlubber for whom
land was the center and ocean was the fringe, suddenly understood why in the
islands one goes "in" toward the sea and "out" toward the moor.

When the weaving started, both men and women spent more time on the
island, but because of fluctuations in the industry, they continued to supplement
their income with other jobs, and many enjoyed the opportunity to leave. One
islander laughed when told about a plan by the Highlands and Islands
Development Board to provide jobs for women so that they could remain at
home. "Young people grow up expecting to get away. You minded your parents,
you weren't wild—you just waited until you got away. Even if home jobs were
available, we'd still leave." Instead of following the fishing, the girls work in
hotels or as domestic servants among the well-to-do families in Glasgow and
other cities on the mainland. The boys find it easy to join the Naval Reserve
because of their fishing experience, and move back and forth between service on

the sea and work at home (a common nucleus of many jokes concerns the frequent practice of sending for an extension of leave). But when the wars came, the long British tradition of using the Highlands as a good source of fighting men resulted in heavy losses. Those who remain—because of aging parents, illness, or the arbitrary quirks of fate—murmur about the Clearances and eagerly await the return of the exiles. In the meantime, they take what work they can get; and in 1970–71, an important source of work was the Harris Tweed industry.

> *Caillean Leobhar was born in 1920, the middle child in a large family. His oldest brother worked for awhile in naval dockyards in Glasgow, and then returned home to start a small business. When it failed, he tried weaving for awhile but returned to Glasgow to work as a security guard in a shipyard. Caillean's oldest sister married a mainlander that she met at a dance while she was working in domestic service. Two other siblings married into crofts in Ciall, and Caillean remained at home with a younger brother to take care of their aged parents. He belonged to the Naval Reserve, and was called up when the war came.*
>
> *"The war was the biggest event in my life. I spent 6½ years fighting for survival. During wartime you had no future. You spent 24 hours on duty, keyed up, and waiting for the enemy to come. When you got off duty, the bombs would be screaming around you but you slept. You got greedy. You were hungry for anything. So when you got into port you drank, you went crazy."*
>
> *Caillean was trained in electrical repair work during his military service. Toward the end of the war he was working in South Africa and planned to stay permanently. "But I threw it over. All of a sudden I knew I had to get back. I drove everybody crazy trying to get a ship as soon as possible. The day I arrived home, my brother, who had been staying with my parents, left the island. Over all those miles, how did he let me know he was leaving? Second sight runs in our family—but perhaps it's best not to talk about it."*
>
> *He started weaving but didn't like it very much. "I was going to leave the island the first year after I got back. But it's hard to leave parents who are old."*
>
> *Caillean's brother eventually returned, and they took care of the parents together. When the parents died, the brother took a 6-month course offered by the Labor Exchange and moved to Glasgow where he married a girl from the mainland. "There's a croft in his name and I take the hay off it for lambs, but he might want to retire there." The best part of the year is the summer, when the relatives return. During that time the large empty house that he built is full again. The women clean out the cupboards, throw out an accumulation of whiskey bottles, and repaper the walls.*
>
> *"I was caught here by circumstance. I was trained not to think of the future. I try to keep occupied. The sheep keep me busy, and I built the house myself, learning to do the bricklaying and joinery work as I went along. The weaving isn't too bad, except you have to be careful you don't earn too much or you'll end up in the poorhouse. I had to pay £90 in tax this year. The tweeds don't come regularly, especially for the last 18 months, but the vans give you credit. You don't need money all the time. The worst expense is the drink. Some people can live on £5 a week and a Bible, but I can't.*
>
> *"I like cities. I'll probably leave when the tweed goes—I give it another 2 years, and then the islands will be cleared because of the rising taxes. But I would hate to start out again, being knocked around. It's comfortable here. The house would be worth much more if it were in a different location, but I wouldn't get what it's worth. I've invested so much of my life in this place."*

DEMYTHOLOGIZING HIGHLAND DRESS

The emblematic significance of Highland dress, and in particular Harris Tweed, constitutes a pattern in which the warp of economics is cross-woven with the weft of luminous metaphor. Everyone "knows" that the national dress of Scotsmen is the kilt, made of woolen tweed woven in a tartan that indicates their clan. This is one of the beliefs that unifies Scotsmen the world over.

Trevor-Roper (1983) ably demythologizes tartan and kilt (although as discussion on the Highlands Listserv and elsewhere indicates, his interpretation is highly controversial,[1] and his reputation scarred by having authenticated the fabricated "Hitler diaries"). The earliest available descriptions of Highland dress, from the 16th century, indicate the Irish pattern of a long shirt (*leine*), a tunic (*failuin*), and a cloak or plaid, usually woven in russet or brown to provide camouflage (there were no distinctive clan patterns or *"setts"*); chieftains meeting Lowland sophisticates wore trews (breeches and stockings).

In the 17th century, when the contact between Ireland and the Highlands was broken, Highland dress changed. The long shirt disappeared, replaced by the Lowland coat, waistcoat, and breeches. In the British civil wars of the 17th century, Highland officers wore trews as lower garments, and the plaid as an upper garment; the common soldiers wore only the plaid, like a sari, wrapped around the entire body and held in place by a belt—the belted plaid (*breacan*). The kilt or "quelt," first referred to in the early 18th century, was simply the lower part of the belted plaid, not a separate garment. The kilt as a separate garment was invented by an English Quaker named Rawlinson, an ironmaster who came to the Highlands in 1727 to turn forests into charcoal. Finding the long plaid too cumbersome for the Highlanders he had hired to cut forests and tend furnaces, Rawlinson commissioned a tailor to produce the abbreviated plaid, the philibeg (*felie beag*) or small kilt, an innovation that spread so quickly through the Highlands it was part of the Highland dress banned after the defeat of the Jacobites in 1745. Once banned, it became the prestigious dress of Highland nobility (who used to disdain the belted plaid and wear trews to distinguish themselves from the common man), and the proud garb of the Highland regiments (who were exempted from the ban on Highland dress). Out of the thick mist of the Romantic movement (promoted, for example, by Sir Walter Scott's Waverly novels, and by numerous societies such as the Highland Society founded in London and the Celtic Society of Edinburgh), the reinvented garb of the Celtic Highlander became a symbol of Scottish identity. When George IV came to Scotland in 1822, the Lowlander Scott, as master of ceremonies, orchestrated the visit as a "gathering of the Gael," and Edinburgh, in Trevor-Roper's words, was

> "tartanized" to receive its king, who himself came in the same costume, played his part in the Celtic pageant, and at the climax of the visit solemnly invited the assembled dignitaries to drink a toast not to the actual or historic elite but to "the chieftains and clans of Scotland." Even Scott's devoted son-in-law and biographer, J. G. Lockhart, was taken aback by this collective "hallucination" in which, as he put it,

---

[1] See, for example, Fraser MacDonald's thoughtful discussion on August 2, 1999, and his useful references to Withers (1992) and Agnew (1996).

"the marking and crowning glory" of Scotland was identified with the Celtic tribes which "always constituted a small and almost always an unimportant part of the Scottish population." (Trevor-Roper 1983:31)

The tartan *"setts"* that distinguished the different clans were far from "traditional." Because of the huge demand that preceded the visit, patterns were assigned to different clans as they came off the loom. The Macpherson tartan, for example, had originally been "No. 155" in the pattern book of the manufacturers, William Wilson and Son of Bannockburn, who had previously found a market only in Highland regiments and were now struggling to fulfill the demand for distinctiveness of the many families planning to attend the Scott's welcome to the first Hanoverian king to visit Scotland.

The Celtic "hallucination" from which Scott and much of Lowland Scotland suffered still affects modern Celtomaniacs who see in tweed, Harris or otherwise, the salvation of the crofter-cum-Celt. A curious example of this "warped" enthusiasm is the case of Mary Elizabeth Perrins, widow of Captain Neil Perrins (a director of Lea and Perrins Worcestershire Sauce/"From the Recipe of a Nobleman in the County"). A thin woman with short gray hair, a finely chiseled nose, and broad mouth, she thought of herself as another Leverhulme (cf. Nicolson 1960) come to save Lewis. Daughter of Sir Ernest Royden of Cunard Shipping and a former nurse and model, she and Captain Perrins came to Lewis in 1960 and acquired two estates with some 19,000 acres of land as well as the woolen business of Maclennan and Maclennan.

While Captain Perrins experimented with sheep, Mrs. Perrins experimented with the tweed business, Maclennan and Maclennan (Ceemo Tweeds). Although initially praised as an entrepreneur who could revitalize the island economy, she was, by the time I arrived on Lewis in 1970–71, a woman whose world had shrunk to a trailer on her deceased husband's former estate where she lived with five dogs and a full liquor cabinet. A woman of aesthetic sensibilities and a vision that outstripped economic sense, she sought to create a tweed business that balanced the "rugged, masculine Harris Tweeds" with "light, airy, lacy, feminine fabrics" (Lubell 1962:93), in many ways foreshadowing the efforts of today's marketing of Harris Tweed by Madonna and the fashion houses of London, Paris, New York, and Las Vegas. But to the people of Lewis, her tweed business combined the worst of Highland conceits (homespun rusticity and aristocratic elegance) as she introduced gold and silver thread into thinly woven tweed from which evening gowns were made.[2] This effort failed in a tremendous debacle that is part of island folklore. According to one version, she placed an order for 2,000 tweeds when she was very drunk. The yarn-making mill in Stornoway brought workers in on night shift to meet the deadline, the local Highland-promoting agencies talked expansively of a new era of prosperity and the entrepreneurial contributions of the landowning class to the survival of crofting, and the crofter-weavers prophesied disaster even as they burned the midnight oil weaving tweed for her. As it turned out, the doomsayers were closer to the truth. Mrs. Perrins, having no actual orders for the tweeds, was afraid to tell

[2]Cecil Lubell, for many years the editor of *American Fabrics,* gives an extremely sympathetic portrait of Mrs. Perrins in his article, "High Fashion on the Hebrides" (1962).

Mrs. Perrins (in foreground) with friends

her husband, and the tweeds were stored in London. When the yarn mill and the weavers began demanding payment, Captain Perrins realized what had happened. His wife's company was declared bankrupt.

But after her husband's death she remained on Lewis, holding court from her small trailer filled with shivering whippets and pugs, crystal goblets, and towering stacks of yellowing files concerned with biblical truths in history, her well-intentioned heart committed to the welfare of the crofter-weaver. It was from Mrs. Perrins, over a glass of sauterne on a wintry evening while a gale battered the tiny trailer, that I first got a garbled version of the 1822 visit of George IV. "It was Sir Walter Scott," she whispered, a breathless conspirator. "After the '45 when Highland dress was banned, everyone forgot their clan tartans. Then along comes King Georgie, magnanimously telling everyone to go ahead and wear their national costume. Everyone was in a panic. Sir Walter saved the day by making up the patterns and passing them out at random." No wonder she was whispering. Any American who had just spent hundreds of dollars on an "official" pedigree search and had received, for his or her money, a coat of arms and a mounted piece of cloth demonstrating clan membership, would feel outraged. Trevor-Roper's version of history is hardly less disconcerting.

HARRIS TWEED

The story of Harris Tweed (in Gaelic, *Clo Mor,* "big cloth") is no less intricate in its mix of myth with concrete events. Like crofting in the field of agriculture, the Harris Tweed industry is a protected species in the jungle of industrialization.

Even its legal definition is connected with the Highland image; its marketing power is a direct result of its "social cachet," as Lord Hunter argued in a court case in 1964 when Harris Tweed was specifically defined as tweed made from 100 percent pure virgin wool produced in Scotland; spun, dyed, and finished in the Outer Hebrides; and handwoven by the islanders at their own homes. According to Grant (1998:26), Harris Tweed "is probably the only industrial product in the world whose methods of production are dictated by social considerations rather than industrial efficiency, as a chartered accountant would define it."

Long before the establishment of the Harris Tweed industry, woolen cloth ("plaiding" or "pladding"[3]) was woven on wooden looms for local consumption, sometimes contributing to the rent. The yarn was hand-dyed with local dyes, hand-spun, handwoven, and waulked—that is, washed to remove the wool grease and shrink and tighten the fabric, usually in a communal setting with rhythmic Gaelic music sung by the participants, often with improvised, teasing lyrics. As Janet Hunter points out in her detailed history of the Harris Tweed industry (2001:21–22), it is ironic that the instigation of a cottage weaving industry on Harris began just as weaving in the rest of Scotland became mechanized in factories (which occurred in relation to development of the woolen industry, promotion of sheep farming, and the Clearances).

Conditions in the first part of the 19th century (collapse of the kelp industry, dependence on the potato, widespread Clearances) had left the local populations destitute at the same time that Highland estates were fashionable (Queen Victoria bought Balmoral in 1848) and Scotland, with the help of Sir Walter Scott, had been tartanized. The term "tweed" became popular as a term to designate woolen cloth associated with Scotland, the river Tweed, and Sir Walter Scott.[4] As Highland landowners, wishing to play the Highland laird, began to dress themselves and their employees in "Estate Tweeds," the custom spread among the gentry. Lady Dunmore, of the Dunmore family that bought Harris from the MacLeods in 1834, is usually credited for developing a market in London and elsewhere for cloth woven in Harris.[5] The romantic image of a cottage industry promoted for charitable purposes contributed to the market value of the tweed, although how much philanthropy and how much marketing shrewdness lies behind this story deserves careful examination (it should be noted that while Lady Dunmore was promoting her tenants' weaving, her husband's Factor was evicting them to make way for sheep). Janet Hunter (2001:24) notes the influence of John Ruskin's home-arts movement on the establishment of the Scottish Home Industries Association and the Highland Home Industries

[3]"A long piece of twilled woollen cloth, usually having a chequered or tartan pattern, forming the outer article of the Highland costume, and formerly worn in all parts of Scotland and the north of England, in cold or stormy weather, instead of a cloak or mantle. . . . The same word as Gael. *Plaide*, Ir. *Ploid* blanket." (Oxford English Dictionary)

[4]As defined by the Oxford English Dictionary, tweed is "a trade name originating in an accidental misreading of *tweel* [a local dialect form of "twill"—see previous footnote] helped by association with the River Tweed."

[5]The Harris Tweed trademark, consisting of an orb topped by a Maltese cross, with the words "Harris Tweed" at its base, honors the role played by the Lady Dunmore in promoting Harris Tweed by taking symbols from the arms of the Earl of Dunmore (Thompson 1969:104).

and Arts Association; and Hendry (1983:80) notes the range of home industries that were promoted in the second half of the 1800s ("lacemaking, wicker work and basket-making, wood-carving, metal work, violin making, Shetland rugs, straw-work, pottery, and sealskin shoes"), of which the only cottage industry to survive into the 20th and 21st centuries was the Harris Tweed industry.

The market for "Harris Tweed" expanded in the second half of the 19th century, aided by ladies of leisure who followed the example set by Lady Dunmore (cf. James Hunter 1976:24–26). The commercial production of tweed spread from Harris southward to South Uist and Barra (1877), and more slowly to Lewis, where the proprietor, Sir James Matheson, provided construction jobs for the islanders. After Matheson died in 1878, people in the parish bordering Harris began to weave for outside markets (commercial weaving started in Lochs in 1881), and the name "Harris Tweed" was used because a market for cloth of this name had already been established. Janet Hunter (2001:47–53) calls attention to development and conflict among three marketing forces: the patronage of a small number of the landed gentry; the more commercial and professional approach of home industries agencies (whose presidents were members of the landed gentry); and local merchants acting as middlemen for the crofter-weavers. It is from this last group that the practice of supplying weavers with yarn to fulfill specific orders developed.

By World War I, all four parishes in Lewis were weaving Harris Tweed. Whereas in 1899 there were 200 looms in Harris and only 55 in Lewis, by 1911 the number of looms in Lewis had increased to 250–300 (Hunter 1976:42).

Producing a tweed at home was a long, slow process. A woman born in the 1870s recalls the difficulties that she and her brother went through in making and marketing the tweed, even when centralization and specialization were already making inroads on the process.

> About 1916 or so it took about 2 weeks to a month to do a tweed. You bought the wool from the Agricultural Board. Sixteen bags of wool, costing about £20, would do four tweeds. You needed four one-stone bags per tweed. Then you would spend a day gathering a bag of crotal [lichen scraped from rocks and used for dye]. One bag of crotal per one bag of wool. After dyeing the wool, it was spread out, dried, and sent to Stornoway to be made into yarn. The weaver wove the yarn when it came back, and about six women did the waulking [the process by which the cloth was washed and shrunk]. In those days the weavers designed their own patterns and sold their own finished tweeds. I remember going into town with my brother, we had two tweeds in the cart. We went into a shop to sell the tweed, and the man said it was poor weaving, he didn't want to pay the full price for it. I told my brother to roll it back up, we would take it somewhere else. As we left the shop, he told me I had "good cheek." In the next shop, the merchant gave my brother the regular price. We went home with £60.

By the late 19th century, domestic spinning and weaving in the mainland Highlands had been taken over by small mills. In the Hebrides, weaving continued to be a home industry, although many Lewis weavers were accused of using millspun yarns, which eventually led to protective steps to establish the Orb mark and monitor the quality of manufacturing. Weaving in the Hebrides was supported by non-profit organizations such as the Highland Home Industries and Arts Association, the Scottish Home Industries Association, and the Crofters

Agency, all established at the end of the 19th century, and by local merchants who had begun to act as middlemen in marketing the tweed. These merchants owned small general stores throughout the island and either bought the tweed from local weavers or, as was more common, gave them goods from their stores in exchange. Many of the tweed firms in Lewis grew from such small general stores using the barter system.

THE ORIGINS OF HARRIS TWEED IN CIALL

In Ciall, a man called Iain Clo had a general store and started a small tweed business in 1915. It expanded and by 1966 it was dyeing and carding wool, spinning yarn and finishing tweed—the only major mill outside of Stornoway. The explanations of his success are numerous: some describe him as a risk taker, a man who "lost the first £50 he borrowed, but he borrowed another and never looked back"; or as a man with physical disabilities caused or aggravated by military service who was unable to work like other men; or as a lucky man who got his first big order by accident because an agent selling tweed for a Stornoway merchant arrived on Lewis for the first time, asked for "John Macleod, merchant," and was mistakenly directed (because of the large number of John Macleods on the island) to Iain Clo of Ciall. "He was an earthy, natural, easy man to get on with. He never changed, even after the money came. He would sit the buyers down with a plateful of cuddies [fish] and say, 'Dig in,' 'Eat up.' He always ate them whole and never spat out the bones. The buyers liked that, they liked his easy manner."

Between World War I and II, the merchant of the general store was an extremely powerful figure. When men and women went away to the fishing, their families bought groceries on credit. "If the merchant thought the fishing season would be good, he let them have as much as they wanted; otherwise he restricted them in their buying." Long after the barter system stopped in Stornoway, it was still going strong in Iain Clo's store. A weaver was paid for his weaving not in money but in goods from the store. "You had to get just the right amount of goods, even down to tuppence in matches. Iain Clo would ask if you wanted a wireless, or would a tweed jacket fit your son. You couldn't refuse, or you wouldn't do any weaving for him for a long time." Iain Clo bought looms for many weavers, and they would weave only for him to pay off the debt. "It was two tweeds for yourself and one for the loom."

The concentration of power in the hands of the merchant brought about the inevitable tendency toward centralization and specialization. One by one the various processes of production were taken over by specialists, and gradually these specialists were brought together under one roof. Wool, standardized by the Wool Marketing Board, was shipped over from the mainland. Chemical dyes, supplied by the Scottish Home Industries, replaced natural dyes. Large boilers for dyeing the wool were supplied by the Congested Districts Board, which was formed in 1897. The most difficult and time-consuming processes were carding and spinning, which small mills on the mainland began to do on commission for weavers around the turn of the century. By the 1920s there were four mills on Lewis, and one brought looms onto the premises.

Susan Parman

The tweed mill in Ciall, 1970

Lord Leverhulme, who bought Lewis in 1918, saw the value of concentrating weavers in one place and improving the technology. He encouraged the introduction of Hattersley domestic looms, which eventually replaced the wooden looms. After World War II, the mills hired warpers to work full time on mill premises. Transporting the tweeds, which used to be the responsibility of the weavers, is now done by the mills. All processes, including design, are handled by the mills, most of which were located in Stornoway until 1990[6]—all processes except the weaving itself, which thanks to the 1964 court decision, is still done by the islanders in their own homes.

Ruaridh Dan came home from World War II, married, and began weaving with his wife's brother, but they had only one loom. At that time the mill in Ciall was buying yarn from other mills in town, warping it (that is, arranging the warp—the yarn that goes the length of a tweed—in the correct order for the weaver, who puts in the weft or cross-threads), and sending it out to the weavers together with the yarn required for the weft. Ruaridh heard that more warpers were wanted and went to ask "the old man, Iain Clo himself," about getting a job. He was hired, and worked with five other warpers in the mill shed, earning 4 shillings apiece for roughly five warps a day. They were paid by piece work rather than on an hourly basis, and received payment once a month.

After warping for several years he was promoted to the yarn store, which kept records of yarn sent to the weavers. He was paid a regular wage, but sometimes had to work on Saturday. "We were cultivating the croft but we still needed the money. It

[6]In an interesting and unusual example of ruralization as opposed to urbanization, most of the Stornoway firms were merged with the Ciall company by 1990.

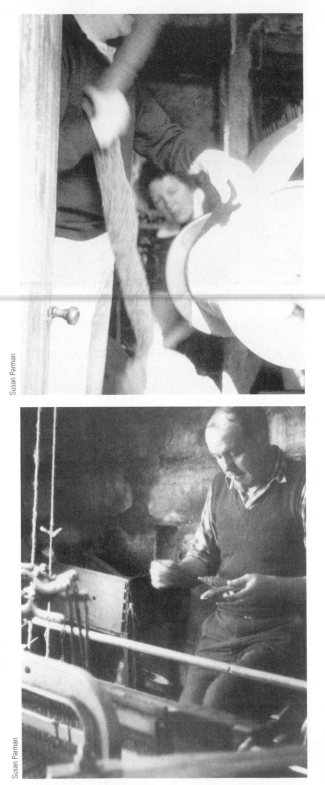

Susan Parman

Susan Parman

After "beaming" the tweed (attaching it to the loom, top), the weaver peddles his Hattersley loom (bottom).

was bad being paid by the month. You'd have a book at the merchant and pay at the end of the month. And of course the merchant was also your boss."

A slump in the industry in 1948 was followed by several difficult years in the 1950s. Iain Clo kept men on the payroll but had them build a garden wall around his house, deepen the drains on his croft, and do painting jobs. Then in 1963, seventeen people were laid off. One of them was Ruaridh.

"I was drawing unemployment benefits, and my sons had started weaving, so we were doing all right. Six months after I was laid off, the mill called and asked if I could go on one of their looms as a pattern weaver. I said I couldn't manage it at all—I had a bad leg and couldn't stand up to weaving for long periods, and in any case I was about to start building a new house. He said that's all right, as soon as you finish the house there'll be a job waiting for you."

During slack periods mill workers usually find other jobs, and many are reluctant to return when the tweed business picks up again. "I came back to the mill for the main reason that I had built this house and wanted to stay on the island. But now we've had a slack period for 2 years, and I don't think it will pick up again. Perhaps the fashion has changed; perhaps people have gone on to other kinds of cloth. The merchants and tailors prefer the wider cloth, but I don't think the mills or the weavers will go for the change. They're trying to hold onto the Orb trademark for as long as they can. But it's more important to have work; and right now the Orb mark is just a white elephant."

Some changes in the Harris Tweed industry make sense to the weavers, who sometimes shake their heads wryly over the waste of time and money associated with current methods. The mills design the tweed and bring out the warped yarn and the yarn for the weft to the road in front of the weaver's house, hoping the crofter is not too busy with sheep, fishing, or a temporary construction job to finish the tweed quickly. An unfinished, greasy tweed woven on the Hattersley loom is about 80 yards long and 28.5 inches wide for two to six shuttles and a weft of 18 shots per inch; it is made from 70 pounds of yarn (which is spun from 100 pounds of greasy wool). When finished, the tweed is 75 yards long and 29 inches wide. In the 1970s a weaver was paid £10 to £12 per piece depending on the complexity of the pattern. A full-time weaver (one who wove 2–3 tweeds a week, which left very little time for croft work) earned £800 to £1,000 per year. The weavers are conscious of income tax brackets, and may refuse a tweed that would bump them into a higher bracket.

When weavers finish the tweed on the Hattersley loom, they put it back on the road where it sits in the wind and weather until a mill van comes to pick it up (or in the case of a larger loom, a forklift comes to pick up the finished tweed). The van or truck might make several trips to pick up the tweed, or to make alternative arrangements if a weaver is not available. But everyone puts up with the delays and expense because the inconveniences of cottage production are what make Harris Tweed special. The tweed is more than a cloth; it is peat smoke and windswept moorland and the image of a free man who has escaped city life and machines and is master of his own destiny—an image that fits very well with the complex of meanings associated with crofting.

Any person can purchase his or her own yarn, weave his or her own tweeds, and sell the cloth; but before weavers can weave for the mills and have that product stamped with the Harris Tweed certification mark, they must be registered

Susan Parman

Susan Parman

Once woven, the tweed waits on a gate post to be picked up by the mill van.

with the Weavers Union. The Weavers Union is a branch of the Transport and General Workers Union, which includes mill workers, lorry drivers, and other employees. It is another anomaly of the Harris Tweed industry that workers classed as self-employed should be required to join a union of employees.

Along with mill workers, weavers bargain with the mill owners for higher wages. But because weavers are classed as self-employed, they do not qualify for unemployment benefit as mill workers do when they are laid off. Weavers buy their own looms and bobbin-winding machines (in 1970 the combined cost was around £400), and pay for lighting, heating, and the maintenance of all equipment. One of the few advantages that weavers have—if this can be con- sidered an advantage—is their freedom from the specific expectations and obli- gations associated with being hired as an employee. Weavers do not have to go through a hiring procedure; they just have to register with the Weaver's Union, which does not test skill or motivation or intentions to devote full time to weav- ing. A weaver is, by implication, an economic pluralist, which sometimes creates difficulties for the mills trying to fill orders within a limited period of time. Theoretically, the mills must deliver tweeds equally, in strict rotation, to all weavers on the island. In actuality, the tweed van meets one variable situation after another: some weavers refuse to do complex patterns; some are busy with croft work and do not want to do "urgent" tweeds; others, recovering from ill- ness, prefer not to handle the heavier tweeds. In the name of expediency, the mills develop their own private lists of reliable weavers and give them a larger share of the work, a practice that the Weavers Union is trying to stop.

A major factor hindering equal distribution of tweeds is the cost of petrol and upkeep of vans, which is born by the mills. Before World War II, weavers were responsible for transporting their own tweeds to the mills, first by cart and horse and then by motorized transport. Independent entrepreneurs began to carry the tweeds in vans and buses at 4 shillings each. The mills began to bear the cost of cartage as the result of a strike during the war when the demand for tweed was high and the number of weavers small, and rather than pay independent drivers a "cartage fee," they started using their own vans to deliver yarn and collect tweeds directly to and from the weavers. Once the mills took over transportation, they tended to deliver tweeds to weavers closest to the mills rather than uphold the principle of equal distribution, which encouraged weavers to live in council houses in town where they could be near the mills. Unequal distribution has con- tributed to Ciall's relative prosperity (since it has its own mill) and to the decline of weaving in more remote parts of the island. The unequal distribution con- tributes to the difficulty of maintaining a large labor force, which in turn limits the growth and development of the industry.[7]

Ironically with the "development" (that is, centralization) of the Harris Tweed industry, public transportation deteriorated. The independent entrepre- neurs who once carried tweeds between weaver and mill before World War II also carried passengers and provided the island with an efficient system of pub- lic transport. When buses were transporting passengers, tweeds, and other goods before World War II, there were four private buses in Ciall alone, and it was pos- sible to go into town by bus at 9 AM, 10:30 AM, 1 PM, 3:30 PM, and 7 PM, and return to Ciall at 10:30 PM (after the pubs closed and the cinema was over). Public transportation has improved since the 1970s but does not compare with this earlier service.

The very conditions that give Harris Tweed its market value—the decentral- ized, nonmechanized human element—also contribute to its instability. After 1934, when the Harris Tweed trademark was stamped on 95,241 yards, the num- ber rose steadily to over 4 million tweeds in 1940, dropped to less than half that amount in 1943, then climbed back up again to over 4 million in 1949, and so on in cycles of depression and prosperity. It peaked at 7.6 million in 1966; but

---

[7]Lewis now has a distribution center that is supposed to reduce favoritism in distributing tweeds.

by 1976, when the vote was taken on whether to shift to power-driven, double-width looms, less than 3 million yards were stamped.

Although industrialization is usually associated with weakening of personal relationships and a widespread adherence to impersonal rules (such as equal distribution), the insecurity involved with the Harris Tweed industry has strengthened rather than diminished kinship and other personal ties, and has increased the intensity of the village gossip network. Questions about "the tweed" permeate every discussion, and often constitute an initial greeting—"Have you got a tweed in the loom?" The movements and whereabouts of the tweed vans are noted and reported automatically by schoolchildren. "Stickey's tweed van just went into the Baile Stigh. . . ." Although technically illegal, some weavers go directly to the mills and request a tweed or two, and the mills support this practice in the name of expediency. Slightly drunk, one weaver confides, "The mills brought me two tweeds and I got two in town myself. I stuck those two in the attic so that anyone who comes in will be none the wiser." Neighbors are in and out of each other's houses and loom sheds, observant and questioning, on the lookout for any indication that they have missed out on some transaction in the competition for scarce goods.

When weaving was done on a wooden handloom, it was more complicated and difficult to learn—"more of an art," as the older weavers remember it today. Not only was the shuttle thrown back and forth by hand, but the lifting of different threads in the warp was done by manipulating four foot pedals in the correct order. Today the process of weaving is greatly simplified and, as many weavers describe it, very boring ("It would be so much easier to attach a motor to the thing, but then it wouldn't be Harris Tweed," one mechanically innovative weaver says wistfully). The weaver pushes only two foot pedals, and the main job is to keep an eye on the automatic shuttle to make certain that it doesn't run out of thread; all other processes have been built into the design of the Hattersley loom (cf. Thompson 1969). In other words, weaving does not entail very specialized skills; it is fairly easy to learn. A sailor, fisherman, or construction worker can learn it in a short time, leave it for awhile, and come back to it without difficulty. Neighbors substitute for each other when someone is ill or called away by some other task. Women sometimes weave, either on their own or to substitute for their husbands. Such low-level specialization and substitutability complement crofting activities and the maintenance of neighborhood ties.

THE FUTURE OF HARRIS TWEED

Despite its positive attributes, weaving is not considered an attractive source of employment—only, under certain conditions, a necessary one. The weavers themselves describe the job as dull, offering no security and no possibilities for advancement. Parents do not encourage their children to weave if they have other options. "I want him to learn some trade, if he's intelligent enough. I don't want him to stay here. The tweed is so uncertain," says one mother. Another comments cynically, "By the time he's old enough to weave, the tweeds will have failed anyway." "There's no future in it," says the father of a young boy. "I definitely wouldn't want him to be a weaver. It would be good if he went in for engineering."

Life histories of weavers show a pattern of shifting occupations. Weaving may alternate with work in the local mill, which is also relatively unspecialized. The Ciall mill must tolerate this unstable labor force, as labor is difficult to find. Eldest sons tend to leave the island for more stable, permanent jobs, leaving the croft and the loom to their younger siblings who remain to care for their aging parents. The table below shows the proportion of male weavers in each age category.

Weaving has not served as an adequate incentive to keep young people on the island. Instead, the industry has provided jobs for those who, for one reason or another, would probably have stayed anyway. The life histories support this conclusion. In 1970–71, of the weavers between the ages of 15 and 24, eight were only sons or sons who had to begin work because their fathers became ill or died; two others lived at home temporarily but planned to work elsewhere. Of those between 25 and 34, two men lived at home because they were disabled; one returned from the Merchant Service for a short period; two were only sons and several were youngest sons or sons whose parents strongly discouraged them from leaving home. Of the 35–44 age group, four remained on the island because of various ailments such as tuberculosis or "mental illness"; one had to leave the Merchant Service because of an injury; at least five stayed or returned because of family ties, the demands of aging parents, or sick siblings. In the 45–54 age category, a number of men served in the navy or other branches of the armed forces during World War II, and returned from shipwrecks and other disastrous events to the relative security of the loom.

Many of the older weavers (at least nine in the 55–64 age category) started weaving after they had returned from the United States or Canada because of the Great Depression. Some recall the horror of wandering through alleys to rummage through the garbage bins of hospitals or other large institutions for scraps of food.

Age Group: Males

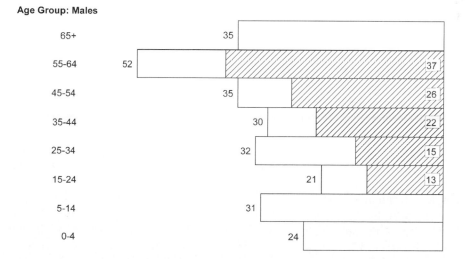

Proportion of male weavers in Ciall, 1971

The Baker was 22 when World War I broke out, and like many of the young men of Ciall he joined up to fight for his country. After 2 months of army service, he was wounded in one lung and discharged. (Tough as salted dogfish and solid as Lewisian gneiss at 78, he pounds his chest and shows visitors his scar.) He married the Ciall girl he had been courting but soon moved to Glasgow in search of work, where he found a job in a factory. The dust in the factory endangered his injured lung, and a doctor advised him to quit. He attended a technical college for 18 months so that he could start his own business, a bakery, but a bakery filled with flour was the worst possible environ-ment for him, said a doctor, who advised him to return to the islands where the air was clean. He returned to Lewis with his family and settled on the family croft.

The Bodach Beag was one of the many Lewismen who left the island in 1924 on the immigrant ship called the Metagama, *and like many of them he returned during the Depression. He joined his eldest brother on the croft, a man who had survived the sinking of the* Iolaire, *the ship loaded with servicemen that sank just outside the Stornoway harbor in 1919, and had never been well afterwards. "He would sit in at night, off by himself. If he had a drink he might come out. When the weaving started, he took that up, and he tilled the croft, kept cattle, and all that—but socially he was a misfit. It was a terrible tragedy, the* Iolaire."

The Bodach Beag bought a Hattersley loom to replace the old wooden loom his brother used, and they wove and worked the croft together. He knew he would get the croft, and for the next 40 years never left the island. He married soon after he returned, and his wife took a 6-month course in keeping poultry and milking. They concentrated on cattle rather than sheep, and sold fresh butter to the mobile vans.

Their family grew up. The eldest son attended school in Stornoway, emigrated to Rhodesia, and married an English nurse. The Rhodesian environment turned sour; he lost his job. They returned to Lewis, where he built a new house on the croft; and then, unexpectedly, he left the island to attend university and become a teacher.

The youngest son became an engineer, married a "Glasgow Highlander" whose parents came from Lewis, and settled in Glasgow. A daughter married a tradesman on the mainland. The third son, unmarried but engaged to a local girl, worked in the local tweed mill and lived at home with his parents.

It is unlikely that Harris Tweed (as currently defined) could survive outside of the context of crofting; and thus far, Harris Tweed is contributing to the sur-vival of crofting by enabling crofters to support themselves in a relative degree of comfort. The Harris Tweed industry does not prevent the loss of young peo-ple as they compare Highland life, unfavorably, with the larger society, which, paradoxically, both reviles and reveres it.

In 1976, the same year the Crofting Reform Act was passed, weavers were given the opportunity to vote on changing from handwoven Harris Tweed to power-driven, double-width looms. With the economic reorganization of the European community looming on the horizon, demand for woolen goods was up; there would be a steady market, even though fewer weavers might be employed, and they would have to travel from the rural areas to centralized loca-tions in the mills. At one of the meetings preceding the vote, one weaver said that he didn't trust the mills; that they would cut the double-width tweed down in the mill and market it as single-width Harris Tweed. When he was asked to sub-stantiate his claim, he replied, "I am only a weaver. What do you think I am?" [I am only a crofter pursuing my struggles against the laird.] A weaver from Ciall said that the number of weavers would be reduced from 600 to 50; Lewis and Harris would be turned into a wilderness; it was the Clearances all over again.

James Shaw Grant, owner of the Stornoway *Gazette*, chairman of the Harris Tweed Association and the Crofters Commission, and promoter of the 1976 Crofting Reform Act, wrote editorials and chaired meetings that promoted the change, but to no avail. With a 94 percent turnout, 497 weavers voted against the change, and 55 in favor. When the results were announced in the local Harris Tweed Association office, only four weavers came to hear the results—like most decisions, it was a foregone conclusion.

HARRIS TWEED IN 2003

In 2003, the company in Ciall that had expanded throughout the 20th century was for sale, and rumors, typically negative, spread throughout the island. One street that held 20 weavers now has only one; he weaves on a single-width Hattersley loom but has purchased a secondhand Bonas-Griffith double-width loom and plans to apply for grants to expand the loom shed and road to the shed ("Thirty-five percent toward the cost of the shed, 50 percent for the road"). Some areas of the island, such as Ness (also the locus of a fervent religious revival), have switched from single-width to double-width looms and increased the number of weavers, despite the high cost of the new looms and the unpredictability of the market. They note the efficiency of the new looms ("It's easier to do patterns, you just insert cards. . . . You can weave six tweeds once the yarn is tied in. . . . It pedals like a bicycle and stops automatically if a thread breaks. . . . No need to change bobbins, you can watch TV if you want to. . . ."). The sight of single-width tweeds sitting on fence posts to be picked up by the tweed van is gone; for the heavier double-width tweeds, a forklift comes to the door.

Harris Tweed is a luxury item, for which the market fluctuates along with other luxury items; and it is dependent on fashion, the guardian angel of which is famously fickle. North America is its largest export market. To survive in the context of the European Union and the global economy, the marketers of Harris Tweed must play a canny game of international sophistication and local authenticity. Harris Tweed's greatest strength resides in its reputation as a quality product handcrafted by salt-of-the-earth natives of the Scottish Outer Hebrides that is both "traditional" and "modern."[8] "On a warm evening in Harris, the air is punctuated by the rhythmic clack-clack of the looms, coming from the outhouses, where weavers work as many hours as their crofts will allow or demand requires" (Frank 1992:44).

In 1993 an act of Parliament created the Harris Tweed Authority. The Harris Tweed Association founded in 1909 was a voluntary association; the Harris Tweed Authority is a statutory body with greater power to protect Harris Tweed. In its argument to change the Harris Tweed Association to a statutory body, the Harris Tweed Association argued that Harris Tweed was a "local resource" with

---

[8]"Today neither its reputation nor the way it is woven has changed," claims an article on Harris Tweed published in *British Heritage* (Frank 1992) that is included in many bed and breakfast reading materials for tourists. "[T]he cloth is still manufactured mainly by hand according to the traditional process."

a "reputation" and "store of goodwill which was the collective property of the community in the Western Isles" (Hunter 2001:351–352).

Charged with "promoting and maintaining the authenticity, standard and reputation of Harris Tweed," the Harris Tweed Authority has a web site (www.harristweed.com); a reorganization plan based on funds provided by the industry, Western Isles Enterprise, and the European Union; and an advertising plan that includes a new book (Hunter 2001) and links on its web site with poetry and Highland tours. Efforts continue to diversify the image of Harris Tweed (from the heavy, hairy sportswear worn by the "gentleman in the country" to softer, lightweight cloth suitable for evening gowns), and to recapture the North American market.

The weavers, however, still tend to be older rather than younger; and the cost of switching to a double-width loom (30 percent of a new loom costing £13,000) is prohibitive to many. The latest debate over single-width and double-width looms is only one of the more recent in the passionate history of *Clo Mor*. But here and there are individual entrepreneurs, like Donald John Mackay of Luskentyre or Leslie Fiona Trotter, tailors of Harris Tweed in Tarbert, who, like Iain Clo himself, have found a whalebone on the beach and choose to erect it in the face of public opinion.

5/The Informal Structure of Leadership, Decision Making, and Social Order

The whalebone arch on p. 98 was erected in the township of Bragar on the west side of Lewis by a crofter who found it on the beach, dragged it home, and erected it with a harpoon hanging from its crest. It is clearly visible from the road and many people stop, as I did in 1970 and many times over the years, most recently in 2003 when I noted that it had been given a concrete-like coating. This durable symbol of idiosyncrasy seems to belie a fundamental rule regarding the presentation of self in crofting communities: keep a low profile. A common form of praise in Gaelic memoria published on the anniversary of someone's death is "His voice was never heard in the community."

This chapter is concerned with informal patterns of leadership, decision making, and social order that lie behind the formal structures of bureaucracy in nation-states in which crofters participate as citizens of Scotland. It explores the pitfalls and strategies of constructing relationships in a tightly knit network in which everyone knows everyone; the management of front stage and back stage representations of self (Goffman 1959); the constraints on friendship and the role of gossip. The chapter attempts to illuminate the paradox that while the general rule guiding behavior is to keep a low profile, those who break this rule do so frequently with an excess of panache.

The statement, "A piece of land completely surrounded by legislation," describes not only the croft but the existence of the crofter in a political system maintained by the nation-state of Great Britain in the context of the European Union. Numerous government organizations affect the lives of Scottish crofters. The Crofters Commission, the Highlands and Islands Development Board (now Highlands and Islands Enterprise), the Department of Agriculture, the Council of Social Services, the Crofters Union, the Weavers Union, the Wool Marketing Board, and the Land Court are only a few agencies in Britain's centralized bureaucracy that specifically affect crofting. Like every other British citizen, crofters pay taxes, are included in census surveys, are affected by legislature passed in London, and submit to the same police, solicitors, and judges who determine the course of law and order in urban environments. However, the

97

The whalebone arch in 1970 (top) and 2003 (bottom)

crofting township has its own informal structure of leadership, decision making, and social control.

In Chapter 3 I described characteristics of the crofting township that make it more of a communal entity than an aggregate of individual crofts. Despite the trends toward individualism in land use, members of crofting townships must act together in developing township reseedings, building township fences, applying

S.isan Parman

"Mullach a bhaile" (the talk of the town)

for grants to improve peat roads, deciding whether or not to argue against a request for an individual apportionment to be taken out of the common grazing, and making other decisions regarding outside agencies, other townships, and internal affairs. (For a recent example of a community decision-making project, see the Crofters Commission 2001/2002 Report discussion of the Barvas and Brue Crofting Consulting Group composed of two shareholders from three townships and a representative from the Community Council and Community Association; also see Issie MacPhail's discussion of her thesis, "Geographies of Crofting, Crofters and Community Action: Case Studies in Assynt, Skye and Lewis," on the Highlands Listserv on July 29, 1999.)

The communal features of crofting are frequently conceptualized in historical terms. Crofters conceive of themselves as a marginal minority, the jetsam of the Clearances, that needs to maintain a united front against outside forces. Symbols of authority are both respected (crofters are interested in the latest gossip about the royal British family, respect education, and give at least token respect to persons in formal positions of leadership) and distrusted, which makes leadership a hazardous undertaking and decision making complicated. Crofters have a cynical disregard for the explicit trappings of authority, are critical of decisions made by formal leaders, and utter dire predictions of failure. A symbol of authority could be anyone, from Mrs. Perrins judging a beauty contest to a county councilman, but the most frequently distrusted symbol of authority is the laird and his or her agents. Although the crofter is guaranteed fair rent and security of tenure, the landlord is authorized to enter the croft to exercise a variety of rights, including mining, quarrying, searching for minerals, using spring water, cutting peat, cutting timber, making roads, having access to sea or loch, and most importantly, to hunt, shoot, or fish.[1] The crofter has no rights to fish for salmon in the laird's river or hunt for deer in the laird's deer forest. As discussed in Chapter 3, the crofter now has the opportunity to become his or her own laird, a situation fraught with ambivalence.

Within the township, most decisions are made in a low-profile, democratic process that either lumbers slowly toward consensus or coughs up a "tyrant." To put oneself forward in explicit positions of leadership is to put oneself above one's neighbors and risk accusations of tyranny; it is a threat to communal solidarity, to the egalitarian code of township life. Nevertheless, the township requires local mediators, people with verbal and literate skills to deal with the elaborate bureaucracy of larger British society. Usually individuals who already occupy prominent positions of high status fill these positions of leadership. The schoolmaster and members of the mill owner family, for example, are constantly being called on to serve on various committees and boards (the minister, although perceived to be a person of high status, should not involve him or herself with such mundane matters). But even as they perform these duties, they are criticized for being "toffs," "too full of themselves." To take up a position of leadership is to offer oneself up for crucifixion, and many people go to elaborate lengths to distance themselves from the negative attributes of leadership, which can make decision making a torturous, indirect process.

In 1971 I was asked to serve as secretary for the Village Hall Committee, a youth club whose purpose was to promote recreation for the young people of the community. When I asked who the other officers were, I was told that there were none, the fault of the area youth organizer who had been lax in getting one started. When I met the area youth organizer, a young man from the island who lived in Stornoway, he told me that it was the responsibility of the community to start youth clubs; his job was to service these groups once they got started. I found out that the Council of Social Services had foreseen the difficulty of recruiting leaders from rural communities and had established an arrangement whereby the local councillor, the grazing clerk, and the postmaster would serve as the trustees for the hall. But on Lewis these persons were usually devout members of the Free Church, which was adamantly opposed to the worldly activities of the Village Hall (see Chapters 7 and 8).

Eventually a member of the mill family agreed to start the club, and I served as secretary for awhile. I was surprised when I was given books of former minutes; no one had told me that the club had a history. But when I tried to reconstruct the events of previous meetings, I ran into a curious difficulty. The minutes were in English, as all formal documents are, which meant that all the names were in English rather than in patronymics or nicknames. In an account of a conflict that led to temporary closure of the hall, at least three different people with

---

[1]A poignant story told in 2003 by the son of a deceased crofter may be idiosyncratic but it also provides insight into the impact of the crofter/laird conflict on the association of crofters with environmental issues. "All that week you could hear shooting along the crofts. The landlords can shoot at anything, they have the right. My father was down at the end of the croft. He found a huge white bird. He didn't know what kind it was, he'd never seen anything like it. He thought maybe it was migrating and got lost or wounded. He used to feed it. Eventually it got so tame it would follow him into the house. And then one day it was gone."

the same "English" name played important roles in the events—but no one could remember (or, more likely, no one would tell me) who was who. Individual contributions to Ciall history had been concealed in a smokescreen of formal English record keeping.

The position of township clerk is difficult because of its visibility. Most individuals take it with the understanding that it is obligatory for all males of the village to take their turn and that everyone should recognize that they are doing it with great reluctance. They emphasize that they are working themselves to the bone for the good of their neighbors.

A few people, however, are carried away with the heady spirit of power; they begin to swagger a bit, become a manifest representation of the bureaucracy with its rules and deadlines. "Here comes Twenty Questions," muttered one man about a township clerk who took seriously all the forms to be filled out. Angry with another clerk who said he would report those who had done less than their share of work on the peat road to the Crofters Commission, one man called the clerk "His Lordship" who was "lording it over everyone in the village." Some were accused of having taken advantage of their position, for example, to get an apportionment. There appear to be two modes of operation in political gear: silent invisibility or aggressive visibility.[2] Only a few people manage to achieve a happy medium, but they need a tough skin.

> *Padruig a Khing (Patrick the King), nicknamed for his willingness to take on visible positions of responsibility, was the township clerk in 1970. An energetic, sociable man in his 30s, he appeared to enjoy the task of visiting the households with information about subsidies, brucellosis testing, and sheep drives, although he described it as an unpleasant chore because of the visibility of the position and the probability of becoming involved with disputes. The clerk provides agricultural statistics for the Crofters Commission, applies for and disperses subsidies, arranges transportation for fencing, sand, and fertilizer, pays contractors, and so on. His most difficult job is to enforce communal participation; all too quickly he will find himself labeled "his lordship," or nicknamed "the constable," his home referred to as the "House of Parliament." Most decisions are made not by visible leaders such as the township clerk but by a few invisible community leaders who mobilize public opinion. All decisions are made in the background rustle of discussion and rumor long before a vote is taken in a committee meeting; most explicit decisions are unanimous.*

CROFTER VERSUS LAIRD

> *On a cold, sleet-hammered day in February 1971, the temporary postman (a cousin of the postmaster, who was sick with pneumonia) walked into my room and announced that I was "summoned to the castle." Mrs. Perrins had called his house early that morning (he had one of the few phones in the village) and asked him to tell me to be at her home by the middle of the afternoon.*

---

[2]In 2003 I asked someone what he thought of the new Land Reform Bill and the possibility of townships acting together to buy land as a group. He replied, "It's like the Balkans here, with cliques in the different neighborhoods, everything run by committees. No one can make a decision except by tyranny and fascism. Uilleam [not his real name] is a little Hitler. All he needs is a mustache. He ignores the rules and attacks people who follow them."

*Intrigued and annoyed (it was decidedly not the type of day I wanted to be out in),
I battled my way through the gales to her "castle"—a small trailer on her deceased
husband's estate. A blast of hot air poured through the door as I went in—there were
four electric burners in the small room, but the five short-haired dogs shivered
pathetically when Mrs. Perrins waved them out of the chair I was to sit in.
"Anthropology is just part of history," she stated without preamble, and launched
into a meandering diatribe about the family tree of Christ, the predictions contained
in Isaiah on the modern state of Israel, and the prehistoric beehive huts on a neighboring estate. She was drunk, and the files of her "research" were piled perilously
close to the electric heaters. "They're sending the new head of the Highlands and
Islands Board[3] out here next month to hear my plans to revitalize the tweed business," she confided. "It's a secret, but I'll soon be starting loom-powered weaving.
The hand loom can't do exciting designs, like diamonds, but it does give Harris
Tweed weavers the finest thighs in the world! The definition of Harris Tweed implies
a muddy quality, since the yarn must mix at least two colors. But I prefer sharp lines
of color. I should have enough orders to keep all the weavers of Lewis busy—to hell
with the Orb mark." From grandiose plans to save the Highlands she went on to
explain "why Hebrideans are fat" (a Lamarckian theory that related long periods of
curing salted meat and fish to water retention). I left the trailer at about 6:00; the
pitch-black darkness of winter in northern latitudes had already descended, and the
small light of her trailer was almost immediately extinguished.*

Britain is a land still obsessed with class based on birth; and while Scotland
tweaks this image with a humor born in part of a poor past and a memory of
exploitation and what Michael Hechter calls "internal colonialism," it participates with an intensity that marks it as irrevocably different from Americans
(who while just as obsessed with the markers of class, such as what school you
went to and what car you drive, believe that the only difference between upper
class and lower class is money, which they expect any day now to have).[4]

Scotland has the most concentrated pattern of private landownership in
Europe. Half of Scotland is owned by 579 landowners, and more than a third of
this land is held in estates of 20,000 acres or more. Much of this pattern of ownership is the result of laws that, over the past 300 years, made it easier in
Scotland to transfer common land to private property (cf. Callander 1987).

---

[3]The Highlands and Islands Development Board, now Highlands and Islands Enterprise, is a
common target of criticism among crofters because of its ambivalence about the contradictory goals
of economic pragmatism and Highland ideology. During the year I was there, a new chairman was
appointed, and the appointment was widely criticized for being politically motivated and totally
inappropriate to the needs of the Highlands—especially because the person was not a Gaelic-speaking Highlander. A month after I was "summoned" to Mrs. Perrins's "castle," I was giving a slide
show on New Mexico to the schoolchildren in Ciall when the new chairman arrived, and I attended
a reception for him at the schoolmaster's. I heard later that he had visited Mrs. Perrins before coming to the school and that she had talked nonstop; every time he wanted to say something he stood
up, prefaced his remarks with "Madam . . ." and sat down again, only to find that one of the dogs
had leaped into his chair. My sympathy for him was sharply eroded, however, when he told a joke
about lazy crofters.

[4]This difference was brought home to me when, during a visit to a rabidly pro-crofter family on
the mainland, the local laird stopped by on a mission of charity. The head of the house literally
doffed his cap and bowed, calling him "my lord." When I commented later on his behavior, he said,
"These people are different from us—their noblesse oblige."

Despite the high concentration of land in a few private hands, significant changes in landownership have occurred over the past hundred years. In the 1870s, when the *New Domesday Book* was published, only 70 people owned half of Scotland. Also, the percentage of land taken out of private ownership and transferred to the state has increased (from about 0.2 percent to 13 percent). The squires of England, the gentry of Ireland, and the lairds of Scotland are essentially anachronisms, feudal lords hemmed in by a government committed to socialism. The symbolic representatives of pomp and tradition and world empire, they are Britain's show pieces, like the royal family that upholds the image of Great Britain while the parliament and prime minister roll up their shirtsleeves and get down to the unadorned business of running the country.

The author V. S. Pritchett wrote several stories about an eccentric rich couple, nicknamed Noisy and the Fairy Queen, who alternately terrified and intrigued the surrounding English countryside. Before living in Scotland I considered the Pritchett characters to be bizarre literary inventions; but after meeting several lairds who seemed to have stepped right out of a Pritchett story, I decided that Pritchett was an observant ethnographer of the peculiar ambience of feudalism that has survived in 20th-century Britain (until the beginning of the 21st century, when it was dissolved in Scotland by an act of Parliament). As Ronald Blythe says in *Akenfield*, "It was the duty of a squire to be meaner, odder and richer than any of his equals in the locality." Officially such persons are looked up to, and often consider themselves the agents of change and leadership; but an enormous gap of confidence, rooted in historical reference points, lies between them and their tenants.

Lewis once belonged to the MacLeods, descendants of the Norse Lord of the Isles, Somerled. In 1612 it went to MacKenzie of Kintail, or the Seaforth family who, burdened with debt in the 19th century, sold it to Sir James Matheson in 1844 for £190,000. The English soap lord, William Hesketh Lever, the first Lord Leverhulme, bought Lewis from Duncan Matheson in 1918 and Harris in 1919, tried to turn the island into the fishing capital of the North Atlantic, and sold it in 1923 after he had lost £1.5 million. Today it is carved up in numerous estates owned by individual lairds, commercial companies, and public bodies and trusts. The main interest of these landowners is not the rent that they receive from the crofters (the Crofters Act of 1886 almost guaranteed that estates based solely on crofting would not be money-making propositions) but the hunting and fishing rights, and, in some cases, the romantic role of feudal lord or paternalistic clan leader. A few "lairds" take an active interest in crofter causes and serve as self-appointed leaders on the island.

Ciall crofters do not know their "laird," who is, in fact, a group of anonymous shareholders in a commercial company, mostly Englishmen who come up to the island to fish and shoot game; but they use the category of laird, "toff," "The Big Cheese" to define what it means, and by contrast, to be a crofter. The existence of the "indolent, stupid rich," as one crofter-weaver described them after he had spent a year as a bagpiper for one such laird, legitimizes all the informal, semi-legal, and illegal economic dealings in which crofters frequently engage, of which poaching is the most popular. Salmon stolen from the laird's river is a delicacy, the most prestigious dish to serve at peat-cutting time, thumbing their noses at historic injustices.

Dinner at the peats

Local lairds are the objects of an ambivalent respect and dislike, a favorite target of barbed humor. Lord Leverhulme is an historical reference point for Lewis residents seeking to characterize the motives and probable outcomes of plans made by modern lairds such as Mrs. Perrins. "She thinks herself another Leverhulme. But she'll fail the same as him." When I first went to visit Mrs. Perrins, a friend told me later, "I thought to myself, what a fool, talking to Perrins if she wants to find out about the islanders." But the county councillor and schoolmaster frequently went to Mrs. Perrins, urging her to use her influence to "save the islands," and she wrote numerous letters, sought signatures for petitions, and dabbled in disastrous economic ventures. As a "local personality," she was asked to participate in prestigious but sensitive village events such as choosing a May Queen (1964 Village Hall minutes). Many of her projects were culturally inappropriate. For example, she sponsored a contest to clean up the "junk" scattered over the island. Much of this "junk" is, in fact, considered a resource, a communal recycling center. Whenever my broken-down, smoke-spewing car needed a part, someone in the village would remember that a car of the same make could be found in some other part of the island, and an expedition would be organized to go over, renew the acquaintance of the tenant of land on which this other car (Perrins's "junk") was located, and retrieve the necessary part. "Junk" is an important resource for strengthening inter-island ties. No one ever says no to a request to cannibalize materials on one's property; and the acquiescence establishes a relationship, an obligation to be eventually repaid. But the crofters are accused of being apathetic when the do-gooder schemes of zealous lairds are resisted or criticized (often appropriately) for their likely failure.

The existence of formal leaders in the community who are already part of the social elite is useful in several ways. They provide villagers with access to resources in the larger society, and criticism of them helps to crystallize the communal, egalitarian spirit of interaction. But when decisions are actually made within the township, the elite seldom make them. The effective decision making occurs through casual discussion, rumor, and the quiet role of a few invisible leaders who mobilize opinion and in some cases carry out direct action.

INFORMAL LEADERS

The ability to generate social consensus is an important symbol of leadership. In fact, the best leader is one who is not perceived as a leader at all, but a reliable person who mixes well and can get a ball rolling quietly and without calling attention to him or herself.

During the early part of my stay, when I was trying to study fishing as well as weaving as alternatives to crofting, I was talking to a 70-year-old man about the local boats that used to go out regularly to fish for cod and ling. I asked: "On your boat, who was the captain?" He replied, "On a fishing boat, everyone is a skipper." "But what about decisions?" I asked. "Who decides when to go? when to cast nets? when to take down sails? when to return?" "They all do," he said.

In the 1950s, a bus company called the Western Lewis Coaches was formed. It was owned by people from four villages, including Ciall, who all took turns being manager. "It got so there were too many directors," said one person trying to explain why the company folded. "All chiefs, no Indians."

In the case of the boat, decisions were made by consensus, by a process I was to witness time and time again during my stay in Ciall. Discursive, slow-moving, and communal as a tide deciding to go in or out, consensual decision making has no visible leader, only indirect suggestions from those whose influence is almost imperceptible in the pre-decision-making discourse. The second case, involving the bus company, was an example of what happens when individuals mistake a position of authority for a license to exercise power. Squabbles erupt, individuals are pushed into a position of uncomfortable visibility, and the tension makes effective decision making almost impossible.

Most sheep roundups are organized through consensual decision making. On one occasion, a decision was made, independent of the township clerk ("He's supposed to notify us of fank dates, but no one can get hold of him, he's always away at meetings"), to bring the sheep in for lambing. I asked one of the participants how the decision was made. "We discussed it and decided" was the laconic reply. I asked what specifically happened. Memory of specific details is a great source of pride, and taking his time he sketched out a process that was like ripples spreading out from the drop of a pebble in the pool. His brother had spoken to him, asking when they should go; after elaborate discussion of past years of lambing, when ewes were brought in either too early or too late, they decided on a date that seemed safe, and both brothers talked to neighbors, who spoke to other neighbors. The date was modified to accommodate people working in the mill; several people indicated they would be away for various reasons. Although authority rests with the township clerk to organize township activities, and to take punitive action if individuals do not participate (for example, writing to the Crofters Commission, or asking them to pay for their share of labor in money), few use this explicit route to decision making. Most decisions are the communal result of the actions begun by informal ripple-starters, those who drop the pebble quietly into the pool and then assist the perpetuation of ripples.

Consensual decision making: Fixing a drain on the peat road

The ripple-starters are those who involve themselves extensively in township affairs, always attending meetings and showing up for projects. With humor, readiness to have a "quick drink with the boys," and skillfulness in conveying significant information without being seen as gossips, such individuals serve as informal leaders. They do not put themselves forward, but they exert an irrepressible force toward decision making. "You've got to do a lot of talking first." "Everyone immediately wonders about your motives—you've got to show them that you won't personally benefit." "You've got to persuade everyone before the actual vote is taken. They have to know that everyone else agrees before they'll risk sticking their necks out to vote." "You have to talk about it first, discuss the merits of it. You must never ask someone outright what he thinks of it, because he might disagree and then he'll have to stick with what he first says."

During the pre-decision discourse, possible courses of action are broached hypothetically—"What if we should do this [for example, have a fank this Saturday]," as if the speaker were distancing him or herself from the suggestion. No one commits to a positive response; the most positive response is something along the lines of "No one has any objections." But to reach this stage of agreement by the default of negation, people float hypothetical objections—"Perhaps the wool won't be long enough"; "Perhaps it will be too wet." If there are too many hypothetical objections that are not resolved by informative comments (such as, "Carloway cut last week; the wool was not too bad"), the decision is postponed. Almost all of the decisions made when a committee or township meets are unanimous. If township members disagree with the decision they know will be made, they stay away from the meeting.

COMMITMENT AND BETRAYAL

A Lewis man living away from the island compared the people with whom he grew up (and to whom he later returned) to "computers that haven't been programmed." I remembered this comment one afternoon, when, after having made an arrangement to meet some people, I arrived to find that they were not at home.

An important part of decision making has to do with attitudes toward commitment, and with expectation of commitment or noncommitment on the part of others. I had always tried to make decisions according to certain abstract principles such as "fairness" or "honesty." If I told someone I would do something, I would do my best to be "reliable" and "trustworthy." But in Ciall I kept confronting situations that felt uncomfortably like betrayals. Were people just being nice, saying yes to avoid conflict, and then doing what they really wanted to do? Why did I often feel that people wanted to avoid making decisions, avoid committing themselves, so that many things ended up being done at the last moment?

"Spontaneous—no preprogramming allowed," I thought, and then remembered the computer comparison, and tried to figure out what all the "betrayals" had in common. I realized that they all occurred when I had made arrangements ahead of time but hadn't been around to nurse the human element along to the moment of fulfillment. It wasn't as if people didn't want to make arrangements and commitments; quite the opposite—they were overcommitted to personalism. A person must never refuse anyone anything—a weaver coming into the mill to request an extra tweed, a neighbor asking his cousin the hotel owner to sell him a bottle when the hotel is technically closed, friends asking you to throw over your own plans for the evening to take them somewhere. If you ask them to commit themselves to a plan of action far ahead of time, you are in effect cutting them out of this web of communalism, asking for a special relationship.

FRIENDSHIP

A special relationship, or "friendship" as an American usually thinks of it, is functional in a mobile urban environment. A "friend" is someone on whom you can depend in a rushing, mobile world; someone who will drop other commitments and come specifically to your aid, in a relationship that competes with all other relationships. But in Ciall, friendship in the American sense of the word would be too intense. People are already surrounded with multiple and equally significant others, in relation to whom they are trying to diminish rather than increase obligation. Every villager is continually faced with overwhelming indebtedness to people he or she will continue to see all his or her life. One result is that no single relationship must be allowed to compete with this generalized indebtedness; another is that people do their best to minimize rather than maximize relationships.

The tendency to stereotype people is one expression of minimizing relationships. Stereotyping is a form of control; it is a process by which you simplify others, reduce their complexity, freeze them into images that can be used for various purposes of interaction, such as object lessons ("Don't be like Inis, he never stops in for a drink when he's in town, he stays to himself, he's odd"). When

Children at a birthday party

people gather information about others through gossip, they do not want information that promotes a compassionate understanding of who someone is; they want to control others, fit them into a category that strengthens their own position. Interaction is a constant battle, an exciting, humor-filled battle, in which information is both the weapon and the goal. Minimize information about yourself; maximize simplified interpretive categories about others.

I was amazed to find that although everyone I talked to knew an incredible amount of gossip about almost everyone else in the village, many villagers had never met each other. Inevitably, when they did meet, their stereotypes changed. "I had always heard he was a bit odd, always stayed to himself and didn't mix much. But when I talked to him at Jonnie's house, he was quite all right." The tendency to reduce information, to speak guardedly, to rely on quotes, stories, and jokes in the performance (rather than the exploration) of communication, creates a sense of distance.

The automatic reflex to minimize information is reflected in numerous ways, not only in discussion. People build houses so that the door through which people enter always faces away from the road. They try to minimize debt by making requests in a last-minute, matter-of-fact way at the end of rather than at the beginning of visits. *"Mo run,"* my secret, is a term of endearment. Discussion itself is curiously involuted and indirect: people want to be able to communicate, but without being accused of having communicated a definite idea. They know that whatever they do (or are thought to do) will be used to link them with the past and the future; the history of community interaction is forged in the white-hot, transforming fire of gossip.

Thus, if I wanted anything done, I could not rely on a promise of commitment or an assumption of friendship but had to generate it from interaction rather than make plans in advance; I had to practice immediate rather than long-term influence in the competitive marketplace of personal, community interaction. If I wanted information, I could not appeal to a respect for science but had to gain it in the context of interaction, as someone who made sense in these contexts, as friend or member of the family rather than as a high-status, authority-symbolizing "anthropologist."

To be immersed in such personalism is both frustrating and satisfying. Said one young woman who had been reviled in stereotypes more cruelly than most, "Whatever else this place means, it means security." "I must leave," many say; but they don't, or else they come back, or at least look on the past with nostalgia. Every day, every contact is full of the immediacy of specific trivia, the malicious interest by which the communal self is constructed. Shortly before I left the island, I was told at a midnight ceilidh, "You have a place here as you will never have anyplace else in the world. Wherever you go or whatever you do, the people here will have an interest." People rarely said "my friend"; instead they said, "Our Jonnie" or "Your Chrissie." When I left, it would be "our Sue."

MAINTAINING SOCIAL ORDER: "THEY MAY BE MURDERERS, BUT THEY'RE OUR MURDERERS"

The police and the courts represent state-level symbols of law and order, but the immediate symbols of law and order in the community are fear of what others will think of you; the chastising, sin-oriented influence of the church; and the control of women as wives and mothers. Occasionally a few men might band together to apply a bit of "friendly persuasion" to someone who had broken township rules. If none of these work, the formal structure of the law may be called on, but this step is taken with great reluctance, for an individual does not stand alone; his or her shame reflects on his or her family and community.

When I first arrived on the island of Lewis, I reserved a bed and breakfast lodging with the tourist association, and was directed to the house with instructions to go on in if no one answered the door, that the lady of the house was at evening service. So accustomed did I become, throughout my stay, to open doors, packages being sent by "the next bus" when they were inadvertently left behind in a shop, and a wide assortment of services based on trust, that examples of "crime" stood out as unusual and interesting deviations from the norm.

The most scandalous crime to have occurred on Lewis "in the last hundred years," as I was frequently told, was the murder of an old woman in one of the westside villages several years before I came. A young man accused of the murder was tried in Inverness; the verdict, "not proven," is an ambiguous decision unique to Scottish law that is the alternative to "innocent" and "guilty." The villagers gave the gruesome, specific details of the murder itself; someone who attended the trial observed that no matter how certain the villagers were of his guilt, they drew together to protect him and refused to give evidence that would convict him. But when the trial was over, "They wouldn't leave him alone. He couldn't face anyone—even if he was innocent, he had been tried and found guilty. He tried to move to Harris, but they found out who it was and refused to sell the house to him. Finally he had to leave the island. But his family—his parents, his siblings, his cousins—they will always be made to suffer for it."

In Stornoway are a chief inspector of police, two sergeants, and four constables; and several police officers are scattered around the rural areas. Their main responsibility, according to the disgruntled villagers, is to lie in wait for people coming out of hotels to trap them with the Breathalyzer. Police officers are generally seen as the representatives of an exploitative system who stick their noses into situations where they don't belong; their behavior is interpreted in personal terms. They have power, get to know everyone in the area, and depending on their experience with these people can put people in tight spots or help them out. "They stopped Uilleam for the Breathalyzer but he didn't register. Uilleam thought it was a personal grudge because he had beat the policeman in a race they had the other day across the moor."

Occasionally crimes of theft, or more rarely, of violence occur. Halfway through the year a neighbor was arrested and charged with stealing. In the ensuing storm of discussion, previous suspicious events were recalled—missing money from a house, lumber from a mill in Stornoway, bobbins from neighboring weavers, salmon from a fellow poacher's net, a check, a fur coat, even peat from various houses around the island. My few inexpensive pieces of jewelry had disappeared shortly after I arrived (and mysteriously reappeared several months later). "He'll say he was drunk and didn't know what he was doing." "His own brother went in to persuade his wife not to marry him." "They should go away where no one knows them." "They should emigrate, but it'll catch up with them. The boys will be haunted by it; they have his blood." "He wanted to borrow the car the other day—thank goodness you had just left with it." When he was let off with a relatively light fine, the gossip channels explored personal connections to explain this, and many were outraged when he was seen enjoying himself at a wedding. A month later, holes were knocked in the bottom of a boat in which his father had a share and that he occasionally used. At the same time, he continued to interact as kinsman and neighbor, being invited in for tea, doing odd jobs, and giving driving lessons.

A police officer who was called in to investigate a missing check told the person who had called him, "I know country folk—somebody will have seen something, but no one will tell." Two months later, after the case was closed, a neighbor reported vital information over a teapot, and this bit of evidence joined the circulating gossip; but gossip rarely extends to testimony in court.

"There are more crimes here than anyone in a court will every find out about," said one person. "If it's taken into a court, innocent people get hurt; it's best to keep it in the community where everyone knows what's going on." On one occasion several young men were beating up the village youth; "They were playing Glasgow Mafia." A fight started, and the truth came out, after which the instigator stayed in his house for 5 years. "When he came out, it started up again, but everyone knew who it was and was ready for them. They may be murderers, but they're our murderers."

People who live alone and behave strangely serve as scapegoats for suspicion when crimes occur. Each neighborhood has its favorite suspect. When people fight, they dredge up things about each others' ancestors. "You're like this because of your granny."

Drink usually plays a role in crime, being used as an excuse for it, as the context in which additional information comes out, or as a contributing factor. One unusual court case involved a man who had gone to the dentist after having several drinks at the hotel in town. The dentist, who had also been drinking, forgot to give him an anaesthetic. When he yanked the infected tooth, the patient hit him and knocked him out. The nurse came in, found both on the floor—the dentist unconscious, the patient fainting from pain—and called the police. The patient won the case.

To help the police, some local people serve as "special constables," but this is interpreted as "spying on your neighbors." According to one man, special constables "are supposed to help policeman at election times, but the bad ones help at other times as well." The tires of one "special constable" were slashed because he had informed on a neighbor. Another quit when he was invited by a police officer to go in to a hotel for a drink with him; he didn't want to be visibly associated with the law.

Other men are appointed "Justice of the Peace." Appointed by the county sheriff, they are people already in a position of authority, either the schoolmaster or mill owner or someone who has served in the armed services. Their major task is to give letters of reference, to sign documents such as out-of-work forms and wills, and "to read the Riot Act to persons of 12 or more who have assembled with the intent to create a disturbance" (this act was passed in 1714; it has never been read in Ciall).

GOSSIP AND THE CREATION OF HISTORY

Lewis is often referred to as *Tir an t-soisgeul,* land of the gospels. It is also *Tir an t-sgeultachan,* land of gossips. *Sgeul* can be meteor tidings or worldly news. A *sgeultach* is a (female) gossip; *sgeultachd* is gossip rendered into history, or tradition.

When I first came to Ciall, I was struck by the sense of space: by the absence of trees, the houses that stood separate from each other in a long line against the sky between the sea and the moor like stone monuments against the weather. Then as I stayed, the sky seemed to be filled with thin filaments of social connection as I realized how much people knew about each other and watched continuously for new information, and how aware people were of the others watching (when I joked about missing a lot of potatoes, as we were digging them one day, someone replied, "Well at least the earth is black"—and I saw him looking out over the crofts, calculating who had dug their potatoes yet and who hadn't). I had dreams of large eyes filling the sky. When a friend returned to the island after many years absence, he said his first impulse was to go out in the front yard and drop his trousers for all the binoculars that he knew would be trained on his mother's house.

It is difficult for people raised in the anonymity of an urban environment to imagine living in a setting in which you are continually confronted with the living memory (sometimes accurate and sometimes inaccurate) of your mistakes and failures. Your actions are woven together and interpreted not only with

Susa Parran

Sharing stories

regard to interpreting your past and predicting your future, but also with regard to connecting you with a vast network of people, past and present, who share your "blood" and thus the tendency to behave predictably.

Gossip is the channel by which community interaction becomes transformed into historical reference points used to interpret and predict past, present, and future behavior. As Goffman (1959) described for Shetland in *The Presentation of Self in Everyday Life,* behavior on Lewis may be described in terms of drama, role playing, front stage and back stage, and audience. An individual plays his or her role before the community, whether he or she is actually in the community or not. Gossip renders people ever-present. If a person is gone for awhile, he meets himself when he returns to the village, often in a form he doesn't recognize.

I was vividly impressed by the speed with which people become appropriated in an incident that occurred during the winter of 1971. The day was bitter, I was fighting a cold, and I stayed inside most of the day working on notes. At about 3:00 in the afternoon I went to visit a neighbor who cried out, "Are you all right? I thought you had been taken to the hospital." Over the next few days, after being greeted by people in various states of alarm, I learned what had happened. A couple from the other side of the village who didn't know me very well were driving back from town. They saw a car stopped at the side of the road. It was gusting a cold rain so they went past, but by the time they got home, they still hadn't figured out who was in the car (cars are a great topic of conversation; even schoolchildren have learned the license plate numbers of cars all over the island). This one was new to them and I was a stranger, so it must be mine. They mentioned this possibility to a neighbor, who asked why they hadn't stopped to help me. This neighbor criticized the couple to another neighbor, saying that for all they knew, I might have had an accident. By mid-afternoon, I was dying in a Stornoway hospital. To this day there must be people who still refer to "Sue's accident" (as in, "I remember when Iain got his tractor, it was a week after Sue's accident, when Mairi and Calum passed her by on the Barvas road, they always were an inconsiderate family").

The pervasiveness of the Eye—the watchful neighbor, the gossiping tongue, the person on the next street with the binoculars—is an important element in social control. Even the thought that someone might think you were doing something keeps behavior circumspect and results in the channeling of deviance. There are stylized, ritualized changes that anxious, frightened people can go through to express their needs, as in the stages of "conversion" and "mental illness" (see Chapters 8 and 9).

The difference between front stage and back stage is clearly defined. "What matters," said one person, "is not what you do, but what people think you've done." I was taught this lesson vividly when I spent all night, in the company of others, in the home of a bachelor. It was not that I had stayed the night—such all-night visiting in company was a common form of socializing—but that my presence was advertised. It didn't matter what had (or hadn't) happened; no one was interested in the truth. My family was scandalized—not because they thought anything had happened, but because they were afraid of how the gossip about me might reflect on them. To compound matters, the bachelor's sister shortly afterwards invited me to cut peats with them, thereby giving public recognition to a potential relationship.

By this time I was annoyed. I had done everything I could to explain the innocence of the visit. I suddenly understood the choice that many people made when fighting the tidal onslaught of a socially defined, erroneous image of themselves: the sear anger that drives a man to the bothan or to extremes of violence, or that molds the character of the village clown or the person who actively breaks conventions; or the choice of the antisocial being who goes out only at night or stays up in a room, always leaving when someone comes in to visit. I was already *mullach a bhaile* (roughly translated as "talk of the town"—*mullach* means top of or eminent, i.e., supremely visible); I might as well enjoy it.

I accepted the sister's invitation and went to the peats in a very unusual state—filled with a kind of blustery to-hell-with-them-all feeling for the whispering sea of gossip that rose and fell in relation to every movement on the vast screen of social visibility. My usual calm state, my detachment, my quiet acquiescence to the social flow was shredded, gone forever. In other words, I had become involved.

The day was angry and wild, a cold, wet day for cutting peat. Rain and hail moved in over the moor in iridescent sheets of pearl. In the heaviest bursts we crowded in under a tent, nine of us, full of crude jokes about the rain puddles we were sitting in. We ate salmon and ginger cakes ("I left behind the currant and apple tarts, they weren't good enough for the peats," said our hostess, making certain that we knew she had honored us; "You're stuffing us at tea time so we won't want any dinner," was the usual distancing reply), rested elbows on knees, shared cigarettes. I was paired with the bachelor, of course; we took turns cutting and throwing the brown buttery slabs of peat onto the bank and compared

Explicit commitments: Cutting peat

notes on our disgrace, like conspirators. Over a quarter of a century older than I, avuncular and possessed of a detachment that mirrored the best of anthropological traditions, he was both embarrassed and amused. I had gone through fire, he said; now I had some idea of what it was all about. I said I had learned that truth is irrelevant; appearance is all. Of course, he said; if you maintain the proper image, you can do anything you want.

There are rules for gossiping. "I told my children when they first started going to dances, if there is a fight or anything going on, leave it there, don't bring it back to the house. Now when I ask them about a dance, they touch their noses to tell me I'm being too nosy." There is such a thing as too much gossip; certain situations should be kept separate. One of the reasons that women are criticized for gossiping is that they carry a major portion of the burden of social control and exercise this obligation by gossip, which is often resented. Fights between men that start over gossip are usually made up in a drinking setting; but the women involved are more slowly forgiven.

As in all societies, there are culturally appropriate modes of deviance, and clear-cut signals for entering into them. So clearly are situations defined that you essentially give over any decision making when you enter them; they determine your behavior. As a result, many people exert control over their own behavior by avoiding getting into certain situations. When the post office was on strike, the mills could not send payments to the weavers so delivered them by tweed van; "If we had had to pick them up in town, we would have drunk the money." "I know I'll drink if I go; best not to go." Carry-outs (buying alcohol to take with you, instead of staying to drink) are popular in part because they limit the amount a man can drink.

Gossip almost always has an edge of malice. "Murdo [the dead brother] was the best of the lot." (As one proverb says, "If you want to be praised, die.") Gossip is often better than late-night horror movies, full of grisly tales of illness and injury ("his hand was black with stitches"; "he lay there with pus streaming out of his ear"). Gossip is often indirect and full of innuendoes; people don't want to be accused themselves of having said something about someone that could itself be the topic of gossip. There is a gamesmanship in gossip: "I think I know what you're talking about. . . . You don't know what you're talking about." The giving and concealing of information is like a jousting match.

Everyone is aware of the differences between front stage and back stage, and people have strategies for bringing concealed behavior out into the open where it may be discussed and rendered into concrete history. A favorite method is asking questions. "People who ask questions already know the answer." One man described giving a ride to a man and his wife:

> The woman started asking me all sorts of questions, finally ending with, "You wouldn't be married to Mairi Macleod, would you?" She knew who I was but never asked me directly. I asked: did you know all that before you started asking the questions? Her husband laughed and said she had told him everything from the time the car had cleared the ridge to when it stopped to pick them up.

If you tell people what they already know, you legitimize their knowledge; they can use it as fact rather than rumor, which is a more powerful coin of exchange in gossip. Gossip contains new information, and it repeats and solidifies

Susan Parman

Mock fight (note the cigarette being rolled in the right hand)

old information, creating a bond between the old and the new in interpretation. Sometimes referred to as "the mythology of Ciall" by the villagers, gossip is a vehicle for transforming the variation of individual behavior into an orderly interpretation of the past and prediction of the future; it isn't done to get at the facts of history but to invent a workable truth that fits with everything else. New events are worked over and over until they are milked for every drop of dramatic impact, and until they can be fit into the existing framework. Probably my greatest coin of exchange, my contribution to village life while I was there, was my unpredictability; I was better than TV. Was I *curamach?* Was I a hippie? I visited with drinkers but didn't drink; I went to church and psalmody class but didn't take communion. The all-night scandalous visit was an explicit piece of evidence by which I could be interpreted. The tidal waves of gossip that spread out from the event marked my entrée into the cognitive fiber of village interpretation. "Now you're part of the mythology of Ciall."

6/Kinship, Courtship, and Marriage

Co leis thu?

Co leis thu? Who are your people? Who do you belong to?

"You know who your relatives are at weddings and funerals. At funerals they know themselves who they are, and come to see you for the last time. At weddings you have to remember who they are and send them invitations or they'll be angry."

From the point of view of most Americans, the kinship group to which all Scotsmen are assumed to belong is the clan. Clan gatherings organized on the basis of last names (the Murrays, MacDonalds, Campbells, MacLeods, and so on) are held throughout the world, and heralded with bagpipes, haggis, and the sale of tartans, family crests, CDs of pipe band and Gaelic music, and usually some written, spoken or sung version of the Highland Clearances.

In anthropological parlance, a clan is a descent group composed of all those who claim descent from a common ancestor (who may be real or fictive). The clan is usually thought of as an extension of the lineage, a residential, corporate descent group whose members know exactly how they are descended from a known common ancestor. The terms "lineage" and "clan" are usually associated with unilineal descent—that is, descent through either male or female linkages. Unilineal descent groups are effective vehicles for social organization because they often take corporate action in owning property, regulating economic activities, and organizing marriages (they are usually exogamous).

Scottish clans, as they exist today in clan gatherings throughout the world, are not unilineal but ambilineal (although they have a patrilineal bias because of the practice by which children take the name of the father). I could consider myself linked to the Ferguson clan because my father's mother's father was a Ferguson (i.e., Ferguson was my grandmother's "maiden" name). Anyone who can demonstrate that they are descended (through male or female linkages, in any combination) from someone whose name is the clan name can claim membership in this group. In fact, such proof is not usually necessary (and in the complicated history of Highland clans never was necessary—lineally unrelated persons often took the name of the person to whom they gave their allegiance

Extended family

and from whom they expected protection), and I would consider Scottish clans more of a common-interest association than a kinship group.

In Ciall, the term *clann* means children, and the descent group to which people in Ciall belong is the same as that with which most Americans are familiar— the kindred, a group associated with bilateral descent, based on ego, with boundaries that are flexible and variable. The quote at the beginning of the chapter expresses the ego-centered features of the kindred: when someone dies, everyone calculates their relationship to the deceased and decides, on the basis of the closeness of the relationship, whether they should go to the funeral; when someone gets married, it is their responsibility to calculate all the relationships that are close enough to deserve invitations.

Knowledge of *cairdeas* (relationships or connections) is a valued skill, and some individuals are said to be especially talented at this, and may be consulted when weddings are being planned. Your *cairdean* (relatives) are, for most purposes, calculated out to third cousins through both the mother's and father's side. Gaelic kinship terms are similar to English categories but are more descriptive (for example *piuthar athar* [father's sister] and *piuthar mathar* [mother's sister] as opposed to the single English word for "aunt").

Many Ciall residents prefer to use the English terms for cousins (as in, first, second, and third cousins), but they also use the Gaelic terms to designate specific types of cousins. *Clann piuthar athar* are the children of my father's sister, and *clann piuthar mathar* are the children of my mother's sister; *nighean piuthar athar* is the daughter of my father's sister. The term "clann" (from which we get the English word clan) is sometimes used to refer to all the descendants of a well-known man, from him through the children of his male descendants (thus, for example, "clann Domnhuill Dubh" would be Donald, his sons and daughters, his sons' children, and his grandsons' children, but not the children of his daughters and granddaughters).

The boundaries of significant kin vary according to circumstances, but as one woman said, "Past a third cousin you don't bother knowing exactly, but you're still a relation." Another woman said, "I've got cousins in Ness getting on into the third generation now." Often people will recognize a link between each other by saying, "I'm related to [ ] in the same way you're related," without bothering to give a kinship term to their relationship to each other. Although kinship relationships may become distant, they are always assumed to exist, and form the primary model by which people explain behavior.

In the middle of winter, I was taken by a neighbor to visit the *Banntrach Clo* (the "widow" of a man nicknamed "Tweed"), the oldest woman in the village. She shook my hand and then held onto it, peering into my face and letting off a spiel of Gaelic, of which I caught perhaps every third word. Still holding my hand, she queried the neighborhood woman, who finally turned to me and said, "She can't understand how you can be here in the village. She keeps asking me who your people are. *Co leis thu?*"

"Keeping up [kinship] relationships" is of primary concern and helps to explain some unusual behavior. One man was teased mercilessly when he sent the excess of his potato crop to distant relatives on the mainland, spending more on the freight to send them than it would have cost his relatives to buy them locally. "Cairdeas," was his oblique explanation.

The interpretation and use of kinship varies in different parts of the Highlands. According to a Gaelic professor at the University of Edinburgh, in the Uists (islands to the south of Lewis), large farms persisted and were not broken down into small crofts; thus, genealogy there means knowing from whom you are descended. On Lewis, he said, genealogy means knowing to whom you are related in the present, so that you may call on relatives for mutual aid.

Weddings are the most important contexts in which you must demonstrate your knowledge of cairdeas. Depending on the number of close relatives, the boundary might be drawn at first or second cousins (these arrangements are always affected by personal factors). It is also important to know your relatives in case you need them during your travels. One man, on his way to join the Merchant Service, said, "I've got cousins in London, Australia, and Houston, Texas. I've never seen them, but I know of them. It's good to know who your relatives are if you need a place to stay, or help in getting a job." One woman in her 30s commented cynically on the young people's lack of interest in learning their cairdeas: "It used to matter a lot more because everyone needed each other; now everyone helps themselves and they don't bother to keep up relations." One man will greet another on the road, "I used to see more of you when you needed me." The largest and most consistent gathering of the kindred occurs at funerals, when relatives as far away as third cousins are supposed to come and attend the wake and then follow the body in a great procession to the graveyard, or today, to the hearse.

According to a member of the Crofters Commission who lives on Lewis on a croft, the Clearances had a major impact on kinship relationships and community integration. His explanation for the murder that occurred on Lewis a few years before I arrived in 1970 was that the town in which it occurred was less integrated. "The people are from Clearances all over the island. Love and land, kinship and a piece of rock—if it weren't for these ties, economic influences would have destroyed the island long ago." In Ciall, many families came from Uig. "They're newcomers, they've only been here a hundred years."

NEIGHBORHOOD AND COMMUNITY

Although people often say about fellow villagers, "We're all the same people here," they distinguish between relatives and neighbors. Although one Gaelic proverb says, "A relative is your best friend," a recent version of it is, "It used to be that your relatives were your best friends; now your best friends are better than your relatives." Another Gaelic proverb says, "A close neighbor is better than a distant relative."

The importance of being able to rely on one's neighbors is reflected in child-rearing practices. Children are trained to see themselves as children not only of a particular family but of the village. They are scolded as often by a neighbor or other member of the village as by a parent. On one occasion the parents of one household were criticized for taking their children's side against other children and parents; they said, "He's teaching his children not to mix with others. One child is as good as another. They may be good one day, but they're likely to be bad the next." A child or adult who enjoys spending time by him or herself is considered odd, and such behavior is often interpreted as indicative of mental illness, or if it happens at a certain stage in the life cycle, as a sign of the *curam* (religious conversion). An important criterion of mental health is whether or not someone "mixes well."

Childless households frequently "adopt" a child of neighbors or relatives. The child sleeps in the neighbor's house frequently, or spends most of the day there; the neighbor might come to the child's house to put him or her to bed at night. If a woman is left alone in a house, the first thought of the neighbors is, "Who's going to go over and sleep with her?" When my family was away for a week in Glasgow, several neighbors offered to send their children over to keep me company, or invited me to sleep in their sometimes already overcrowded households.

Whatever is asked must be given. Parents loan their children to neighbors if they want company or need an errand run; people borrow vacuum cleaners, cars, and even each other's medicine and reading glasses, often without asking; they babysit, give rides, repair cars and appliances without expectation of payment (although many prefer to pay to minimize their indebtedness). On one occasion, someone was criticized for not offering to loan me his tape recorder (it hadn't occurred to me to ask for it). "I wonder what he'll do when he needs something?" was the often-heard comment. When I was attending the reception for the head of the Highlands and Islands Development Board at the schoolhouse in 1970, I received a phone call asking me to drive a neighbor to the other side of the island, and left immediately to do so ("See there, now, she's like one of ourselves, she doesn't set herself apart"). One negative side of this preparedness to offer mutual aid is the susceptibility of the villagers to outside salespeople. Many villagers have ordered magazines they didn't need, and light bulbs they didn't want, simply because salespeople asked them to.

When wedding invitations are sent out, it is just as important to remember one's neighbors as it is to calculate cairdeas. The uses of and changes in the rel-

Susan Parman

Susan Parman

Women who welcomed all neighborhood children into their home in 1970 are now being cared for by relatives and neighbors.

ative significance of kin and neighborhood ties become visible on occasions when people are forced to make explicit requests for aid, such as at peat-cutting time. Because of the rules that make it difficult to request aid and that emphasize maintaining a low profile, it is difficult to tell what relationships are important; but at peat-cutting time, the relationships stand out loud and clear—the close relatives that don't help because of a recent or long-standing feud, the distant relatives that have "kept up the relation," the emergence of new friendships, and

Before the divide begins

stages in the development of a courtship. Who is cutting peats with whom is as common a topic of discussion as is the location of the tweed van.

MALE AND FEMALE

"Women are evil, the root of wickedness, because they tell things that should be kept a secret. A man will keep a secret to his grave, but a woman will gossip. With men you can do foolish things and keep your dignity. A woman is there to remind you of shame with her shameless tongue. You can tease a woman, you can court her, marry her, have a family by her; but you can't talk to her and be friends with her."

This particular view of male-female relationships, expressed by a man at a midnight ceilidh, may be stark and melodramatic, as such midnight pronounce-ments often are; but it captures the flavor of the divided world of male and female. In the light of day, males and females avoid each other. Even married couples tend to prefer the company of their own sex, the women siding with each other against the men in some argument or discussion, and vice versa. Boys and girls are seated separately in school and go around together in separate groups. When describing the children in a family, an informant will usually list the boys first, and then the girls, rather than naming the children in order of age.

The roles assigned to men and women are separate and distinct, and the dif-ferences are assumed to be rooted in biology. "Women are catty, cruel, and untrustworthy," said one bachelor. "It has to do with their biological makeup, a way of protecting their families." It is "natural" for a woman to care for cattle, and "natural" for a man to care for sheep. A man is expected to enjoy only the company of other men; a woman seeks the company of "her own kind." A man can wander the island freely, but a woman's place is in the home. "In the old days, if a woman were seen out alone late at night, people would think she was a witch out to do harm to the cows." "I realize now why most women are such nags," said one young woman who yearns for the unrealistic romance portrayed in novels, films, and soap operas, "A man can come and go as he pleases; a woman is supposed to knit and gossip while she waits for him to come in. When he does come in, he sits by the fire, has his tea, and goes to bed without saying three sentences."

It is generally accepted that women are a source of social control and divisiveness, whereas men emphasize communion and solidarity. If a woman is away, a man blames her if he gets into trouble—"after all, she left me alone." Whereas in England a man is in charge of finances and gives his wife her housekeeping money out of his paycheck, in Scotland "the manly thing to do is hand your pay packet to your wife unopened." If a man is in a hotel and doesn't want to drink, he will give his money to a female companion rather than trust himself with the temptation. The nature of a woman is to gossip, nag, criticize, and mother, that of a man to compromise, resolve conflicts, give and take within the male fraternity. "Men are like a secret club."

SEX AND COURTSHIP

During the summer when many young people in their late teens and early 20s return to the island for holidays, they congregate at the Gate or by the seashore, the girls clustered in one group and the boys in another, surreptitiously eyeing each other but keeping their distance. It would never occur to a courting couple to walk hand in hand down the road together where they might be seen. No matter how exciting courtship may be, it is a hazardous process, hemmed in by guilt and gossip.

Although sex education is sometimes provided in the schools today, it is a subject about which people are extremely reticent, except in the sometimes crude but more often lyrical and metaphorical excess of the late-night ceilidh. A woman in her 50s was first given sex education classes when she was in the forces. "I trembled as I listened to the lectures. I didn't want to have anything to do with that." Another woman recalls that her mother never told her anything about where babies came from; she just told her to stay away from boys, because if they got at her they would leave her and not care for her. "I never looked at them, even when I was 18—I hated them sometimes. Even after I got married I felt my husband wouldn't like me." I once got into an awkward discussion with a 9-year-old about humans being mammals that carried their babies inside instead of laying eggs. She asked with wide surprised eyes, "Do they get big?" Her mother said her daughter had never asked where babies came from.

Menstrual periods, if mentioned at all, are referred to indirectly, as they are in the United States—"I've got my grannies"; "Visitors have arrived"; "Have the doo-dahs come?"; "Has the ship docked?" Many older women were unaware that pregnancy could occur only during certain times in their monthly cycle and were too embarrassed to inquire about or use contraceptives. Even the younger ones feel awkward about using contraceptives. "I had three kids and was really worn out. My doctor gave me the pill. But it made me feel sick, so I threw them

Susan Parman

Girls go separately to the beach and sit apart from the boys.

all down the toilet and never mentioned it to my doctor. That's why I was glad when my husband was away so often." Some women are referred to as "very strong": it is believed that they can get pregnant even when they're old or using contraceptives.

With all the strict segregation between males and females, I wondered, when I first arrived in 1970, how courtship ever managed to occur. Several weeks after I moved to Ciall, one of the neighboring girls, home for the summer, invited me to go with her to a dance. Promising to come for me in the evening, she had to wake me up at 11:45 in the evening—I had gone to bed, thinking she had changed her plans. We went to the Village Hall. The lively strains of accordion-dominated dance music burst out through the door as a couple emerged and went to sit in a car. Inside, clusters of boys and girls circled and watched each other, sometimes joining in group dances or shedding individual members that paired off. At around 4 a.m., groups piled into cars and gathered in nearby homes for tea, talk, singing, and the rare expression of affection as girls sat on laps or rested with their elbows on a man's knee—these might be courting couples, or an older man flirting safely with a neighbor's child, or the woman of the house joking with a teenage boy. No English was spoken; this was the heart of tale-telling, humor-filled, musical, Gaelic communitas. Before dawn, the groups dispersed. In the short nights of Hebridean summers, dances begin when the darkness finally arrives, and last until the light brings visibility once again to the watchful countryside.

When families were large, boys courted girls in large groups, in a custom called *ruith na h-oidche* (night-visiting). "Boys came in packs of about six to a house where there were several girls sleeping together. They came in to talk in the darkness after the old people had gone to bed, and sometimes they lay down beside the girls under the covers, fully dressed. It was dark and sometimes it was difficult to tell who was with you. Sometimes girls would dress up as boys to tease another girl, especially a straight one. The boys would come home with their trousers covered with bed fluff. In the morning you would be teased about your *caraid na h-oidche,* your night-visitor." A woman born in 1925 remembers when a group of young men came to her bedroom one night, and she was sleeping with her mother. "They went out and told the next gang to go in, that I was in bed with my *bramar* [sweetheart]. When the gang came in to see the fun, they got quite a shock. It was always a good laugh—the parents angry, the father shouting *Mach a seo* [Out of here!]."

Courting is irregular; couples meet by chance at a dance and rarely plan a next meeting, never speak to each other during the day. A man who comes to visit a girl during the day is making a visible, explicit statement of serious intentions. Courtship usually involves meeting at a dance and walking to the end of the road and back, or "going behind a peat stack for a wee cuddle," since you each came with different rides; but now that many boys have cars, they court more regularly, and the girls go with them and are starting to drink, something that women are not supposed to do. Men and women automatically assume the other to be untrustworthy. "You go with one this night, someone else the next night." One girl in her late 20s who was being courted described her feelings about men: "The only thing between men and women is sex. There really isn't anything else that keeps them together. They only come to women because they have to—it's as though women are a weakness. If I marry, it will be for a house and money, when I am almost old." One young man, rendered monosyllabic with drink at a late-night ceilidh, expressed his feelings about courtship quite succinctly: "Women grrr; men grrr."

On the other hand, once a commitment is made, there is a strong emphasis on commitment to one spouse. "If you love someone, you love them till they die." Men in particular are thought of as being capable of great loyalty, of never marrying if the one they love has married someone else. "Boys don't get over broken hearts." "A boy will try the first night to go to bed with a girl. If she won't, fair enough; if he likes her he'll go with her for years." A tale is told of a man at the turn of the century who came back from the fishing to have a *reiteach* [engagement party] with a girl in Ciall. Her father didn't approve, so he had to go back to his home in Uig. "He stopped at Callanish and got a reiteach there, but when he was old and bedridden, it was the first girl's name he kept calling."

A woman is expected to be a virgin when she marries; if a man is not, it is not his fault but the fault of the loose woman he was with. "It's not a man's fault when he gets involved with a girl. It's up to her to indicate whether or not she wants something to happen." "It's natural for a man to give in to temptation." "If a man spends a night with a girl, it doesn't mean a thing; in fact, just the opposite—he'll never go back, because if he was there one night, he knows that someone else was there the night before." If a young woman has a child out of wedlock, her parents are blamed ("They didn't watch her closely enough"). Once a woman has had a child, she is expected to stay away from dances, even if the father does not step forward and marry her. "That's her finished."

When a woman becomes pregnant before marriage, enormous pressure is exerted on her to tell who the father is, and the man is pressured to confess his sin and admit his guilt. (He is not necessarily expected to marry the girl, and in fact

Susa Parman

Conquering the divide.

his parents argue that their son should have nothing to do with her. A girl is considered "lucky" if he marries her.) On one occasion, a doctor in the hospital in Stornoway, who had recently come to the island from Lowland Scotland, was surprised to find girls being visited in the hospital by elders from their community who had come to find out the name of the father—"It's like an inquisition," she said, and banned the visitors. One unmarried girl who had just had a baby received a call from a neighbor: "I've been praying for you to be forgiven your sins."

Sex out of wedlock is not uncommon, given all the barriers to marriage; but sex that results in pregnancy threatens the web of kinship. *Co leis thu?* Who do you belong to? A child must know its father or the web is rent. To carry a name in which you are identified by the house of the mother's father, or where the child is raised, carries with it the aura of shame, of not belonging to the full range of kinsmen on both sides. The greater shame is the woman's ("The lad had a dram, he meant well"); to be pregnant out of wedlock, without the father identifying himself, is a great embarrassment. The child grows up ashamed not so much of being illegitimate (many marriages start this way) but of not knowing who his father is; the gaps in his identity loom large during the intense discussion of the details of cairdean.

Social pressure to admit paternity lasts forever. One man (who was married to another woman) was rumored to have fathered a child that was stillborn. The man and his wife refused to go to the child's funeral, and the mother married another man. Years went by; the suspected man could not have his children baptized or take communion (his wife did it in her name), and finally he admitted his guilt before the kirk session. When a child is baptized, the parents (if they are married) or the mother of a child conceived out of wedlock must stand up in church and be lectured in front of the congregation.[1] Many women prefer to leave the island before they will consent to endure this public shaming.

Despite the shock and upset of unwed pregnancy, this explicit statement of relationship forces many marriages. Some explain the frequency of this event by saying that the tendency to behave this way is "in the blood."

"When you look at certain families, you see it happening over and over again. If you look at one person, you'll see it throughout the family—her mother, her aunties, her sisters. Parents should teach you, that's true; but if they fail to teach you, it's because something in their heredity is wrong; there's something missing upstairs. Sex is like stealing; it's taking something that doesn't belong to you. Some people steal and others don't."

The tendency to explain all behavior as rooted in hereditary inclinations is widespread; but in fact the major contributors to delayed marriages, the high frequency of unwed pregnancies, and prolonged courtship are social and economic factors. One contributing factor is the definition of the croft as an agricultural unit rather than a place of residence, which inhibits the development of adequate housing. The various family arrangements in Ciall reflect a tendency for children to remain with their parents and extended kin; and if they marry, to marry late in life after family obligations have been fulfilled (to care for aging parents or sick siblings, to raise the children of sick siblings, and so on). Some couples marry and live with their in-laws, but the arrangement is not considered ideal.

Teaghlach is the immediate family, which includes a married couple, their children, and the children's grandparents (and great grandparents if they are still living). Teaghlach also means the household, which is usually a nuclear family but may include some of the next generation up or down (grandparents or grandchildren) depending on various factors.

Of the 169 households in Ciall, 78 were nuclear families (married couples, or a widow or widower, with unmarried children living in the house), of which 46 had a household head who was 55 years or older. Sixteen households consisted in married couples with children living away, of which 14 had a household head 55 years or older. Another 16 widows or widowers lived alone, and 16 unmarried persons lived alone. Thirteen households were composed of siblings who remained in the family home after the death of the parents; in two of these households, one of the siblings had married but was a widower or widow.

The desire to remain within the community, and scarcity of housing, often leads to extended family arrangements, which are not considered ideal. It is difficult to marry when other unmarried siblings live within the household, and as indicated above, some households are composed of aging, unmarried siblings whose parents have died. Often one child will remain to take care of the parents, and may marry late in life; twenty married couples, without children, lived with parents. In several cases an unmarried daughter with children lived with her parents.

---

[1]Standing in church to be told off by the minister was widespread throughout Presbyterian Scotland. Brown (1997:72) reports that during the 18th century, "In addition to being fined, and in many ways more important, fornicators and other transgressors had to 'purge their scandal' by rebuke. This took the form of standing before the congregation for up to three Sundays and being subjected to a 'rant' from the minister. This public humiliation might take place whilst standing or sitting on a special repentance stool at the side of the church or beside the pulpit, and in a few places wearing sackcloth." By 2003, this practice had stopped in Ciall.

Engagements are often long. One woman was engaged for 17 years, and her son for over 10 years because her daughter-in-law had to raise the children of her sister, who had TB. One woman began dating a man when she was 19; she is now in her 40s, still unmarried but still "going with" the same man. A woman in her 70s, who was 35 when she married, said, "Twenty-nine or thirty is a decent age to think about getting married; any younger is too young. You need to learn to care for a house, and how to keep a man in order." People hesitate to disturb existing family arrangements. One girl in her late 20s agreed to marry someone, but panicked when his relatives tried to pin her down on an exact date; she said 5 years "to hold them off." Another girl described the importance of pregnancy in forcing a decision to marry or not marry. She described a couple who "had to get married": they had been going together for 6 or 7 years, and she was a bit older than him; "she probably realized that this was the only way she was going to catch him." After the youthful days of caraid na h-oidche and Village Hall dances are over (a woman becomes a spinster in her mid-30s and is considered too old to go to dances, whereas a man remains a boy until he marries), courtship continues in a quieter way that often becomes locked into a steady pattern of inconclusive visiting.

The jobs that men and women get affect the high ratio of aging unmarried people. Women have a better chance of marrying away from the island. More girls than boys seem to attend school in Stornoway and then go to the mainland for further education. They work in hotels and domestic service on the mainland, go to dances and other social functions, and are more likely to marry an outsider. The men go to sea, and their major contacts are with the village where they spend their holidays and send their money and letters. Being at sea does not lead to many new contacts with potential mates and job opportunities off the island.

REASONS FOR MARRIAGE

Men are expected to get married because "they don't take care of themselves. They need a woman to look after them." If they are in a house with their mother or sister to do the housekeeping, there is less need for them to get married. As for a woman, "A woman's lot is to be married." If by her late 20s a woman is not married, they say there must be something wrong with her.

Marriage might be spoken of in the abstract as a love match, a bonding of two souls, but no actual marriage is attributed to such pure motives. Marriage is pragmatic; it is done because of convenience and social expectation.

A Gaelic proverb says, "Marry health." One woman was engaged, but when she had to have an operation on her leg, which left her with a permanent limp, her fiance's sister came to get back her brother's engagement ring. An ideal wife is someone who is never sick, and who can provide you with good family connections; and if she comes with a house and/or croft, so much the better.

"Marrying into a croft" is looked down on by other villagers, but it happens often enough to constitute one of the recognized ingredients in matchmaking. A man born in 1920 who "married into" a croft in Ciall explained, "I came from a family of 10 children. Everyone had to leave, or marry a girl with a croft. Only one son could inherit the croft." There was little room for romanticism in the fight for scarce land among the sons of large crofter and non-crofter families.

"The most important thing about courting was the land. If a girl was going to get a croft, she could have the pick of anyone." Stories are told of broken alliances and the interference of parents, all related to the inheritance of the croft. A woman born in 1900 recalled that her father married her mother because she had a croft; he had been engaged to a beautiful girl, but had left her, saying, "Never mind beauty, just a bit of land." A man might hike 14 miles across the moor to buy a jug of beer required for the reiteach (engagement party), only to come back and find that his beloved was having a reiteach with someone else, especially if her parents didn't approve of him (in this story, the man had a reiteach "with the first one he met—he wasn't going to let the jug go to waste"). Tales of witchcraft, such as magical reiteach parties on moonlit nights to get a spouse, are exceeded in number only by stories concerning the bewitchment of cattle.

BARRIERS TO MARRIAGE

Ma tha thu airson do mholadh, baisaich; ma tha thu airson do chaineadh, pos.

(If you want to be praised, die; if you want to be criticized, marry.)

Despite the pressures to marry, the barriers are almost insurmountable. All villagers have an enormous amount of information about each other, some of it false, some of it true, and most of it exaggerated. Any sign of physical or emotional disability in someone prompts a critical word of discouragement if that person is known to be considering marriage.

Every individual is a representative of a family unit that through many generations has manifested certain physical and behavioral traits. Characteristics such as shyness, a tendency to drink heavily, an interest in reading, or "the gift of the gab" are thought to be inherited. A single moment of behavior—succumbing to the urge to steal a piece of candy, or refusing to lend money—is immediately linked to some remembered bit of family history, even if that behavior is uncharacteristic of the person. *Tha e anns an t-fhuil.* It's in the blood. It's in the people, it's "natural," so it is likely to crop up again in future generations. A person is seen not as an individual with a fresh start but as part of a family, a manifestation of a history of family interrelatedness with the community; and because it is important that good relations be maintained, the community is alert to its "bad seeds."

The relentless pressure of gossip can threaten and destroy a budding relationship. One bachelor who was courting a girl until 5 a.m. "walked away over the crofts and straight into a bog up to his neck, and was so embarrassed he hasn't been back since." "After he proposed to her at New Year, he took to his bed for a month." Both girls and boys are mercilessly teased, and they return the banter with strong expostulations about the worthlessness of their presumed lovers. Everyone is on the lookout for signs of commitment, which is sufficient to keep eyes glued to the ground and positive statements about a person of the opposite sex to a minimum.

Stories are told about engagements being made and broken. "They were engaged for about a year when she started up with someone else. The other fellow came up every Tuesday night, when she was supposed to be washing her hair." "She was engaged to this one fellow, wore his ring and all; then all of a sudden she was going to marry someone else. They say the first fellow found out from other people." Marriage proposals made in a drinking situation are usually "forgotten" in the sober light of day.

REITEACH (ENGAGEMENT PARTY)

The word "reiteach" means disentanglement, putting in order, reconciliation. In the context of marriage, it refers to the social celebration that announces the engagement. The reiteach functions to "pour oil on troubled waters," to smooth the relations between the two families. "In the old days, a father didn't know that his daughter was going to be married until the young man came in with a bottle." Often couples met during jobs away from home and might be from different communities; even if they were from the same neighborhood, the parents were unlikely to be aware of the night-based process of courtship. The reiteach was an opportunity for the two families to meet and discuss matters; it was also the opportunity for the parents to interfere with the match.

The reiteach was at one time even bigger than the wedding reception ("Everyone came to the reiteach; the wedding was just for family and friends"). Today, with increased transportation, the couples are able to visit, and the parents are more likely to know who their children will marry; the reiteach, when it occurs, simply underscores a foregone conclusion. It serves primarily as an explicit statement to the community. After this occasion, the two are the focus of endless jokes. "So-and-so has a new bed with reinforced springs—it must be for the new couple."

Since relationships are circumspect and changeable, the villagers look for explicit statements of intention. Engagement is a serious step, not lightly broken. The most common indicator today is the wearing of a ring by the woman (many girls get three rings: engagement, wedding, and eternity—"the keeper"). She wears it casually to work or to some social function and waits for it to be noticed; the word spreads quickly. The arrival of the ring is usually the occasion for informing the two families. At some point after the arrival of the ring, the reiteach is held. On Lewis, this is usually a small affair involving only the close family members, and is referred to as a *reiteach bheag* (small engagement party). The prospective groom brings in whiskey to the house of the bride. In the past he used to be accompanied by someone who knew both families who helped to "smooth things out."

Other areas of the Highlands remember the *reiteach mor,* the big reiteach. On mainland Harris and the island of Scalpay, an elaborate drama is played out with great merriment. As described by Morag MacLeod of the School of Scottish Studies (1971), the groom is seated while two men from the groom's side and two from the bride's side conduct a humorous banter concerning some theme— for example, sheep. Although the explicit topic is sheep, everyone knows the real topic, which is the upcoming marriage, the personalities of the two people involved, and sex. The bride's people bring out a series of girls, beginning with someone who is the least related to the bride, and the groom's spokesman must find something wrong with her, along the lines of the chosen theme (her hair is too curly, her hooves are too sharp, etc.). The next girl, more closely related, is a bit better, but not quite all right, and so on, until finally the bride is brought out, whereupon the groom's spokesman finds that she fills the bill.

Elements of the reiteach mor remain in the humorous speeches given at Lewis wedding dinners.

POSADH AND *BANAIS* (THE WEDDING)

Gaelic has two words for wedding: *posadh,* which is the marriage service in church, state of matrimony, or bonds of wedlock; and *banais,* which comes from *bean* (woman or wife) and *feis* (feast), and refers to the wedding parties, the feasts that celebrated the event. The posadh was usually on a Thursday; but there were at least three wedding feasts. Anyone can attend the church service, but an invitation is required to attend the banais.

I asked a young woman and her mother if the bride's parents were expected to pay for the wedding. The young woman said that both the bride and the groom shared expenses. Her mother laughed and said that a couple would wait forever if they waited for the parents to pay. Parents help out with expenses, but most couples pay for their own wedding. In the old days, much of the expense was born by the village in a communal house wedding. According to some people, the communal house wedding actually consisted of three "weddings" or "feasts"—a "big wedding" with additional feasts on the night before and the night after.

Female friends and relatives planned and carried out preparations for the wedding. Those who had been in domestic service were in charge of cooking the wedding supper. Furniture was removed from the house ("even the loom was dismantled"), sheets covered the sooted walls of the "black house," and huge tables were covered with food and drink—whiskey, beer, port wine and sherry ("We had our first drink at weddings"), cold sliced chicken and mutton, scones and pancakes, trifles and puddings.

For a month or so ahead of time, visitors were invited to come in to view the presents and trousseau; men were served whiskey, women sherry. A couple of neighborhood boys were given the task of delivering the invitations; they went to every house in the village. Hundreds of people were expected to attend the big wedding. In the entire village, and in villages that had relatives of the marrying couple, "recognition flags"—white cloths, such as dish towels—were hung to signify their relationship.

On the day of the big wedding, the best car in the village came to get the bride to take her to church. When it turned around to drive out, it found the road barricaded with old carts and barrels. The church service itself was less somber—less hellfire and brimstone, and even a few jokes from the minister— and the wedding feast that night was a wild, all-night celebration of eating, drinking, and dancing. At some point during the night the bride and groom were prepared for their wedding night together. "The girls undressed the bride and put her into her nightie, and tucked her into bed with a hot water bottle. They had some sherry together, and then the girls went out and the men brought the groom in. Oh there was a lot of fun and joking."

"The third night was for the old folks. That was the best time for the old stories, a quiet time, after everyone was tired out from all the celebrating."

Wedding reception

When the bride and groom returned from their honeymoon, they went to church with their bridesmaid and best man in a ceremony called "kirking" (Gaelicized as *kirkeadh*)—a general recognition ceremony conducted for any important change in status ("kirking the council" when a new town council is elected; "kirking the provost" when the newly elected provost attends church in his robes).

According to one family, the house weddings stopped when the white house replaced the black house—"The new houses would be too difficult to clean." But this use of the past camouflages the real reason for the change, which is to avoid the potential conflict of not remembering all the relations who should be invited. A wedding in a hotel in Stornoway, or at Peel House in Partick Hill, Glasgow, has higher prestige, and it imposes an external constraint on the number of people who can be invited (Peel House, for example, sits only 70 people for dinner). Said one nervous bride, "I was going to have the wedding in Stornoway [where the hotels can accommodate over a hundred people], but by the time I got to 200 people to invite, I decided to have it in Glasgow." People still make an effort to fulfill their obligations, but there is less conflict if some people are excluded. Collateral relations out to first cousins should be invited, and second cousins if there is enough room; and every house in the neighborhood should be represented. Thus it is not unusual for a husband or a wife to attend a wedding without his or her spouse; the person goes as a representative of the family.

Only if weddings are held on the island are recognition flags still flown. The presents and gowns are still displayed, with everything carefully labeled, and visitors discuss and compare the accumulation of gifts ("All she needs now is a

Hoover"; "She has five lamps"). Wedding gifts go in and out of fashion—a bride one year might get lamps, whereas next year the going thing is wall plaques.

The church wedding is relatively profane (the minister stands in the lower pulpit where the presenter usually sits, and jokes of "tying the knot" in the wife's tongue); the minister's sermon emphasizes the importance of a wife's submission to her husband and that she should enter into the union without shame, a husband's responsibility to care for his wife, and their mutual responsibility to raise children and live a good life according to the Bible.

Although the wedding feast has been reduced to only one night, it contains speeches that are reminiscent of the battle between the groom's side and the bride's side in the reiteach mor. In one wedding that I attended in Glasgow, the master of ceremonies, who happened to be the minister ("This would never have happened on Lewis unless the minister were a close relation of the couple"), set the theme for the speeches by referring to the enmity between Ciall and the neighboring village that was to be overcome by this union. Most of the "replies" were in fact separate speeches (such as that made by the spokesman for the groom who began with, "Help! Help! Help!").

The high point of most weddings today is the reading of the telegrams by the best man. Wedding telegrams are an opportunity for those not present at the wedding (either because the wedding is held on the mainland instead of the traditional home wedding, or because they are part of the community of "exiles") to display racy humor and verbal dexterity. Everyone agrees that the Gaelic ones are the best; but most telegrams are in English. One explanation for this is that telegram senders don't usually speak Gaelic and so the messages were getting scrambled; but it may be that many are hesitant to commit their Gaelic to written form. Telegrams are part of the English-speaking context. At the wedding I attended, 56 telegrams were read, only one of which was in Gaelic (*Ged nach eil sinn aig a banais, biod sinn aig an urstean* [Though we're not at the wedding, we'll be at the christening]).

Many telegrams do little more than convey best wishes, but a large number of them are full of sexual humor and references to an expanding family. "Peas and barley fill the ladle, but it's up to [husband's name] to fill the cradle." "Heartiest congratulations. Very pleasant celebrations. And don't forget the multiplications." "In his arms tonight, in his pockets tomorrow." A man who used to ride his bicycle from 6 miles away to court the girl he eventually married received a telegram "from the bicycle," expressing its relief at no longer being the one to be punctured. Many of the telegrams draw on nautical knowledge. "Congratulations. Report position at midnight." "New captain, new ship, maiden voyage, 9 months trip." "[Husband's name] the captain. [Wife's name] the mate. Crew to follow at a terrific rate." The humorous telegrams immediately make the rounds of the village, the best ones are repeated endlessly, and favorites are used in future weddings. When my sister was getting married during my year of fieldwork, a neighbor brought out the telegrams that she had saved from her own wedding, saying, "Do you like this one? You can use that for your sister." The entire wedding is discussed in such detail that even those that did not attend repeat the stories as if they had been there—"You should have seen the bridesmaid, her colors were awful."

The top layer of the cake is put aside and saved not for the first anniversary but for the christening. Who is included in wedding pictures is a topic of much discussion. At the wedding I attended, it was decided not to include the husbands and wives of the bride's brothers and sisters (the in-laws) in the formal pictures. I was invited to join the group for one of the informal family pictures, but when the pictures came out, all that showed of me was my arm.

Co leis thu? In old Anglo-Saxon kinship terms, I was not even a *Nagerbruder.*[2]

---

[2]"Nail brother," or distant cousin, according to a system that counted distance in relationship by referring to the parts of the body, from head to fingernails.

7/Supernaturalism

The Gaelic-speaking Highlands were once closely linked with Ireland, and many stories, magico-medical practices, and calendar festivals have their parallels in Ireland; but most of the explicit discussions of "Celtic survivals" occur in the context of nationalism or in exaggerated romantic literary expressions promoted by Lowland Celtophiles. In Ciall, supernatural beliefs are expressed primarily in two domains: the institutionalized church (the Free Church, an evangelical off-shoot of the Church of Scotland), and the noninstitutionalized, less freely discussed contexts of community interaction in which beliefs in witchcraft and second sight are expressed in particular contexts and for specific uses.

THE REFORMATION IN SCOTLAND

The Church of Scotland was established during the Reformation, recognized by the Scots Parliament in 1560, and legally made the national church in 1690. It was conceived of in explicitly theocratic terms as a "covenanted country" (Reid 1988), the Church of the State, a fulfillment of St. Augustine's image of a "City of God" whose government policies would reflect divine discipline as dictated by scripture interpreted through individual faith and direct experience ("By faith alone, by scripture alone"). The church established its austere, puritan policies first in the cities, gained the support of the gentry, but for several centuries had very little effect on the Highlands, which continued the Catholic practices introduced from Ireland. Lowland missionaries entered the Highlands in the 18th century in part to suppress Jacobitism, paganism, and episcopacy in the Forfeited Estates following the Jacobite Rebellions; Brown (1997:91) notes that the Highlands and Islands were Scottish Presbyterianism's "first 'foreign' mission, and a 'dry run' for the great work in Africa and Asia." He also notes the irony of the fact that the church was a vehicle to absorb Highland into Lowland culture and that today it is the Gaelic-speaking Highlands that uphold "the religious heritage of the seventeenth-century Lowlands" (Brown 1997:92). Today the northern half of the Outer Hebrides (North Uist, Lewis, and Harris) is Protestant, most of which is Free

Susan Parma

A bank in Edinburgh is tiled with the maxim, "Thrift is blessing."

Church, Free Presbyterian, and Church of Scotland. The southern part of the Outer Hebrides (South Uist, Barra, and Eriskay) is Catholic. Unlike Ireland, there are no economic and political underpinnings to these religious differences that create serious conflict. As one travels from the northern tip of the Outer Hebrides to the south, the Gaelic-speaking townships remain the same but small roadside shrines begin to appear, with Gaelic salutations arching over small statues of the Virgin Mary—*Failte Dhuit a Mhairi*, "Hail to thee, Mary." Catholic townships are considered less strict with regard to recreation; dances may be held on Sundays, sponsored by the church. In the sterner north, many a fiddler broke his instrument over his knee when he converted to the evangelical Protestant churches. On Lewis, ancestors who broke their fiddles or bagpipes are remembered with pride, but the southern Catholic isles interpret the history of the Reformation not as salvation but as destruction.

The important thing to remember about the Reformation is that, unlike Catholicism that has maintained a remarkable unity for hundreds of years because of its elaborate priestly hierarchy, bureaucracy, and procedures to maintain conformity (from threats of excommunication to the Inquisition), the Reformation is about reform and has therefore generated continuous fragmentation.[1] Luther's attempts to reform Catholicism unleashed a spirit of stubborn

---

[1]The fragmentation continues in the 21st century on a large and small scale: from the establishment of alternative websites to the official Free Church website, to the formation of the Free Church of Scotland (Continuing), a secessionist movement that has split Ciall and many other Free Church congregations (see Fraser MacDonald 2000 for a review of the empirical evidence leading up to the split, and for his interpretation of this event as "ecclesiastical theatre").

Catholic shrine in the southern part of Eilean Siar

righteousness by individuals and congregations to discern the absolute truth of God's will, by which continuous reforms of reforms became inevitable (see Bruce's 1985 application to Scottish "fissiparousness" of Wallis's 1979 theory about why the Nazi Party was less prone to schism than Marxist parties[2]). The Free Church (conceived of as a purification of the Church of Scotland that, through "Moderatism," had lost sight of its mission and was enforcing patronage, or the right of the State to choose ministers, onto resistant congregations) is an evangelical offshoot of the Church of Scotland (which derided their critics as "the Wild Evangelicals") formed during the Disruption in 1843. In 1893 the Free Church fragmented, with thousands of Gaelic-speaking Highlanders deserting to form the Free Presbyterian Church, and in 1900 the Free Church split again over a proposal to unify the Free Church with the United Presbyterian Church of Scotland to form the United Free Church of Scotland; 26 ministers and some 50,000 people remained in the Free Church. Additional realignments occurred during the 20th century, of which the most recent is the formation of the Free

---

[2]Wallis argues that "the propensity to schism increases directly with the availability of means of legitimating authority" (quoted by Bruce 1985:597). Since the means of legitimizing authority in conservative Protestantism rests in each individual's interpretation of the Bible (all of these individuals have a straight line to the Word of God), schisms are inevitable.

Church (Continuing).[3] (See Collins 1974; MacDonald 2000; MacLeod 2000; Stewart and Cameron 1989; Wylie 1881.) The sense of personal enlightenment, purity, and power that infuses reform movements may be found not only in the formation of new churches but all the way down to the lonely dissenter who withdraws into his house and is rarely seen for the rest of his life.

THE FREE CHURCH

History

The Free Church is an evangelical offshoot of the Church of Scotland and reflects the ideology of Calvinist Scotland. The interpretation of historical alliances among the branches of Christianity varies among the interpreters (see Meek 2000). According to one Free Church minister on Lewis, the Free Church is descended from the Celtic Church founded by St. Columba, which never obeyed Roman Catholic law. Members of the Free Church on Lewis consider the Free Church to constitute the heart of Celtic/Highland/Scottish purity. Not only is it given historical priority, but it is considered the bastion of the common people, and the source of the spiritual and moral superiority that makes Lewis *Tir an t-soisgeul,* Land of the Gospel.

Beliefs and practices found today in the Highland Free Church, such as belief in the base sinfulness of human beings (including children), belief in the doctrine of predestination and that almost everyone is doomed to damnation and only a few are saved, stringent adherence to the Sabbath, the view that theatrical and musical forms of recreation are worldly temptations of the devil, distaste for ornamentation, public condemnation of sinners (such as having women who had conceived or given birth to children outside of wedlock stand up before the congregation, confess, and be lectured for their sins), and scriptural examinations of congregational members in their homes by ministers and elders, were common throughout Lowland Scotland but gradually declined there. These beliefs became symbolically appropriated by the Highland Free Church as part of an evangelical movement that, although widespread throughout Scotland in the late 18th and 19th centuries, was particularly prevalent in the Highlands, which were reeling from a series of devastating economic ills.

In the 1820s, kelp was no longer a money-earning proposition, landlords were deeply in debt, and Clearances were widespread. In the words of one villager, "During the Clearances, the Church of Scotland ministers said the Clearances were the will of God, a punishment of the people; they didn't help at all." The Free Church minister of Ciall, describing the Assembly in Edinburgh, said there was an "ecclesiastical Berlin Wall" separating the Church of Scotland and the Free

---

[3]Although the FCC (Free Church Continuing) justifies the split as a doctrinal issue (the right of spiritual independence in disciplining a straying member of the flock that was confirmed during the Disruption of 1843), financial issues are also clearly at stake. The Model Trust Deed of the Free Church requires that one-third of the ministers of the Free Church must agree to a split to get a share of the assets of the church. The assets involve much more than the sessentation fund; Americans give more than $1 million a year to promote evangelism in Scotland, and the FCC (Free Church Continuing) is perceived as targeting these funds. (See debates on websites and *The Monthly Record.*)

The Free Church in Ciall

Church. "The only thing they share are the dignitaries, like the Queen, who attend both assemblies." According to one person, finding a minister in the Church of Scotland is like advertising for someone to fill a vacancy; but in the Free Church, a minister must give testimony and explain why there was a change in his life. The giving of testimony, and the experience of conversion, is what distinguishes the congregation in general (which includes most of the village) from the select chosen few who have been "saved," who are said to be *curamach* (converted). Of the latter group, most are "communicants" who take Communion twice a year.

A book about the Reverend Alexander MacLeod, the first evangelical minister on Lewis who arrived in the parish of Uig in 1824, was loaned to me by a Ciall man in his 70s whose life history followed a pattern common to many Lewismen: an early life at sea characterized by hard drinking followed by dramatic religious conversion. In handing me the book he said I should pay special attention to the reforms that overwhelmed Lewis: "Four years after he came, 7,000 people came to the Uig Communions."

In fact, he had underestimated the number. According to Beaton (1925), 9,000 people came, and his description of evangelical fervor applies to many Communions today. "When the elements were presented, there appeared as a shower of revival from the presence of the Lord through the whole congregation. . . . It was a night ever to be remembered in this place, in which the whole of it was spent in religious exercises, whether in private or together with others, in cases mingled with unusual instances of joy and sorrow" (Beaton 1925: 9–10; see Meek 1987 for a discussion of the relationship between Highland evangelism and agitation for land that led to the Crofters' Holdings [Scotland] Act of 1886).

Although some families in Ciall today belong to the Church of Scotland and other Protestant churches, and a few describe themselves as agnostic or atheist, most villagers attend the Free Church, which is the only church now in the village. The present church was built in 1883, after a conflict with a village 5 miles away

where Ciall villagers used to attend church. According to one version of the conflict, an old man and a young man from Ciall were repairing the minister's glebe
fence in Inisbay, and asked the minister's wife for some boiling water to put in
their tea or oatmeal "which they had brought with them to keep hunger at bay."
When she said she didn't have time to give it to them, the old man said to the young
man, "It's time we were going," and returned to Ciall where they started work on
a church of their own. The Ciall people were helped by four families in the neighboring village, and today the congregation includes a "side" for each village.

Organization of the Free Church

The Free Church is supported by congregations (one-fourth of the Free Church's
income comes from Lewis), and all ministers are paid an equal salary. The salary
comes from the "sessentation fund" that the deacons collect from the Free Church
households in their neighborhoods and send to Edinburgh. Ministers also receive,
as part of their salary, the use of the church manse, and from the villagers, contributions for fuel—either money to buy coal or oil, or in some areas, contributions
of peat. At Communion time, the villagers contribute eggs, potatoes, or other food.

The democratic, individualistic ingredients of Presbyterian religious organization are evident in the organization of the Free Church. The congregation
elects the minister, who receives a "call," or request from a congregation in need
of a minister. Congregations have many opportunities to hear a variety of ministers preach, either during Communions or by special invitation. The entire congregation votes. "The minister can refuse the call—that's between the man and
the Lord." Ciall had just gotten a new minister when I arrived in 1970; he was
the third to be requested, and the village had gone for a year without one.

Elders and deacons handle church business; deacons and elders are members
of the community, elected by those who have taken communion. Deacons handle worldly affairs pertaining to the running of the church, such as collection of
the sessentation fund. The elders constitute the kirk session and handle more
sacred matters, such as examination of those who wish to take communion or
have their children baptized. They sit separately from other members of the congregation in seats below the pulpit (*an suidheachan mor,* the big seat).

Church services are held twice on Sunday, a combination of sermon, singing
psalms, and prayer that lasts about 2 hours ("the previous minister kept us for
over 3 hours; he would say, if you were at a dance you wouldn't mind the passing of time"). The deacons select a precentor, a good singer who is usually an
elder, who sings out the lines of the psalms to the congregation, who then take
up the line in pentatonic harmony, drawing out the line in a swelling, droning,
communal sound.

Those who are "following"[4] (*leantail*) the church also attend a Wednesday-
night prayer meeting, and twice a year Communions (*na h-orduighean,* the ordi-
nances) are held, at which time those who are converted (curamach) and whose
request to join the communicants has been accepted by the kirk session partake
in the "Lord's Supper" of bread and wine (Parman 1990).

---

[4]From Mark 8:34, to take up the cross and follow Jesus. In Gaelic usage, to "start following"
refers to a new convert.

The Free Church minister with bridal party outside the church

Na h-Orduighean (pronounced "ordion," as in "accordion"), the Gaelic term for communion, refers not only to the act of consuming bread and wine but to a set of rotating 5-day ceremonial periods held twice a year (in fall and late winter). For 5 to 6 weeks, communion services are held among Free Church congregations, and many members move from village to village to follow the services,[5] staying in the homes of villagers who open their doors to communicants. For the 5-day period, services are held twice a day, usually in Gaelic, and reach a crescendo of intensified separation of converted (curamach) from unconverted on Sunday when the curamach take communion under the watchful and envious eyes of the unchosen.

The 5-day period begins on Thursday with a "day of humiliation and prayer" (*Latha Irioslachaidh*) in which the congregation is reminded that man was born into a condition of total depravity and sin. Friday is *Latha na Ceist,* day of questions, also referred to as the day of "marks and signs" or "Men's Day" (*na Daoine*), so called because the elders give testimony on their experience of conversion, the signs by which they knew that they were saved. It is a day of questions because, after the service in which the elders give testimony, members of the congregation are invited to meet with the kirk session and give evidence of why they should be allowed to take communion.

[5]For example, in 2002, the communion dates as described in *The Monthly Record: The Magazine of the Free Church of Scotland* (February 2002) were as follows: March 3: Glasgow-Dowanvale, North Tolsta, Lochbroom, Urquhart, Kiltarlity, Kilmallie, Dumfries, Carloway; March 10: Cross, Park, Scalpay-Harris, Portree, Knockbain, Livingston, Lennoxtown, Glasgow-St. Vincent Street; March 17: Dunbarton, East Kilbride, Barvas, Kinloch, Inverness-Greyfriars, Creich, Kincardine and Croick, Rogart, Bishopbriggs, Dunblame, Dornoch; March 24: Greenock, Lochs, Olrig, Rosehall; March 31: Back, North Uist.

The "curamach" at a psalmody class, 1970

Over the next 24 hours the lives of these hopeful communicants are subjected to intense scrutiny. Is there a shred of gossip[6] that casts their testimony in doubt? Are they truly good-living people? Many people who are widely considered cura-mach choose not to subject themselves to such close scrutiny and never take communion, in part because by doing so they will cross the line from low visibility to high visibility; they will have taken a position that puts them at odds with other members of the community. They will have to give witness, to lead public prayers, to be counted on to take a stand on a variety of issues related to conceptions and applications of scripture. Wives might have to give testimony against their husbands, parents against their children, to uphold a commitment to purity.

Saturday is a "day of preparation" (*Latha Ullachaidh*) in which members of the congregation are called on to examine themselves for the signs of behavior, state of mind, and knowledge of the Bible that mark them as saved. On this day, successful applicants for communion are given tokens[7] by the kirk session that permit them to attend the sacred table on Sunday.

On Sunday morning, Feast Day (*Latha na Feille*), the church fills early in preparation for the communion service. Rarely used, the balcony fills quickly, as it provides a bird's-eye view of the pews at the front of the church that have been

[6]At the level of the General Assembly, gossip is glossed by the ecclesiastical term *fama clamosa,* a widespread rumor, such as the one on which the FCC split was based (see MacDonald 2000:132).

[7]In Ciall, tokens are square pieces of metal with the name of the Free Church on one side and a verse from Corinthians—"Do this in remembrance of me"—on the other. Communicants receive these tokens from the elders of their street. The tokens may be round, and in Gaelic or English (see Mitchison 1978:42 for an illustration of locally produced tokens of lead or pewter given out by the Church of Scotland for their annual communion service in the 17th and 18th centuries).

marked off with white sheets. Who has declared themselves? Who has been accepted? As the communicants come in, give their tokens, and take their places, separating themselves from the rest of the congregation (and in many cases from their spouses, children, parents, and friends), the news spreads more quickly than the flow of boiled sweets, mints, and horehound drops during the third hour of a boring sermon. Fraser MacDonald (2002:55) calls attention to the importance of spatial organization in Presbyterian churches and the Free Church in North Uist, quoting Lefebvre (*The Production of Space*): "What [space] . . . signifies is dos and don'ts . . . above all it prohibits." The communion service on Sunday follows a rigid order of spatial symbolism, condensing the 5-day structure that in turn reflects stages of the life cycle (see Parman 1990:300).

The communion service on Sunday is divided into four parts, the first of which, called "fencing the table," is considered the most sacred. At each stage of the communion service, certain passages are read and specific psalms sung. During "the fencing," believers are separated from nonbelievers; during "strengthening," believers are encouraged; during "the elements," communicants consume the bread and wine (the plate and goblet are passed along the pews, not controlled by the minister). On Monday, the Day of Thanksgiving (*Latha Taingealach*), the communicants are exhorted to go out into the world and give witness. The groundwork for conversion is laid in the training given to children in learning their catechism.

Children are taught their catechism, or series of questions to which they give memorized responses, at home and in Sunday School, which is taught primarily by curamach women who may or may not be teachers. Before World War II, classes were taught in Gaelic. After the war it was decided to give instructions in English. Catechism was once taught in the schools as well, and the ministers visited the schools regularly to examine the children. This practice has recently been discontinued. In the past, teachers preceded class with prayer practice. There were "catechism nights" on every street, in which the minister drilled parents on "the question." Parents drill their children in parrot-like memorization of catechism that they will be asked to repeat in school drills and examinations by the kirk session for baptism and Communion. "Remember," said the minister, who was visiting the school in 1971 to examine children on their catechism, "Remember . . . what does that remind you of?" A small voice came from the back of the room, "Remember-the-Sabbath-Day-and-keep-it-holy." These memorized phrases lay the foundation for later experiences of "talking with God" and conversion. They are deeply embedded and surface sometimes as unbidden thoughts, as a voice external to themselves. This uncontrolled flow has the thumbprint of supernatural intervention, as something non-normal, as proof of the divine.

The Church and Conceptions of Human Nature

Q. 19. What is the misery of that estate whereinto man fell?

A. All mankind by their fall lost communion with God, are under his wrath and curse, and so made liable to all miseries in this life, to death itself, and to the pains of hell for ever.

—The Shorter Catechism

Sunday school picnic, 1970

Hilda, the teacher from Detroit: "I didn't see Ciall until I was 20, when my father decided to retire here; but as soon as I came, I saw, magnified, the feelings that I had grown up with: the feeling that I was doomed; that everyone is sinful; it's the human burden of original sin, and there's nothing you can do about it. It's 'in the blood' or God's will; and people sit around saying *'oich, oich'* and waiting to find out if they've been chosen for salvation."

As I was struggling with the Gaelic, recording sermons, and asking people to translate them for me, I was asked if I noticed that in Gaelic the sermons seemed more somber and dire. On one occasion, I was asked during a visit that followed an English sermon for summer visitors that included, as part of the text, "Even the ground groans under our feet and wants to be rid of us. We are a weight, an encumbrance." My host commented, "In the Gaelic it's all hellfire and brimstone and doom. *'Bas . . .'* death—ach, they're all prophets of doom. If you're not converted, you're going to be burned. 'How long have you been coming here?' says the minister. 'Have you gone gray coming here, and still without Christ.'" In Gaelic or English, the psalms and the text are full of suffering, sin, the wrath of God. "The harvest is done, the summer is gone, and you are not saved." Bedside reading in 2003 included sermons, meditations, John Bunyan's *Pilgrim's Progress,* and daily devotionals. From John Blanchard's *Ultimate Questions,* I learned I was "debased. Sin has invaded every part of your nature and personality. The heart is deceitful above all things, and desperately wicked. You are defiled. Out of the heart of men proceed evil thoughts. Who can say, I have made my heart clean, I am pure from my sin? Hell is factual, fearful, final, and fair. Religion can never satisfy God. All our righteousness are as filthy rags. God demands perfection."

> *We are by nature unlawful. The natural man is the man without the curam, the man who sees God and the law as a burden, the man who wants to be "free." Strife will*

end when man and the Creator agree. The law is a burden because man does not keep any of it; what he wants is so utterly different from what the law allows.

—Minister, communion service, March 1, 1971

There are some people in Hell tonight who once listened to the gospel in this church.

—Sunday night communion service, March 2, 1971

The Free Church reflects the Calvinist emphasis on predestination. Some souls are saved and some damned; to find out which you are, you must look for signs. To be curamach is to be circumspect in behavior, careful; there are definite signs that everyone watches for, which indicate that you are among the saved. All behavior is a sign, a marker of your status. When I visited communicant households, I was typically told, "This cup of tea was meant for you." One person commented on the tendency of many people to turn at random to some point in the Bible to help them make decisions. "If you can't find anything in the Bible to help you, it is foreordained that you are not to get help. If a desperate man looks in the Bible and finds nothing and the next day commits suicide, it was foreordained that he was going to die." Some villagers debate the concept of predestination. "If I'm predestined to not be saved, I'm doomed even before I was conceived; so Christ didn't die for me. But he was supposed to die for everyone. Then why isn't everyone saved?" Elaborate debates are held on whether the Bible should be interpreted literally or symbolically.

Q. 60. How is the Sabbath to be sanctified?

A. The Sabbath is to be sanctified by a holy resting all that day, even from such worldly employments and recreations as are lawful on other days; and spending the whole time in the public and private exercises of God's worship, except so much as is to be taken up in the works of necessity and mercy.

—*The Shorter Catechism*

In the report of the Committee on Public Questions, Religion and Morals to the General Assembly of the Free Church of Scotland (*The Scotsman*, May 14, 1970), the committee railed against the lawlessness propagated by the larger society through TV, cinema, and stage.[8] It condemned the ecumenical movement and attributed world problems to God's desire to humble and chastise a world fallen from grace. It condemned sex education in the school, stating that it hoped that the subject would not be taught from a relativistic point of view, from a "purely humanistic and pagan view, which would in due course debase our society." Sounding very much like the antihumanistic Moral Majority movement in the United States, the Free Church has a witch-hunting, moralistic reputation

---

[8]*The Monthly Record: The Magazine of the Free Church of Scotland* reviewed the film, *The Lord of the Rings*, in February 2002, comparing it to *Pilgrim's Progress* and the Narnia books in its treatment of basic Christian themes of evil, sin, forgiveness, sacrifice, redemption, faithfulness, and love. It criticized the film for its "post-modern tendency toward psycho-babble" (Aragorn would never have the self-doubts shown in the film; he knew "the right and wise path"); and for its portrayal of Arwen saving Frodo from the Black Riders ("The whole point of that scene . . . is that little Frodo of the Shire stood alone and resisted temptation"). On the other hand, the Harry Potter books are attacked as being based on real occult practice.

even in dour, sabbatarian Scotland. The Sabbath is kept more seriously here than in any other part of Britain.[9]

Tourist brochures warn visitors of the strictness with which the Sabbath is maintained in the rural parts of Lewis. Most Ciall families contrast the laxness of the present day with their father's time when the hot food for Sunday was prepared the previous night, no children could be out past twilight on Saturday and certainly not out after midnight, and Sunday was spent attending two church services and reading the Bible in between. "No cooking or washing, not even knitting. You shined your shoes for church the previous night."

When the Reverend Alexander MacLeod came to Uig in 1824, he was scandalized by the "polluted remains of Popery" and paganism (the people prayed that wrecks be cast ashore for their use), and by the laxness with which the Sabbath was observed. Occupants of Ciall today remember stories that they identify with their great grandfather's time concerning the change to a more strict observance of the Sabbath; "Even tethering a cow on a Sunday was prohibited. But now the young people go to a wedding in Glasgow and see the shops open on Sundays, and they ask why can't the shops be open here too." Said one man in his 30s, when a church meeting was held in the middle of the week when he was a child, all work would stop and people would stay inside. When a Stornoway resident first came to the island 20 years ago, he was told of a minister who warned his congregation not to get Sunday papers (but they got early editions on Friday, which was all right); another told his congregation not to read papers on Monday because they had been printed on Sunday. Lewis girls working in mainland hotels refused to celebrate New Year's Eve if it fell on a Saturday night; Lewis men were fired for refusing to work on emergency construction jobs on Sundays. "When television came to the island, my father went to bed and pulled the bedclothes over his head when my brother—still living at home but too old to smack—watched it on Sunday." One mother, who allows her children to watch TV on Sunday, "keeps an eye out for the holies. We draw the curtains and turn down the volume."

Today few people would dare to be seen out visiting after midnight on Saturday, but meals are prepared and nonreligious books are often read, and attending one of the two services is considered sufficient. The male head of the household is supposed to lead the family in morning and evening prayers. Many younger men have not kept this up; some say they cannot read the Gaelic easily. But wherever people are, they are very conscious of the restrictive presence of Sundays. "Wherever I am, I always stiffen up on Sunday. Once a Glasgow fellow took me to a dance and I sat there as rigid as a post, certain I would be sent straight to hell." In Stornoway, strict churchgoers refuse to pay fares on the bus going to church. A minister in Skye organized a sit-down strike against the ferry operating on Sunday. One boy wrecked his car rushing home to beat the Saturday midnight curfew. A plan to show "Lord of the Isles," a film about Leverhulme, on Sunday night in the village hall was rejected. Although I spent many Sundays using the quiet, restful days to catch up on notes and reading, I

---

[9]Much against the efforts of the Lord's Day Observance Society, in 2003 MacBrayne's now provides Sunday ferry service to Stornoway and drinks are served in the airport bar.

was careful not to use my typewriter, which might have been labeled "worldliness" by someone walking down the road.

CHURCH AND COMMUNITY

The Free Church oversees and marks the passage of its congregation from birth to death.

Baisteadh (Baptism)

Supposing a father were given the whole world, all the money he wanted, he wouldn't part with his child. But the child's soul is far more valuable. You must stand up for the child's soul before God, confess that you have brought him up in the Christian faith. Don't let it be said that you came home drunk and swearing, but that you set a good example, and don't be like a certain woman who when she was on her deathbed on the Isle of Skye called her father and told him it was his fault that she was lost, because he had never brought her up right.

—Minister's comments during a baptism, October 17, 1971

Before a child can be baptized, the father (or mother, if she is alone or the father refuses to come before the kirk session) must approach the neighborhood elder with a request for baptism. The parent(s) must go before the kirk session on the Monday night following Communions. The service occurs as part of a regular Sunday service, with the fathers sitting in the front of the church separated by several rows from the rest of the congregation. After the sermon, the mothers bring in the babies and sit in front of their husbands. The men then take the children; the minister questions each father whether they are going to raise the child in the church and set a good example for them. He asks each child's name, dips his hand in the water brought to him in a silver bowl by one of the elders, and places his hand several times on the child's forehead ("Not in the sign of the cross—that's the Catholic church"). The fathers return the children to the mothers.

Most people refer to this event not as a baptism but as a christening, because of the importance of naming. Baptism is not relevant to being saved (your salvation or damnation is preordained; "Only the children of the covenant are saved"). "It means that now you're a member of the Free Church," said a non-curamach member of the congregation. A visiting minister qualified that statement, saying, "In the strict sense of the word, baptism should make a person a church member; but in the Free Church, membership depends on Communion." Almost all villagers have their children baptized (said one person, "It's almost like you're not legal until you've been baptized").

You have brought shame upon yourselves, shame upon your children, and shame upon your parents. I cannot erase your shame; I can only hope that you ask Christ to forgive you, and that from now on you follow closely in the ways of the church.

—Minister's lecture to couple standing in church, 1971

The village has extensive knowledge, through the channels of gossip, about whether the parents of a child have conceived, or contributed to the conception of, a child out of wedlock. Before such parents can have their children baptized, they must go before the kirk session, like everyone else, to be questioned about their religious beliefs. A man who impregnated another woman besides his wife, a couple who conceived a child out of wedlock (even if the child miscarried), a woman if she is unmarried or if she conceived the child to be baptized by a man other than her husband—they all as responsible sinner(s) must be called on for their sins at this time by the elder of their street, asked to confess, and asked if they are willing to stand up in church before the congregation and be lectured by the minister.

A woman, of course, cannot evade culpability, but the question of who the father is may be debated for generations. The public confession of paternity validates gossip that may have gone on for years; it achieves a sense of social and psychological closure. If it does not occur at baptism, it usually occurs when a man wants to take Communion.

Some couples have left the island or had their children baptized in Glasgow before they will consent to endure the shame of standing in church (*seasadh*). The elders are usually blamed for this practice; but if an elder does not ask a father to stand in church, the elder is blamed for allowing him to "get away with it." When one person had his child baptized without having to stand in church, several people commented that he had undermined the law of the church and that in the future others might refuse to stand. On one occasion, the minister forgot to lecture the sinful couple, and sent a note later to apologize; because he had forgotten, he said, they would not have to stand. But the father insisted on having to stand; he said that people would talk about him and say that he was getting special treatment. One man justified this practice: "If I go to jail for stealing something, after I've paid for my crime no one can call me a thief."

When the previous minister left the island, Ciall had no minister for a year, and the new minister had to lecture quite a few couples before their children could be baptized. Everyone worried ("What will he think of us?"), but consoled themselves with a discussion of ministers they knew to be illegitimate themselves.

Posadh (Wedding Service)

All members of the congregation may attend a wedding service, which, as described in the previous chapter, tends to be lighter in vein. If there are irregularities in the marriage (if the bride is known to be pregnant, or has already had a child, for example), the jokes are fewer, and the minister may take the opportunity to give the couple a lecture on their responsibilities.

Death

When a member of the community dies, the church services on the Sunday following his death are usually more somber, full of frightening visions of the misery that awaits sinners after they die ("Death is the wages of sin . . . We are all going to die, this isn't really our home . . . Only those who have been quickened will be saved . . ."). Dances in the village are cancelled, and usually the *bothan* is closed, especially if the person was young or well liked. The minister is expected to give a prayer meeting in the house of mourning on the evenings that precede burial; but death is primarily the responsibility of the community, and the minister may or may not accompany the body to the cemetery.

Susan Parman

Susan Parman

Neighbors gather to celebrate the dead with prayer and stories, after which men take turns carrying the coffin either to the graveyard or to a waiting hearse.

For several days preceding the burial, neighbors keep watch over the body in a communal wake, a *tigh aire* or house of watching. "Every house must send someone to show respect." "When something happens to one person, everyone feels it; we're all so interconnected here." The body is laid out, neighbors bring in food, endless cups of tea are prepared by relatives for the visitors, and amid occasional outbursts of sorrow and *"oich oichs,"* happy memories of the deceased are recalled. At one wake, the antics of a village character were remembered. "He used to have 'Mods' for the children. He would put a pound note on the hearth as the prize for the best singing; he would sing himself, and claim the

Susan Parman

Susan Parman

Cemetery in 1970 (top) and 2003 (bottom)

prize." "When his wife started weaving, he would bring other people's tweeds and hang them in front of the house so everyone would think she was weaving one tweed a day."

It is at the *tigh aire* that you hear accounts of premonitions, of dreams foretelling the death, of second sight. "There was a patch of white in front of the house." "I saw two Land Rovers beside the house out of the corner of my eye; but when I looked straight, they weren't there. The next week, after the death, the Land Rovers were there for the wake."

There are endless discussions of who the dead person's relatives are, and whether they have come to show respect. Detailed accounts of the deaths of others are recalled ("His wife was 13 months older than himself, much frailer than he. The weather when she died was bad, like this year—2 weeks of bad weather followed by sunshine in June"). Often the descriptions of the dead person are graphic ("It was a bad death . . . . turned all black"; "a liver disease . . . the corpse was an orange color").

Today few wakes are held through the night; the minister arrives at around midnight, gives a long prayer ("To keep things from getting too hilarious," said one minister), and the watchers usually disassemble. But in some cases the watch continues throughout the night. "All the visiting paralyzes your brain; you're too exhausted to think. It keeps you going."

On the day of the funeral, all the males of the village assemble to carry the coffin. The women remain in the house, a solid body of weeping, commiserating watchfulness as the body is carried away by the men. The coffin lies feet-first on a wooden-slat bier and bears a simple plaque labeled with name and age. The chief mourner (usually the eldest son) walks at the head end of the coffin, the younger sons, uncles, and other close male relatives at the feet. The line of bearers may be a quarter of a mile long, and everyone takes a turn, even if it means parking the hearse, which now drives the coffin to the graveyard, some distance away. Two by two, the bearers at the back of the bier are displaced by those behind, and move up, finally displacing the two at the front, who step out of the way and remain standing at the roadside, or join the procession at the end when it finally passes them. One of the last funerals I attended was in the middle of summer—the long black line of somber men showed starkly against a sea of green that foamed with yellow flowers.

Traditionally a dram of whiskey was given at the house and the graveside; in one village, where the coffin had to be carried five miles, the bearers stopped for tea and biscuits along the way, and a "piggy *uisge beathea*," an earthenware jug of liquor, was carried "to keep out the cold." Said one minister about his previous calling, "I went into one house, and the table had bottles of whiskey on it. In the next sermon I told them that they could only invite one of two people to the wake service, myself or Johnny Walker, and after that the practice went underground." In Harris, there are cairns, or heaps of stones, from the days when bearers piled stones to mark where they stopped to rest.

The grave is dug the night before by neighbors and relatives ("Someone has to know the graveyard well so you won't dig down to another coffin; you use a long pole to make sure"), and the deceased lies in death as he lived in life—as part of a layer, which holds 6–8 coffins. An unmarried woman is buried with her parents; a married woman goes with her husband, but "she gets her name back when she dies." A woman is buried with her maiden name, and her age, on her coffin. Jokes are told about complications in social life that make funeral arrangements difficult. When a man who had outlived three wives finally died, his family puzzled over which wife to place him with. "Just put him down anywhere," commented one of the gravediggers, "He'll find one of them during the night."

A funeral committee keeps the cemetery clean, organizes the building of retaining walls to keep off the sea; and a "West of Lewis Funeral Association," started in 1911, assures that Lewismen will not be buried among strangers. Daughters wear black for at least 6 months; widows traditionally wear black for the rest of their lives.

Functions of the Church

All members of the community participate in some or all of the religious rituals that mark the passage of life from birth to death. Sermons remind the congregation that the Bible contains everything that people need to know, that it never needs to be updated or revised. Many people in the village use the Bible as an historical framework in which all events since the dawn of creation to modern times, in all cultures, can be placed. Like those who prefer to use encyclopedias, or those who claim that for every illness there is a healing plant, there is an assumption of the fixity and containment of knowledge, a finite wholeness that can be packaged and held in the hand.

The church also plays an important role in maintaining social control. Just as Robert Ekvall (1968) described Tibetan lamas serving as "research centers" for processing the gossip that flows rapidly through the countryside and using it in divination, the minister once described the manse as the office to which every one brought information. "They tell the minister everything," complained one young woman. "The previous minister used to use this information in church— who was out after midnight on Saturday night, who was seen having a drink on Sunday." Church is also the setting in which gossip is verified when public confessions of sin and error are made.

The church is the one place where almost everyone in the village goes, and thus it is a center of information regarding changes in status or geographical movement. A newly married couple go to church with their best man and bridesmaid when they return from their honeymoon. When the exiles return, they joke, "I'd best go to church and announce my presence."

The church keeps up one end of a continuous dialectic between the Bible and the bottle. If some consider the Free Church, and in particular the in-group of the curamach (those who are saved), to be the core of Celtic/Highland/Scottish purity, others credit whiskey with the same role (see Chapter 8).

WITCHES AND GHOSTS

When I first visited Lewis and was introduced as an anthropologist, many people assumed that I was interested primarily in archaic folklore and exotic beliefs. A writer from the island said he had some information about witchcraft, if I were interested. Expecting to be given an idiosyncratic, romantic concoction of historical fragments that he found useful in his own writing, I told him that I wasn't, particularly, unless the beliefs were meaningful in everyday interaction.

The first time I ever heard witchcraft mentioned was when I was out with a group that was bringing back the peats in a truck, and the truck got stuck and had to be partially unloaded. One of the men that I didn't know very well looked in my direction and muttered, *"Buidseachd"* (witchcraft). The man who had invited me to accompany them was embarrassed, and later explained that women did not usually go out to bring home the peats.

Witchcraft at the Peats

I did not ask about or bring up the topic of witchcraft, but I found it being discussed on various occasions without my bringing it up, usually with some self-consciousness ("It's a backward notion, no one really believes that sort of thing any more"), and often with humor. In most people's minds the term "witchcraft" connoted rural superstition. Many stated, however, that witchcraft did tend to run in certain families. "After all," said one person, "Did you ever stop to think why [some example of good fortune] came to a particular family?" Then out tumbled a series of stories about various members of the family, both living and deceased. As I listened to the stories, I began to classify them as a form of gossip with supernatural ingredients—the same touch of malice, the embellished tale, the explanation of why some have more than others ("Things always seem to fall their way, into their laps"), the imposition of order by weaving past, present, and future. "Whenever something unusual happens, especially if it's to someone's advantage, out comes the buidseachd [witchcraft]." An illegitimate child born dead, three brothers married to three sisters, an overturned peat truck, wishful but unsubstantiated plans for a marriage that never came off—several examples woven together around the explanatory thread of witchcraft create a trend, a characteristic "in the blood," one more tie with which to bind your neighbor. In the old days cattle were always getting bewitched, and spinsters gave magical reiteachs on moonlit nights to catch husbands. Today husbands are still in scarce supply (and a good topic for speculations about witchcraft), but tweeds and tourists have replaced cattle as items of envy and manipulation. As in other societies, certain families are more likely to attract accusations of witchcraft, in particular those who consistently do well and those who manifest antisocial behavior.

Stories of second sight, ghosts, and witches are used for social control, intimidation, and recreation, and to reflect a sense of connection to deceased kinsmen. Adults use ghost stories to persuade their children to stay in at night; friends tell the stories they heard at midnight ceilidhs to spook their peers.

> *One day a woman came across a man killing a sheep, which was a dreadful offence. He killed her to keep her quiet, and threw her into a loch. Much later a boat was out fishing. An arm bone kept coming up with the net. The captain said that this bone must have something to do with someone in the boat, and made each of the three crewmen hold it in turn. When the murderer's turn came, blood gushed from the bone.*

("The gorier the better," said one young woman who told me this story. "We were raised on ghost stories."[10])

Scotland in general is renowned for its ghost stories. Many of these are associated with castles and significant historical figures. Many of them draw on the romanticized history of the clans. The following story, told in the context of a midnight ceilidh, contains a number of interesting cultural ingredients, such as attitudes toward strangers, the close connection of an individual with his kinsmen, mother-son relationships, and second sight.

---

[10]When I saw the same woman in 2003, the first memory she brought up was a night we were walking together and saw a light on the moor. "I've always wondered what that was."

Susan Parman

Witchcraft at the peats

Seventy years ago a boy was fishing in Stornoway; he was 15 or 16. He used to walk home across the moor every second week. One night he noticed a man walking beside him, some distance away. The next time he went with a friend and didn't see the man, but he was back whenever the boy was alone. Finally he grabbed the man, who told him, "Your grandfather was the first to walk in my blood after I was killed." The man was a stranger to the island who had been killed by local people who didn't want strangers there. The man told him many things, including the fact that he would die a violent death; but he must not tell anyone else these things. The boy went home in a daze and told his mother everything. When he woke up the next morning, he realized what he had done. He begged his mother not to say anything, and left the island forever. As the ghost had prophesied, he died a violent death in Glasgow as a policeman who fell off a bridge.

I had my own private, idiosyncratic encounter with a supernatural being that reflected my romantic immersion in the stories that were told to me when I was out on the moor looking at the ruins of the shielings. I had gone about 6 miles out on the moor alone, something I had been warned never to do, and was finishing some mapping when a downpour began. I rigged my rain cape between the walls of a shieling and as I sat there, waiting for the rain to let up, I started thinking about a story I had been told, called "The Shieling of the One Night." In one version, two girls had been caught in the rain and slept there overnight; but in the morning one girl had vanished, never to be seen again, and some said she had been captured by an *each uisge*, a water horse who lived in a nearby spring. Another version had her lying dead in the shieling with blood pouring out of her ear, having been murdered by the same *each uisge*.

It got warmer and darker. The fog rolled in over the hills. When I finally started back I couldn't see more than a yard in front of me and began to think seriously of the warnings I had been given, warnings I had dismissed as the concerns of people who never slept alone, never walked alone, who always lived in the midst of others. If there had been cattle, I could have followed them home; but the cattle were gone.

I kept the hill slope on my left and moved slowly across the uneven ground, looking for the saddle-like break between two hills that marked the line of descent to the peat road. I couldn't find it; I felt as if I had circled the same hill several times. Then my foot broke through the deceptive surface of green moss, and I sank up to my hip in water. It was one of the springs that had once provided fresh water for the shielings, so seldom used now that it was almost overgrown. When I pulled my leg out, the peaty bottom glurked and bubbled.

The fog seemed extraordinarily thick and filled with uncanny noises. There were eerie whispers. And then I heard the sound of hooves scrabbling over stones and rustling the reeds.

It was the water horse—I could almost see him through the viscous gray of the fog, like a patch of white above me on the hillside. I turned and walked, with sudden furious energy, down the slope. I found the break in the hills; and as I slid down a shallow ravine the hoofsteps grew louder and more insistent, more nervous and frantic. I reached the peat road. The fog, blown by winds off the sea, thinned considerably. I looked back.

When I was about 12, I asked my parents for books that would terrify me; I wanted to be really frightened, I said. They recommended Bram Stoker, Algernon Blackwood, and H. P. Lovecraft. *Dracula* I found dull, but *The Dunwich Horror* gave me the shivers I was looking for.

I had known on the hill that if I looked back I would see something terrible, a cultural blend of my old nemesis, the Dunwich Horror, and the water horse. Now, on the safety of the peat road, I saw only brown peat banks, gray-green hillocks, and lichen-stubbled boulders, against which moved the black-faced sheep, now grazing quietly after I had startled them with my frantic rush down the hill and sent their small hooves scrabbling over the stones and through the reeds. For a moment I had clothed in Hebridean garb the universal human tendency to tinker with emotional and cognitive boundaries—archaic garb at that, for who but an anthropologist would be interested in water horses when steamrollers and fast-moving cars streaking over the moor roads were available? I thought of what would happen if I told my experience to anyone. It would reintroduce the water horse to currently discussed lore; and in a hundred years, when a folklorist was looking for old tales, he would collect various versions of one that began, "Well, you see, there was this anthropologist out on the moor . . . ."[11]

SECOND SIGHT

Gaelic Scotland is associated with the gift of second sight (see Cohn 1999 for an historical review of ideas and examples of second sight in Scotland), or the ability to be aware of things outside the normal range of vision ("a distortion of the time-space continuum," explained one well-educated islander. "Usually second

[11]Sometimes fiction conveys the reality of experience more vividly than the remembered events. For a fictionalized version of this experience, see Parman (2001).

sight involves a prediction of the future; sometimes it means being aware of something in the present—a friend on his way to see you, a death that has just occurred"). Second sight is usually associated with the prediction of unpleasant events: someone missing, the onset of illness, and particularly death. It is also associated with marriage. Second sight usually occurs in dreams, but may be experienced in visions, or be associated with a general feeling of unease. "I was feeling upset for 3 days. I knew something was going to happen, that someone in the house was going to die. On the third day a first cousin died, and I felt immediate relief."

Second sight is usually associated with people to whom you feel very close, usually kinsmen. Even if the predicted event is nonlocal, such as the loss of an ocean liner at sea, the prediction is explained as resulting from the influence of relatives who were experiencing the crisis. Many dreams of second sight involve the sea.

Persons who have this ability are said to have inherited it. "I inherited the ability to predict events through dreams from my mother," said one man. As one would expect in a bilateral kinship system, the ability can be inherited through either the mother's or father's side.

> My mother's father was dating a girl in Breasclete. One night he dreamed of a beautiful girl that he had never seen before. He told his friend to go and see his girl, that she was all right in everything but he couldn't marry her. His friend married the girl within the year. Several years later my grandfather met the girl of his dreams coming off the shielings in Inisbay, and they were soon married.

Dream symbolism associated with second sight is sometimes thought of as universal, and sometimes as idiosyncratic. For one man a white patch in front of a house signifies a death in the house, but he considers this a personal signal. For one woman, dreams about meat always indicate that you're worried about someone, as do dreams about young children and babies; gray is a bad color, and so on.

Many people make efforts to reconcile second sight with scientific concepts. Various explanations for its increase or decrease are given. Some people believe that it declined when electricity came to the island; "the light" interfered with the ability to see. But the ability is considered a biological fact that exists in certain families, and it has no difficulty incorporating technological changes such as the introduction of cars. Many modern examples of second sight involve cars. For several weeks during the winter months, when darkness reigned, I heard variations on the following stories. "The other night a boy saw car lights coming up the hill straight toward him. He couldn't move. They went right through him. He's terrified that he's going to be killed in a car accident." "She saw a steam roller with a man sitting on it in the headlights of an approaching car; but when the car passed and they turned on their lights, it wasn't there."

Although second sight is not spoken of or condoned in the context of the established church, the church is considered an arena of the sacred in which such events may reasonably occur. In the summer of 1971, a young man died suddenly of a heart attack. The minister, during the evening service on the Sunday that preceded the young man's death, had spoken of men who tear down barns to build better ones ("that is when their souls are called for"). The young man who died had just torn down his own house to build a new one; financially he was doing well by driving the fish van, bringing liquor to the bothan, and carting tweeds. This was a clear case, many people said, of second sight; the minister had predicted his death.

I asked if ministers or the curamach were more likely than others to have this power. One man said he thought this likely, and tried to remember if the person on his street who was credited with being a prophet ("He said there would be no German flag in Britain") had this ability before he became curamach. Another person said, "Many of the people here have it," but agreed that the Bible itself was a concentrated form of prediction that could stimulate already existing tendencies; he himself had stopped reading the Bible at night because he was having too many predictive dreams. Still another person disagreed, saying, "God chooses who has it, but God's people aren't more likely to have it than anyone else." In general people agreed that second sight was an ability peculiar to Gaels; and in this context a few fragments of the history of a famous prophet called the Brahan Seer were recalled by some who prided themselves on their knowledge of Gaelic folklore.

I asked the minister if he knew that second sight had been attributed to him by his congregation, and was teased about my anthropological quest for the pagan and primitive. He said that some ministers believed that these visions went out when Jesus came. His concern, he said, was to remind people that they could die at any time; that they should not invest in worldly things, especially material goods that made them look better than their neighbors.

8/Creating Culture in Ciall
The Bottle and the Bible

WHISKEY AND SCOTLAND

In his book *Whisky and Scotland,* first published in 1935, Neil Gunn credits the Gaels with giving whiskey to the world (the word "whiskey" comes from the Gaelic *uisge beatha,* the water of life). His book is a nationalistic treatise that places whiskey at the core of Scottishness in a roundabout symbolic construction linking selected aspects of history. According to Gunn, the boundary between Highland and Lowland, between Celt and Anglo-Saxon, was marked by the whiskey still. In 1787, Scotland was divided into Highland and Lowland by an act of Parliament that distinguished two different methods of collecting duty on whiskey: per gallon of spirits in the Lowlands and England, and per the capacity of the still in the Highlands (Gunn 1977:106). Simple pot-still distillation was a family affair in the Highlands, a method of converting surplus barley into cash and hospitality. Smuggling whiskey, or evading the whiskey tax, was as much a symbol of Gaelic integrity and Scottish distinctiveness as was poaching salmon from the laird's river. At the time of the Clearances, say many of the smuggling stories, the chiefs used smuggling as an excuse to turn people out of their homes.

"Freedom and whisky gang thegither," Gunn quotes Robert Burns, and then adds, "Quite clearly Burns, though a Lowlander, has never taken to the feudal system, any more than the crofters of the Highlands who kept on fighting the alien enslavement until they gave it at least a partial check by forcing the Government to pass a Crofter's Act embodying the ancient right of 'security of tenure'" (1977:111). With this and many other statements, Gunn forges a symbolic link between crofter, Gael, the common man, and Scottish cultural distinctiveness. The crofters represent the Celtic spirit, "the heart of native strength"; Burns's Kailyaird School "derives directly from the ancient Celtic source."

Another whisky to drown the memory of that impertinence! If not in fact, still in spirit, Scotland is a nation, and the Kailyaird School is her true Celtic Twilight. (Gunn 1977:112)

Slainte!

Eventually, "the ordinary Highlander, who has forgotten most of his Gaelic and has never worn a kilt, aware of the unspeakable slum life . . . will begin to demand less glamour and more barley, less intoxication by windy rhetoric and more by the true water of life" (1977:189). Whiskey, says Gunn, will provide employment, save the Highlands, preserve Scotland from English domination, and restore the promise of Gaelic distinctiveness, like the pure, raw taste of neat whiskey, to the Scottish soul.

For Ciall residents, paeans to whiskey are also sung, but in a different context, and with different intentions. Less concerned with being perceived as the symbols of Gaeldom and Scottish purity, the consumers of the "barley bree" are participating in rituals of hospitality, manhood, and profane communion in one of several systems of cultural resolution.

WHISKEY AND COMMUNITY

Rituals of Hospitality

Whiskey is an important ingredient in Scottish, Highland, and village hospitality. I remember being surprised, during my first stay in Scotland when I was an undergraduate attending the University of Edinburgh, when an 80-year-old landlady, serving me tea at the fireside (all lace and tea cozies, the essence of respectability), handed me a whiskey. In Ciall it seemed that the offer of whiskey was a welcoming gesture that represented the beginning of a visit, whereas the serving of tea symbolized its end. Although women are not supposed to drink, and never to act drunk, they hold and sip drinks as part of their participation in a convivial evening of conversation and song.

Whiskey is associated with special ceremonial occasions, with the birth of a child, weddings, and wakes. Jokes are told of the man who came with two *osdean,* the drink to celebrate the birth of a child, within a single year. An engagement party requires whiskey, and many wedding receptions are held in hotels for the explicitly stated purpose of cutting down on the drink expense; and when a married couple return from their honeymoon, they must go visiting with a bottle. Having whiskey at a funeral was once considered so important that many widows sold their cows to provide it, "so that people would not say it was a bad funeral."

New Year's Eve is the occasion for the greatest expenditure on drink. Sometimes lasting for as long as a week, with excessive and elaborate reversals in behavior (cf. Parman 1979), this holiday represents the most extreme example of culturally patterned drinking outside of alcoholism, a problem that is widespread throughout Scotland.

The Men's Club

Serious rather than ceremonial drinking is considered a masculine activity; indeed, it is almost required of males, especially if they are adult and unmarried. A man who avoids drink is not praised for his self-control or his ability to abstain; rather, people say, "What's the matter with him that he doesn't mix?" When a young man was sent to the mental hospital near Inverness, a statement used to validate his diagnosis as mentally ill was that he didn't drink with his age mates.

Women are not expected to drink, and if they drink, they are not supposed to get drunk. Women are agents of control. "It's a men's club," said one woman, describing the disappearance of her boyfriend from a *tigh ceilidh* (a house where both men and women were visiting) to go with other men to the hotel or *bothan* (small, unlicensed hut where liquor is sold).

Lewis has gone through cycles of "dry" and "wet" periods when liquor could be sold in certain parishes. Around 1930, men from Ness (many of whom were sailors and used to having drink easily accessible) began to bring kegs of beer back to their communities, and would drink in barns or in tigh ceilidh, the houses in which people gathered regularly for evening visits. Eventually they built huts of stone or concrete, or used shelters already available, such as the shells of old buses or Nissen huts. A few men brought liquor to these shelters, called bothans, and sold the drinks at cost. In 1963 the police raided a bothan and fined the men; but in 1967, another court case decided that the men were not guilty of trafficking in excisable liquor because there was no evidence that money had changed hands. The drink was not "for sale," argued the lawyer, because drinkers made "voluntary" contributions to a common kitty.

The first bothan in Ciall was started after World War II by a sailor home on leave. The men met in an old Nissen hut, and then, overnight ("if anyone knew it was being built, they would protest"), replaced it with a small concrete hut built inside the Nissen hut. "They were tearing down the Nissen hut when the minister passed by and praised the Lord that his prayers had been answered."

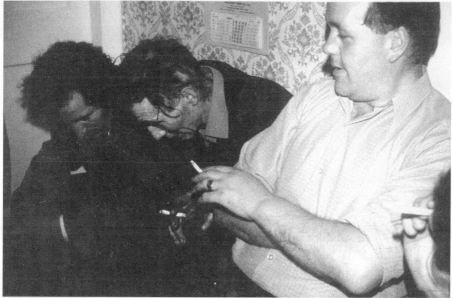

Susan Parman

Men at a ceilidh

A hotel 5 miles away is operated by a Ciall man, but many men prefer the bothan, where the drink is cheaper and the atmosphere less formal. Drinking situations provide opportunities, rare in the self-conscious, low-profile arena of village life, to express emotions and ideas. Because these expressions are often retracted in the cold, sober light of day, many contrast the warmth and good feeling expressed at this time with the fellowship of the converted. In fact, Bible and bottle are often seen as antagonists, as partners in a dialectic duel for commitment.

> *The Bible says that you cannot have two masters. It's dangerous; it will mislead people if you go to the church meetings during the week and then go drinking in the pubs on Friday night.*
>
> —A man lecturing his girlfriend who has been trying to convert

> *The only places where people can talk and sing is either in church or when they're drunk.*
>
> —A converted woman in her 50s

When I returned in 2003, the bothan was gone but in its place was a restaurant, within full view of the manse, whose primary business was the sale of "carry-out" liquor. The two buildings stand together as a visible representation of the statement made by a man who, after 40 years of hard drinking at sea, returned to the village and converted: "When God made the Bible, he also made the bottle. The Bible drives many a man to the bottle, but it's the bottle that makes him come back, in the end, to the Bible."

Standoff between the Bible (the manse) and the Bottle (a restaurant that provides "carry-out" liquor), 2003

THE PROCESS OF CONVERSION

In 2003, a woman described her husband's conversion:

He was gone for his usual visit to the hotel, and on his way back he went in to speak to a friend who was in at a prayer meeting up the road. He saw them sitting there praying, all the young men, and he started crying. They looked so clean; he felt so dirty. I was at the window with his mother looking out for him. We saw him coming in the road staggering and I thought well he's drunk again, and when he comes in I'll make sure he doesn't go out again, I'll lock all the doors. But then I saw he was crying. My heart went out to him; it was filled with tenderness. I said, "What's wrong?" but he just cried and went into the bedroom and lay down. He lay in bed for several days, very depressed, the handkerchief over his eyes. Then I knew what it was—it was conviction of sin. His mother was annoyed. All her life she had been a Christian, and he was the one who converted. You have to be plucked. Plucked like a brand from the fire.

"We're a God-fearing people," said one woman, shaking my hand after church during one of the intensive religious services of the Communions. "Lewis is *Tir an t-soisgeul*, Land of the Scriptures."

The word *soisgeul* comes from *sois* (meteor) and *sgeul* (which in different contexts can connote sacred tidings or mundane, worldly gossip), and means "gospel" or "heavenly tidings." A *soisgeulaiche* is an evangelist, or someone who brings good tidings. Ever since the Reverend MacLeod came to Uig in 1824, Lewis has reverberated with evangelical fervor.

A visiting minister told me that in Sutherland on the mainland (the region where Nancy Dorian conducted her study of "language death"), no one under 40 years of age had experienced conversion. The phenomenon of conversion is most common in the Outer Hebrides, and in Lewis in particular; it also occurs among Highlanders in Glasgow. Some villages are said to have more conversions than others; it comes and goes in waves. In the 1950s, revivals in Shader had people chanting, collapsing, and speaking in tongues; in 1970–71, revivals occurred in the vicinity of Ciall; in 2003, there were rumors of revivals in Ness. One minister explained the intensity of their conversions as due to a history of genocide: "They have been driven to the edge; they are defending their church, their language, their way of life."

Curam (Conversion)

A converted person "has the curam" (has been saved, or is in a condition of conversion), or is curamach (converted). The word "curam" means care, anxiety, responsibility; it means to be "under concern" for one's state of mind and spiritual condition. The word "curamach" means to be careful, solicitous, anxious, and attentive. In ordinary conversation the word may be used to mean being careful with your clothes; but in a religious context it means being careful and circumspect in behavior, evincing by your behavior that you are living the "good life"; your circumspect behavior is a sign that you are among those chosen to be saved.

Some non-curamach villagers refer jokingly to "the Big K" (from the brand name, Kellogg's, which appears in television and radio advertisements). A definitive sign of "the big K" is when girls wear their hair in a bun[1] and men stop drinking, and when they begin going twice a day to church and to Wednesday-night prayer meetings. The ultimate statement of conversion is to become a communicant or adherent by taking Communions. Not all those who are curamach wish to take the highly visible step of becoming a communicant; but all those who do so must be curamach.

As you get older, you are expected to become more circumspect; but the change is quiet. "Old people usually get one form or another of the curam." "Most of New Ciall has the curam. It's an old street." A woman, as the primary agent of social control, is typically more circumspect than a man, and her eventual conversion is expected. Joked one man, "Only recently were women allowed souls. Now they're outpacing the men in being saved. From the looks of the Communion table, only women are going to heaven." Usually women move quietly and predictably into conversion, whereas men, who are expected to "mix well" with other men in drinking groups, and who are expected to be less able to control themselves, often provide examples of dramatic conversion.

Dramatic conversions usually occur among the young, who convert in groups, and at middle age. "She got it suddenly. She left halfway through a dance." "He converted suddenly, in the middle of a drink in the bothan." Of the examples of dramatic conversion among females, most are associated with women who have lived away from the island and have returned to nurse an aging parent or to retire. "I was working in the hotels. Then my mother got sick and I came back to nurse her; and when she died I couldn't leave my father there alone. Within a year I was converted." Another woman lived for many years on the mainland, where she never attended church; when her husband died, she returned to the island and converted shortly afterwards.

---

[1]"Good-living" women should also not wear trousers or makeup, and should always cover their heads in church.

People are often converted by specific preachers. Some have been refused communion because the presiding minister did not approve of the person who converted them, or because they were converted in another church. I asked if the minister were needed in conversion. "The Bible tells us that God uses the foolishness of preaching to show the way to conversion. God can do it that way or a number of other ways." The process of conversion often starts when people hear the minister read the Bible, and something he says starts them thinking. Phrases, learned so thoroughly from childhood, drift through the mind. The actual conversion or intense vision may come days later. Several people said to me, after an English sermon in church, "I was hoping you would convert since it was an English sermon tonight."

Young people between the ages of 17 and 30 often go to meetings and church together, and convert around the same time; but sudden conversions may fade, and people may find that they are going along with the crowd without feeling as involved as they expected to be. One woman who began attending Wednesday meetings was puzzled when people came up to congratulate her. "It's nothing you've done yourself; supposedly you're chosen." She was inundated with calls and visits; but she felt bothered by the difference between social pressure and what she expected conversion to be like.

Said another woman, "I started going last spring with my neighbor when there was a lot of interest; it seemed everyone was converting, and you didn't want to be left out. But then I stopped trying—it just wasn't what I expected." "She was frightened, wouldn't go to bed alone, and stopped going to dances after she heard the Reverend MacMillan. This extreme fear lasted only 2 weeks; but once she started, she couldn't stop. She was on the path. People expected it of her; and she expected it of herself, it was better than the path she was following."

One young woman, trying to convert, described a dream she had had in which a line of people came down the aisle of the church dressed in white but not wearing a veil. She realized later that as time went on, all of these people were becoming converted. I asked if she were in the line. "Yes, I was at the very end—but I was naked, and kept trying to cover myself." She says she is afraid of everything. Not a day passes but that she doesn't think of death. She wants to pray but doesn't know who to pray to. "I've read too much. I'm afraid of praying to one god and then when I go to the afterworld I'll have to pray to someone else."

People watch each other carefully for signs of conversion, and the status of their progress or regression is a topic of extensive discussion. "Mairi has been under suspicion for a few months. But she goes to the Nicolson, and you tend to lose the curam in town." "He has started going to the weekly meeting; this is his fifth time. Since his wife is going with him, they'll probably both convert." "She's been under suspicion for years; she's very quiet. But she doesn't go to the weekly meetings." "He's been under suspicion for several years; he goes regularly to church. He's not very wild, but he will take an occasional drink." "He had it for awhile, but then he lost it." "She converted during the past 2–3 months, after the crowd converted. She's been ill for years with TB. You could see it coming."

"There are definite symptoms of conversion," explained a young woman. "A person who has been looking bored in church suddenly begins to pay attention. The women go all weepy, sigh and say *oich, oich;* the men only sigh. They wait around outside the church and don't leave so quickly; you see them shaking hands with the converted. I saw Catriona crying outside the church one night and knew that was her away."

Often people are suspected of being curamach who are not. "I fainted in church. The elders gathered around to pray, thinking I was converted. I could hear the old *cailleachs* talking about me like it was a wake. That skunnered me. I haven't been back to church since." After the schoolmaster had a heart attack, the rumors spread that he had gotten the curam. I visited him in the hospital and found him his usual agnostic self, joking about snoring in church and carrying a hip flask to make him feel more relaxed.

Someone who gives confusing symptoms is "half and half." I asked one of these "half-and-halfs" if he thought he was a sinner. He said the important thing was if a man had a good heart—if he didn't do any harm, if he gave things to people and helped them, if he didn't lie or steal. Those with a bad heart were gluttons and misers, they didn't help anyone, they kept everything for themselves. "Religion doesn't change your heart. If you have a bad heart when you convert, it will still be bad."

Conversion often occurs in association with death and the fear of death. "Before his wife died, he was like an animal. When he saw his wife's coffin, it started; and in 6 months he was taking communion." "Everyone's going to die. We came bare into this world, and we leave it bare."

In dealing with the certainty of death, many go through trauma and doubt but these experiences do not necessarily end in conversion. Anxiety and raving may be interpreted as the onset of mental illness, as second sight, or as the onset of the curam, and many see them as substitutes for each other. "If he hadn't gotten the curam, he would have ended up in Craig Dunain [the mental hospital near Inverness]."

Conversion may be accompanied by feelings of fear, anxiety, restlessness, inability to sleep, alienation from normal surroundings, and occasionally visions. Scriptural passages may run like broken records, uncontrollably inserting themselves into mundane thought.

> Around the time of the Ciall Communions, I was lying in bed around midnight, not thinking about anything in particular. Then all of a sudden I felt God talking to me. It's the strangest feeling to describe. All of a sudden I didn't feel safe. I felt I was going to die; that with each tick of the clock, time was running out, the universe was rushing toward its end. For 4 days I was in a dazed, uncertain state, a state of not feeling safe. I was talking to God but I didn't know what to do. I was in the mill working but I didn't know what I was doing most of the time. Then all of a sudden I had a vision, of Christ on the cross who died for us. I had been praying to God and here was my answer, trust in the Lord Jesus Christ. God does everything for you. He makes you breathe, lifts your lungs in and out, makes your blood flow. After I realized that, I could take the days as they came, from one day to the next. God can do anything. I saw the blackness of the life I was leading. I used to drink a lot, but I didn't lie or steal. I used to rub shoulders with everyone, but that life was leading me nowhere. I was black as that coal in the fireplace, then lifted to light.

A converted person expresses the feeling that he or she has become separated from the mundane world. One curamach woman quoted a sermon in which a minister compared the process of living and becoming involved in the church (one's spiritual progress through life) to a boat tied to the pier. One by one the ropes fall away. "There is only drudgery in this life. Any joy I experience is fleeting, a shadow of that ultimate joy; everything is a shadow. The only pleasure I get is being in the company of good-living people."

Fencing the Lord's Table

The most sacred moment in the communion service is the "fencing of the board" (*cuir garadh mu'n a bhord*) that bars some and invites others to come to the Lord's Table. "It is then we see most clearly the difference between the fruits of the flesh and the fruits of the spirit," said one communicant. "There is a barrier around those people who are saved." Husbands are exhorted to leave their wives behind, children their parents. One man, looking down from the balcony to the table where his wife was taking Communion, felt overwhelmed by the minister's statement that he was now cut off from his wife, and 6 months later had joined her at the table. Coordination of conversion may make or break a courtship. "He converted first, and she left him. Then she converted and that got back together. Then after they married he de-converted. She's still converted." "She's not converted, which is unusual, since her husband has the curam, and everyone else in the family has it too." "When the husband doesn't have it, the wife usually gets it later. Like marries like—converted marries converted, nonconverted marries nonconverted, and change occurs later." The nonconverted often express feelings of jealousy—what have they got that I don't have? I was asked: "Wouldn't you like to be like the converted people, to feel as they do? They seem to be more satisfied."

"This is the last fling," said one young man. "The next time you hear of me, I'll be in the church parade." He spoke of his sister who recently got "full military honors" (she took communion for the first time). They were sitting by the fire one night and she said, "I've got something, have you? I've got Christ." He felt very hurt when his sister took communion, because he hadn't "got it." He goes to bed at night and something is over his bed saying "This isn't your bed, this isn't your place." He tells people, "You won't have me with you long."

Deeds are not supposed to cause conversion, but they are a sign of being saved. You have no choice about whether you are chosen or not chosen. It's God's choice to cut you off from your neighbors, to fence you off, to remove you to a higher plane. The in-group is justified; the non-curamach resent being excluded, but feel it is justified, and enviously await the signs that they too might belong.

The Chosen People

Once the person accepts that this inner turmoil is a sign that he or she has been chosen, and concludes that conversion has occurred, there is a sense of peace and certainty; and the person begins associating primarily with other curamach, finding in this close, warm group the same familiarity and lack of restraint and conversational flow that characterized the drinking group. Explained one voluble communicant, "I don't mind giving my testament to you. The Bible says not to hold anything back, but to give testimony about how we were saved."

The curamach *gathered for a psalmody class*

Entrée into the clique of the converted opens up a wealth of social activity and connections. The curamach meet for special prayer meetings, and the Communions (*na h-orduighean*) are held twice a year. Services are held for 5 consecutive days in a particular village, during which time several ministers speak and villagers from other parts of the island come to visit and attend the services. The ministers and traveling congregation then move on to another village; this continues for 5 or 6 weeks. Communions are a very important way for people to establish ties throughout the island. "East side knows west side because of the Communions. Not because of the dances—you're alone at dances." Often these ties are maintained throughout the year and used for mundane purposes, such as selling cattle or cars, and receiving the yearly delicacy of the *"guga"* (the salted goslings of the solan goose) and gossip.

Not only does a converted person become part of a closely knit and accepting group ("You feel so close to them, you could marry any one of them"), but the sense of marginality and inferiority vis-a-vis the larger society melts away. Lewis is *tir nan t-soisgeul,* Land of the Scriptures; a center of holiness in an unholy world. Also, the converted become linked with a worldwide network of evangelism. A converted merchant seaman finds a home wherever he goes, becomes part of an international unity. Those who have never left the island read literature or pump the "exiles" for news of evangelical activities in Chicago, Hong Kong, and New Guinea as if they were discussing events in the next parish. All people—the handicapped, the exiles, those with a history of drinking and violence—all may find a place in the welcoming arms of the curamach. One man is deaf and mute, and never learned to read or write. He converted when he was about 30. "He can't understand the sermons, but he picks up the feelings."

When the minister asks him to pray, he makes a high, moaning, unintelligible noise, and people use him as a validation of their belief that God can reach out to anyone.

Effect of Conversion on Community Interaction

When a person undergoes conversion, he or she takes seriously the admonition to declare by thought and action his or her enlightened state. In effect, a communicant is given a context of expressiveness, a network of people with whom it is impossible to be shy, with whom it is required to "give witness." As in a drinking group, talk is easy and physical distance reduced; and "everything's fresh, not like the stale old jokes and stories." "There's much more enjoyment in church than in a ceilidh. When you're with religious people you can hear someone give testimony, or sing psalms, or share experiences."

> You can talk with the converted all night, see them the next day, and still go on talking, because you're always talking about something new. Now before when you were telling a yarn or hearing a tale, I'd say to myself, I've heard that before, I don't want to hear it again. But when you're talking about Christ, the conversation is always new.

Also, the word of God is one thing that can be given away and "it doesn't take anything from you." Your relationship with God is unalterable and equal. "He shows no favoritism."

Obligations of communicants to their new, demanding network often create conflicts with township requirements. When they follow the Communions from town to town, they often miss township duties such as sheep fanks and road work. Their work is done for them with much grumbling, except when the work involves a small group who bring along a bottle—and then they are relieved that they don't have to be on their best behavior.

Among neighbors, relationships are often strained. The development of a special in-group of those with the curam creates dissension in a community that expects equal access to personalism. "I had visitors in, and a couple who had just gone through a blue-flash conversion came in and invited one of my visitors, and none of the rest of us, to come to a prayer meeting. And you call that good-living?" "I say 'How are you,' she says, 'I'm fine but how can you be fine when you're not saved, when you might die at any moment and know you're going to hell?' They're fanatics. All they think of is death. When they're talking to you, a line from a psalm might come into their heads, usually it's very negative, and they say it's a message for you."

The converted are sometimes accused of being hypocritical and two-faced. "They do whatever they want to do—take a drink on the sly, sing a song." "That man broke township rules by bringing in his sheep 2 days before the fank—and he takes Communion. See there, now." "When he hurt his hand in the garage, he swore, which no really religious man would do. Ministers have gotten their fingers caught on fan belts and they squeal like bloody pigs but they don't swear." "When women leave here, they deposit their curam in the left luggage department at Stornoway, and pick it up 50 years later."

Children of the curamach tend to win contests, even beauty contests. "Considerations of family enter in very strongly. The judges are always the upstanding members of the community, and they take things into account—if your father is an elder, if your parents are curamach, you've got it made. If your parents aren't religious at all, you've had it. There are strong class distinctions here, which is a funny thing to say, because there isn't any class, except for the tweeds; it's religion that's the important thing."

"It's really a social club more than anything else," said one woman. "The biggest social climbers belong to the religious clique. I told one of them, 'You wouldn't be caught dead speaking to me. At the church you all shake hands with each other, but never with me—how about passing some of it on?' They are the greatest gossips, always the first to condemn someone. Other people are quicker to perform Christian acts."

The excitement and sense of festivity that permeate the village at Communion time affect profane as well as sacred arenas. Although the nearby hotels are closed during Communions, the bothan is usually open. On the first night of the Communions in February, I was wakened to join a midnight gathering where, amid singing and discussion of the new faces seen in the village, one man began to speak incoherently of Christ. "It's the bottle tonight," one person joked, "but he'll be taking communion within 6 months."

A Lewisman living on the mainland observed that the Free Church plays cat and mouse with members of the community who drink heavily. The temporary pleasures of drink are contrasted with the eternal joys awaiting those who have been saved. The "false" friendships of the drinking situations are contrasted with the more lasting, consistent relations that characterize the clique of the converted. "You have lots of friends when you get converted, and they don't change overnight the way your drinking companions do." "With the drink it's easy to get started and just not be able to stop drinking, especially with the money there is now. Everything's unsteady here except religion."

Many of the most deeply religious male members of the church were once heavy drinkers. One villager observed, "If a man went to extremes as a sinner, he'll be just as fanatical when he becomes holy." The most dramatic examples of conversion usually come from men whose lives are used as object examples (of what not to be like) for the young.

He was a hard worker but everything went to booze in the bothan. He slept in the same room as his father, and his father used to lecture him, but he closed his ears. Then his father died. One day a letter came for him. A relative who had never sent him any money before sent him £10. He had been trying to buy a suit on installment, but always spent the money on drink. He went into town, got the suit, and wore it to church the next Sunday. They saved his glass in the bothan, but he never went back.

In the 21st century, the hold of the churches appears to be less strong. Stornoway now has public art (for example, fountains and boat structures planted with flowers) and puts up Christmas lights and decorations (the commercial aspects of Christmas having bypassed the papish connotations). The Stornoway airport has recently begun flights on Sunday, and to the consternation of the Lord's Day Observance Society has also begun bar service. Couples whose children were conceived out of wedlock no longer have to stand in church during the baptism service, and more people live together without getting married. Sweets still circulate during the sermon and no woman would enter a church without a hat, but English sermons are replacing the Gaelic, no precentor stands to lead the English psalms, and the music is tamely melodic rather than fiercely individualistic. It is possible to hang your washing out on a Sunday without receiving a delegation of church elders at your door; and instead of sleeping on Sunday afternoon, people read or watch television.

At the same time, the church retains its passionate intensity for reform, an extremism that is both hated and admired. When asked if the communion services were still held in Lewis, a minister replied, "How many Lewismen does it take to change a light bulb? None, because nothing ever changes." Lewis is idealized as the last bastion of Calvinism, and people of all denominations make pilgrimages there.

The passionate intensity with which the boundaries of good and evil are pursued is reflected in the rapidity with which a congregation pounces on communicants who are suspected of sin. Trials are held for those suspected of drinking, adultery, or other forms of falling by the wayside. Many feel they have the *curam* but are afraid to step forward because of the intense scrutiny of their behavior, not only during the period leading up to the taking of communion but also afterward, when a fall from grace is treated as such—as disgrace to themselves and to their family. The rules are harsh, and often split families. A man brought to trial for drinking was convicted on the testimony of his wife, who, as a communicant, had been asked by the elders to speak against him (the marriage ended soon afterward). The suggestion that people might have adapted the idea of Christ to their own ways (a "culturalized Christ vs. Christ in a culture") is sure to provoke anger; they are right and certain of their righteousness.

At the same time, the Gaelic psalm singing provides one of the best metaphors of Highland life (and would benefit greatly from a narratological analysis, as per Tarasti 1979, 1994). The power of psalmody is in the grace notes. Given the emphasis on kin and community, one might expect harmony, but nothing could be further from the reality. Each member of the congregation tackles the tune with intense individual concern—with sharp, forceful, personal interpretation. The result, as a whole, is cacophony—a metaphor for community as a loud, raucous whole: all individuals strong and beautiful, forming their own version of the universe, and by intent brushing their musical lines hard against their neighbors under the veil of worship. Psalm singing in the Gaidhealtachd is the essence of William Robertson Smith's totemism, better known to sociologists and anthropologists as Durkheim's church-as-society. As the Gael sings, so is his society—piercing ("They always seem to be biting at each other"), intense, lyrical, and full of grace.

The harsh bitterness, the dense musical individuality, is part of the piercing sound, like Sorley MacLean's bog pierced by radiance:

> 's eol dhomh seirbheachd gheur an spioraid
> nas fhearr na aoibhneas luath a' chridhe[2] (MacLean 1999:76–77)

---

[2]The darkening sourness of the spirit—Not joy—is what I most inherit

9/Stories and Silence

The "culture of crofting" has been discussed in this book from two different points of view: (1) what the culture of crofters means to outsiders and how the system of meaning is communicated and maintained; and (2) what the crofters themselves do to communicate and maintain a meaningful way of life.

It is clear that the crofter has been used and maintained for historical, political, and social reasons that transcend the existential concerns of the crofters themselves. The Celt has been variously defined and invented, has played different roles in history (for example, as learned, barbarous, uncouth, and romantic), and now exists, in the form of the crofter, as one of the bastions of Scottish nationalism, a symbol of European distinctiveness, of rural, independent man, of the egalitarian commoner against the hierarchical laird, and so on, by various audiences that sometimes but not always include the crofter himself.

The crofting way of life is frequently conceptualized by both outsiders and crofters themselves as an anachronism, an irregular glitch in the processes of industrialization and urbanization in Scotland, a doomed contradiction. In attempting to define themselves, crofters are continuously confronted with the image of themselves as marginal, members of a fringe society. Associated with economic marginality is a sense of social marginality, of being technologically backward and socially uncouth (the *siarach* stereotype, the image of the Highlander as portrayed in the comic strip "Angus Og"). In response to these interactive cues, the crofter has forged what might be called a culture of anomaly, a set of strategies for dealing with marginality, a cultural system by which crofters create significance out of their anomalousness. There are various cultural solutions to this anomalousness, including both effective and ineffective routes by which a sense of historical destiny is created.

CULTURAL PATTERNS OF INVOLVEMENT

As discussed in Chapter 8, there are two primary arenas for creation of significance using historical symbols, one profane and the other sacred. The first, the arena of the tigh ceilidh, the houses of visiting where drink often plays a significant role, and in particular the men's drinking group, is often an arena in which Gaelic is enjoyed and praised, family genealogies are reconstructed, and village history is renewed. Whiskey has symbolic significance for the Scots in general; for crofters, it is an avenue for cultural resolution.

In the second arena, the process of conversion establishes strong affective ties and assures members of their historical importance and destiny in a decadent, doomed world. The Free Church, for outsiders as well as crofters, is evocative of the Celtic heritage. Conversion is participation in this heritage, a method of resolving the contradictions of an anomalous life. Through conversion, the historical importance of the culture of the participants is enacted.

Both of these arenas are characterized by intense involvement with social interaction.

> *Cha cumair tigh le bheul duinte.*
> *"No household can go on without somebody arguing" (a Gaelic proverb that, roughly translated, means "You've got to say something," usually said after someone says something provocative, joking, teasing; the proverb is intended to take away the sting).*

"Mixing," the most important criterion of mental health, is like swimming in shark-infested waters. It is invigorating and life giving, but you have to know how to swim and use shark repellant. Mixing is a double-bind situation: if you don't mix, you're declared insane; if you do mix, you're torn to pieces, shredded with gossip. But this gossip is what creates identity. There are many methods of staying alive in the feeding frenzy of interaction: subterfuge, limiting information, and perhaps most important, a sense of humor and the ability to joke. The following joke, first heard in 1970–71, is still being told in 2003.

> *A two-faced elder, one who pretended to be holy but really wasn't, came to lecture a man who had been drinking. On the way out he stumbled over the dog who was sleeping by the door, and was about to give him a kick when his host called out to him, "Don't you kick that dog. He has far more of the gospel inside of him than you do— he just ate the cailleach's [old woman's] Bible."*

The search for and construction of meaning goes on in different arenas, with a variety of symbols. The arenas of Bible and bottle involve intense community interaction. But another type of solution to the problems of marginality and anomalousness occurs as well, that may be characterized as withdrawal. Withdrawal occurs in two primary patterns; they are standardized enough and occur frequently enough that they should be recognized as part of the culture of anomaly.

CULTURAL PATTERNS OF WITHDRAWAL

> *If you can't stand the heat, get out of the kitchen.*
>
> —American President, Harry Truman

It is possible to survive economically as a crofter, but the life is unpredictable and full of dire prognostications. The "canny" crofter who poaches from the laird's river (and also, occasionally, from the Unemployment Exchange) is, like the image of "Br'er Rabbit" that emerged in the context of plantation slavery, a humor-filled trickster who survives in a hostile environment.

The economics of crofting are hazardous, and the cultural requirements no less so. As in any forge, great heat is necessary in the process of creating a viable form. The forging of an effective system of survival and meaning, a sense of historical destiny and personal significance, requires enormous energy. Besides the requirements of participating in a crofting township (which includes working out alternative methods of supplementing one's income), the crofter is an architect of meaning, and his participation in communicating, gossiping, arguing, and so on, requires energy and risk taking. For many, the risks are too great, the requirements exhausting.

A common method of resolving the problems of economic (not to mention social) survival is to become an exile. The second is to assume the label of the "mentally ill."

The Exiles

As discussed in Chapter 3, the category of the "exiles" must be included in a description of township organization. The decision to become an exile is one method of resolving the problems of economic and social survival while still retaining strong ties to the cultural center of home and community. Glasgow, especially Partick Hill, has become a reconstructed Highland community that has the added advantage of providing community warmth and support in the midst of the anonymity of the city. Although many people are more involved with village-related gossip than they would be at home ("Gossip is ten times worse in Glasgow, someone is always on the phone"), they have the option to withdraw from interaction ("I moved out of that area so people weren't calling and coming over all the time"). Island weddings are usually held in Glasgow; and dances are often described as "more Highland than those at home." Every summer, and often at New Year's, the exiles return. Abroad, the exiles form Highland Associations, Celtic Societies, and Scottish Clubs that promote the Celtic-Scottish image, and many exiles return to their home base to retire. The existence of these exiles fuels the sense of personal significance at home. Many siblings who have remained on the island to care for aging parents are reluctant to leave, even if they have the opportunity, because to do so would destroy the home base, the symbol of significance that keeps both exiles and village residents going.

From the point of view of culture as a system of meaning, the preponderance of old people in a Highland village is not necessarily a sign of cultural decline. It reflects a continuing commitment of a far-flung network of cultural participants to a centered community.

At the same time, every community must solve the problem of continuity (the religious organization of the Shakers resonated with significance but died out because they practiced sexual abstinence), and from this point of view, Highland communities are fighting a losing battle. The Shakers survived for awhile by adopting children, and in some parts of the Highlands adoption was common. The recruitment of new members to the crofting cause is another

Susan Parman

Susan Parman

*Two cousins visit (the
father of one emigrated to
the United States and the
father of the other
remained in Ciall, top); a
family welcomes a
returning visitor (bottom).*

source of replacement. Whether or not a member of a crofting community has a "true" claim through Celtic affiliation is irrelevant. People reconstruct elements of their history that are relevant to the present. When, halfway through my year of fieldwork, I mentioned that my father's mother was a Ferguson, extensive discussion eventually connected me, by a tenuous but possible link, to the Fergusons of Uig. I was invented as an Uigeach, and took a fictional position, beside the MacIvers of Ciall, as a latecoming but nevertheless kin-linked member of the community. My English, German, French, American Indian, and other potential historical reference points (some of which, in my parents' creation of history, were emphasized, some were probably fictional, and many I've forgotten) were not relevant and therefore ignored. In the construction of a meaningful present, it is incredible how quickly and creatively humans pick up, modify, reinterpret, distort, deny, discard, and invent.

Mental Illness

A relatively unsuccessful resolution to problems of social interaction within the community is the invention of mental illness. The label, "he's mental," is a frequent element in the maelstrom of gossip and may be embraced and used by individuals to refer to themselves.

Several studies of mental illness concluded that rates of mental illness were no higher for the Highlands than for the rest of Britain (e.g., Whittet 1963, Brown et al. 1977), but found some differences in the pattern of problems reported. Whittet (1963) found high rates of alcoholism and depression in middle age. Brown et al., comparing the pattern of psychiatric disorders in London and North Uist, concluded that women who were culturally most well integrated in North Uist had a higher rate of anxiety and lower rate of depression; those least well integrated had higher depression and lower anxiety. These figures reflect but do not explain a highly complex set of strategies for resolving social-psychological problems in the context of community interaction.

The label "mental illness" is one of several interpretations used to resolve personal difficulties. In resolving feelings of anxiety, depression, and alienation, some people interpret these feelings as signs of mental illness, but in some cases these same feelings are interpreted as second sight or as signs of conversion. The choice of interpretation is worked out in the arena of gossip, as people try to create a meaningful pattern for purposes of effective interaction.

A person who withdraws from community interaction is usually labeled as mentally ill. The ability to mix—whether in a drinking group or in the clique of the converted—is the major criterion of health ("He's not quite gone—they bring him out for wakes and funerals").

Some people choose to withdraw. The choice to become an exile removes a person from the continuous impact of gossip; but people who withdraw while remaining at home are subjected to extensive gossip and pressure-filled social interpretation that in itself can create a self-imposed definition of madness (cf. Szasz 1961), especially if they reject other cultural explanations.

In case studies of individuals who are given the label of mental illness, one can catch glimpses of personal attempts to deal with the problems of marginality. In one family that I visited regularly, a daughter existed that I had never met because she never came down from her bedroom when people came visiting. When a neighbor went to bring her down, he found her unkempt and in her nightgown, saying, "What is there to get dressed for in this place?" In another family, the onset of "mental illness" is indicated in one woman when she begins to speak in English.

Perhaps the most heart-wrenching example of culture-linked mental illness was the case of one young man, prevented from leaving the community because he was the only son, who read widely and refrained from drinking, only to be told that the books would drive him mad, he was strange because he didn't drink with the boys, and the tendency to go mad was "in his people." He once attended Gaelic plays, but stopped because he said no one really cared about Gaelic, that it was dying out. He became very upset, experienced a kind of free-floating anxiety in which he talked about Gaelic speakers who "don't like to speak Gaelic; they don't like the image of the Gaels" and other things that didn't make sense to the family. The doctor gave him sedatives and suggested he go to Craig Dunain "for precautionary measures." A neighbor took him over by boat and reported that he "kept saying he had to get away from here." The neighbor, who considered the visit a minor matter, was upset with the doctors for not letting him shave himself. "The last thing he asked was, would I help his father bring in the sheep from the moor for dipping."

The young man was in his mid-20s, and this was his second visit to Craig Dunain. During his first visit, he was given electric shock treatments and sent home with medicine cabinets full of sedatives. I had spent several afternoons on the moor near the shielings with him and his cousin from America, and we had listened to him expressing his bitterness over not being able to leave the island. When I left, I gave my car to someone who said they would teach him how to drive and then give him the car so he could at least have some mobility around the island; but within the year I received letters filled with the tragic news that the young man had thrown himself off the cliff and was dead. "He ran out of the house. He said the stars were giving him shocks." But it was not the cliffs that killed him; it was culture.

For a few individuals, "going for the cure" (for alcoholism, or for shock treatment to cure depression) is almost like a holiday, a change of pace, and is done regularly, especially when the long, dark winters set in. But for most people it has the flavor of despair and tragedy. In many cases anxiety is resolved culturally; it is associated with second sight or religious conversion.

NARRATIVES OF THE LIFE CYCLE IN THE CONSTRUCTION OF CULTURE

The construction of culture occurs in part through the construction of the self through narratives that use historical references. If "man is an animal suspended in webs of significance he himself has spun," then each self is a spider born to a patterned web, using the ingredients of past-spun webs to weave his or her own.[1]

---

[1] And not to neglect the requisite postmodern footnote, the ethnographer is just another spider, weaving another web, hopefully with local-web ingredients although inevitably adding alien, self-referential web material.

Susan Parman

The cliffs of Ciall.

As new spiders enter the web, they give their own interpretive "spin" on the narratives of the past, integrating the past into the present in contextually meaningful ways. Culture is not a passive entity but a continuously created system of meaning, and an important vehicle of culture- and self-creation is narrative. Humans are inveterate storytellers.

What is an "historical ethnography"? Does it refer to digging in the detritus of cultural midden heaps and "cultural survivals" in search of archaic origins? Sometimes "the past" signifies irrelevancy to the present, as when the Taylor Commission reported in 1954 that "the history of the past remains vivid in the minds of the people and, in some measure, conditions their attitudes to current problems." Jokes about light bulbs and laziness reflect a contestive narrative told from the perspective of mainland/urban/bureaucratic contexts ("Why can't these people get on with it?" "I'm tired of hearing about the Clearances/the Highlands/the Celt, etc.").

An "historical ethnography" is not about the past but about the uses of the past in the present. This idea relates to Moore's (1987) discussion of the present as current history (focused on the process of how the present is produced), but is different in its discrimination between cultures that make extensive use of the past and those that do not. Some cultures invest a lot of energy in imagining the future (Americans, who continuously invent themselves, take extensive license in manipulating the past as they focus on a constantly changing future) and some (such as Scottish crofters) draw heavily on the past as a resource, and are more likely to view it as factually accurate rather than metaphorically true. Cultural patterns of bringing the past into the present in narrative structure deserve further treatment, but such an analysis is beyond the scope of this book. What I have attempted to do is to tell the stories of Ciall in an organized framework of meaning, to capture contextualized speech events, to explore the relationship between action and significance while staying as close to the raw data of experience as possible.

A narrative still being told in Ciall concerns a man named Sonny Piseag. His life reflects the five days of *na h-orduighean:* an early life of depravity and sin (*Latha Irioslachaidh*), a period of withdrawal, anxiety, and self-examination (*Latha na Ceist*), a reorientation and growth of conviction (*Latha Ullachaidh*), a triumphant stepping forward to take his place in history (*Latha na Feille*), and finally a return to the world and to Ciall, where he spent the rest of his life giving witness to his conversion (*Latha Taingealach*). The narrative reconstructs the life cycle of many men in the Presbyterian northern islands: the period of exile, the wild life of the communal drinking group, and then the gradual sacred separation from the profane, the fulfillment of Celtic specialness (second sight and conversion), all of which is validated within the social hierarchy of Britain by the Queen's award.

> When Sonny was a young man, he was a humor-filled, hard-drinking participant in the men's drinking group, and when he joined the Navy as a sailor he became wild, "completely out of control. He was a wild character; he used to drink a lot; he liked the gay life. He was always a bit of a harum-scarum before he was converted. Now he's quite the opposite. He doesn't like to be reminded of the sins of his youth, when he was sowing his wild oats."
>
> During the war he was on a ship that had been away from port for some time. He began to have difficulty sleeping, and phrases began to come to him, unbidden, from the Bible. He said strange things, and the other sailors "thought he had gone berserk." On one occasion he told the captain they were going to New York, which was not their destination at all.
>
> A collision with another ship forced them to stop for repairs, and the captain sent Sonny to a mental hospital while they were in port. "When he returned, they told him things hadn't gone right since he left the ship, and they wanted to know, how did he know they were going back to New York? The captain had received a message to return to New York for repairs."
>
> On their way back, the ship was torpedoed. Sonny was the only one who was calm. "He got dressed, put his Bible in his pocket, and went about the ship helping people. He saved a man from the engine room. He swam free just as the ship was sinking. He took charge of one of the lifeboats. Oh, there were officers but they weren't practical seamen same as Sonny was; and he was used to sails. The captain, who was in another lifeboat, wanted to make for Newfoundland, but Sonny decided to make for Ireland. The captain's boat was never seen again, but Sonny's people were picked up by a destroyer when they came into the shipping lanes. He kept everyone calm by reading to them from the Bible. When they were rescued, he was the only one able to climb the ropes; the rest had to be carried. After that he wasn't the same man; he knew he had been chosen, and wherever he was in the world, he found true believers like himself. For his bravery on the ship he was awarded the British Empire Medal by the Queen herself."

This narrative is told frequently, by many people, in situations that vary widely. It is told by the curamach as proof of theological convictions, and as a lesson to children and those heavily involved in "the Men's Club." It is told in drinking contexts with varying degrees of derision ("He doesn't like to be reminded of the sins of his youth, when he was sowing his wild oats"), admiration (the physical and moral strengths deriving from his convictions, his second sight, his being awarded the Queen's Medal), and self-reflection (Is this what lies ahead for me? Will I too undergo the Change? Well, at least I won't be lonely.). Women emphasize how creative and gender-flexible he was after his conversion and return to the village: he set up a sewing machine alongside his lathe, and designed and made clothes for his wife from the extra tweeds he wove. Kinsmen argue about whether he learned to sail from his mother's people or his father's people. The story functions as a symbolic capsule that organizes many of the elements of culture in Ciall, such as separation and belonging, ethnicity and nationalism, home and exile, kinship and community, gender and class, concepts of supernaturalism, and choices of how to live. In different versions of the story, the contents vary—the examples to illustrate his wildness and conversion, and even the award given by the Queen (was it the MBE or the OBE?). The structure of all the stories appears similar—a life of extreme wildness followed by dramatic conversion, with a transition period of "mental illness" and second sight, all framed within the British hierarchy—but the narrator picks and chooses, selecting what is personally relevant, and in doing so both re-creates and modifies culture.

CONCLUSION

In the prologue to her beautifully written but controversial book on Ireland, *Saints, Scholars and Schizophrenics,* Nancy Scheper-Hughes borrows from Levi-Strauss to identify anthropologists as necrographers, or people who record "the death rattles and attend the wakes of those cultures sadly but rapidly on the wane" (1979:xv). In contrast with her and many writers concerned with things Celtic, I do not see my role to be one of a necrographer but of a celebrator of culture in all its transmutations. Neither do I intend to serve as an apologist for the social, economic, and ecological disasters that have wracked Scotland. Change occurs everywhere and is inevitable, and humans are incredibly inventive in creating new structures. Life happens and we make up stories about it. Only when the stories stop (as, perhaps, among the Ik described by Colin Turnbull) can we talk about necrography.

This ethnography has described the relationship between historical representations and the construction of "crofting culture" in Scotland. Scotland has a long literary tradition in which many people have written histories for various reasons, investing certain people and lifestyles with meaning, creating linkages between past and present groups, and between those groups and themselves. The people themselves use these ideas in various ways to derive meaning.

This relationship between outsiders who invest in certain historical conceptions of the Celt, and the Celt who uses these historical concepts to survive and derive meaning generates an enormous display of healthy humor. The Celt jokes about the Sasunnach who dresses up in a kilt; the Englishman jokes about the anomalousness of the tweed van traveling for miles to pick up a single finished tweed on a lonely, rain-swept moor. The dialogue of humor is, I would argue, an indicator of cultural health. From this perspective, the culture of Scottish crofters is far from dead/past/anomalous, no matter how it might seem to an outside observer. Such judgments indicate that the observer doesn't understand the meaning of the story.

A culture cannot be judged to survive by virtue of how many historical ingredients it retains, for cultures always change. What is important in the long run is not that they have a history but that they survive—and if they use history to do so, more power to them.

Recommended Reading

Anderson, B. *Imagined Communities*. London: Verso, 1983.

Cameron, Ewen A. *Land for the People? The British Government and the Scottish Highlands, c. 1880–1925*. Phantassie, Scotland: Tuckwell, 1996.

Chapman, Malcolm. *The Gaelic Vision in Scottish Culture*. London: Croom Helm, 1978.

Cohen, Anthony P. *Whalsay: Symbol, Segment and Boundary in a Shetland Island Community*. Manchester: Manchester University Press, 1987.

Darling, F. Fraser (ed.). *West Highland Survey: An Essay in Human Ecology*. Oxford: Oxford University Press, 1956 (1955).

Goddard, V., J. Llobera, and C. Shore (eds.). *The Anthropology of Europe: Identities and Boundaries in Conflict*. Oxford: Berg, 1994.

Goffman, Erving. *The Presentation of Self in Everyday Life*. Garden City, NJ: Anchor, 1959.

Hechter, Michael. *Internal Colonialism: The Celtic Fringe in British National Development*. London: Transaction, 1999 (1975).

Herzfeld, Michael. *Anthropology Through the Looking-Glass: Critical Ethnography in the Margins of Europe*. Cambridge: Cambridge University Press, 1987.

Jackson, Anthony (ed.). "Anthropology at Home," *Association of Social Anthropologists Monograph No. 25*. London: Tavistock, 1987.

Macdonald, Sharon. *Reimagining Culture: Histories, Identities and the Gaelic Renaissance*. Oxford: Berg, 1997.

MacLeod, Finlay (ed.) *Togail Tir Marking Time: The Map of the Western Isles*. Stornoway: Acair and An Lanntair, 1989.

Poliakov, Leon. *The Aryan Myth: A History of Racist and Nationalist Ideas in Europe*. New York: Basic, 1974 (1971).

Smout, T. C. *A History of the Scottish People 1560–1830*. London: Collins, 1969.

Stevenson, Robert Louis. *Travels with a Donkey in the Cevennes*. Avon: Bath Press, 1879.

Wilson, Thomas, and M. Estellie Smith (eds.). *Cultural Change and the New Europe*. Boulder, CO: Westview, 1993.

Wolf, Eric. *Europe and the People without History*. Berkeley: University of California Press, 1982.

Bibliography

Agnew, J. "Liminal Travellers: Hebrideans at Home and Away," *Scotlands 3* (1996): 32–41.

Anderson, Alan O. *Scottish Annals from English Chroniclers A.D. 500 to 1286.* London: David Nutt, 1908.

Appadurai, A. "The Past as a Scarce Resource," *Man 16* (1981):201–219.

Beaton, Reverend D. *Diary and Sermons of the Rev. Alexander MacLeod, Rogart (formerly of Uig, Lewis).* Inverness: Robert Carruthers and Sons, 1925.

Blake, G. R. *Scotland of the Scots.* New York: Charles Scribner's, 1919.

Boon, James A. *Other Tribes, Other Scribes. Symbolic Anthropology in the Comparative Study of Cultures, Histories, Religions, and Texts.* New York: Cambridge University Press, 1982.

Borofsky, Robert. *Making History: Pakapukan and Anthropological Constructions of Knowledge.* Cambridge: Cambridge University Press, 1987.

Brown, Callum G. *Religion and Society in Scotland since 1707.* Edinburgh: Edinburgh University Press, 1997.

Brown, G. W. et al. "Psychiatric Disorder in London and North Uist," *Social Science and Medicine 11* (1977): 367–377.

Bruce, Steve. "Authority and Fission: The Protestants' Divisions," *British Journal of Sociology 36* (1985):592–603.

Buckle, Henry Thomas. *On Scotland and the Scotch Intellect.* Chicago: University of Chicago Press, 1970 (five chapters from Buckle's *History of Civilization,* published in 1857 and 1861).

Burnett, John. *Liquid Pleasures: A Social History of Drinks in Modern Britain.* New York: Routledge, 1999.

Caird, J. B. Unpublished Survey of Crofting (Geography Department, Glasgow University).

Callander, Robin Fraser. *A Pattern of Landownership in Scotland.* Fort William, Scotland: Haughend, 1987.

Cameron, Ewen A. *Land for the People? The British Government and the Scottish Highlands, c. 1880–1925.* Phantassie, Scotland: Tuckwell, 1996.

Campbell, R. H. "Too Much on the Highlands? A Plea for Change," *Scottish Economic and Social History 14* (1994):58–76.

Chadwick, Nora. *The Celts.* New York: Penguin, 1970.

Chafe, Wallace L. (ed.). *The Pear Stories: Cognitive, Cultural, and Linguistic Aspects of Narrative Production.* Norwood, NJ: Ablex, 1980.

Chapman, Malcolm. *The Celts: The Construction of a Myth.* New York: St. Martin's, 1992.

_____. *The Gaelic Vision in Scottish Culture.* London: Croom Helm, 1978.

Cheape, Hugh. "The Communion Season," *Records of the Scottish Church History Society 27* (1997):305–316.

Clifford, James. "On Ethnographic Authority," *Representations 1* (1983):118–146.

_____. *The Predicament of Culture: Twentieth-Century Ethnography, Literature, and Art.* Cambridge, MA: Harvard University Press, 1988.

Clifford, James, and George E. Marcus (eds.). *Writing Culture: The Poetics and Politics of Ethnography.* Berkeley: University of California Press, 1986.

Cohn, B. S. "History and Anthropology: The State of Play," *Comparative Studies in Social History 22* (1980):198–221.

Cohn, Shari A. "A Historical Review of Second Sight: The Collectors, Their Accounts and Ideas," *Scottish Studies 33* (1999):146–185.

Collins, G. N. M. *The Heritage of our Fathers.* Edinburgh: Knox, 1974.

Condry, Edward. Personal communication, July 31, 1979.

_____. *Scottish Ethnography.* Social Science Research Council, 1983.

Cregeen, E. R. "The Changing Role of the House of Argyll in the Scottish

Highlands," in I. M. Lewis, ed. *History and Social Anthropology.* New York: Tavistock, 1968, pp. 153–192.

Crofters Commission. *The Acquisition of Crofting Data: A Baseline Study.* Inverness: Ekos, 2001.

———. *The Way Forward: The Role of Crofting Communities*, 1998.

Darling, F. Fraser (ed.). *West Highland Survey: An Essay in Human Ecology.* Oxford University Press, 1955.

Day, J. P. *Public Administration in the Highlands and Islands of Scotland.* London: University of London Press, 1918.

Devine, T. M. *The Great Highland Famine: Hunger, Emigration and the Scottish Highlands in the Nineteenth Century.* Edinburgh: John Donald, 1988.

———. "The Rise and Fall of Illicit Whisky-Making in Northern Scotland c. 1780–1840," *Scottish Historical Review 54* (1975):155–177.

Dodgshon, Robert A. "Strategies of Farming in the Western Highlands and Islands of Scotland Prior to Crofting and the Clearances," *The Economic History Review, New Series, 46, 4* (November 1993):679–701.

Dorian, Nancy C. *Language Death: The Life Cycle of a Scottish Gaelic Dialect.* Philadelphia: University of Pennsylvania Press, 1981.

Fabian, Johannes. *Time and the Other: How Anthropology Makes Its Object.* New York: Columbia University Press, 1983.

Frank, Bryn. "Harris Tweed," *British Heritage,* December/January (1992):40–45.

Gillanders, Farquhar. "The Economic Life of Gaelic Scotland Today," in Derick C. Thomson and Ian Grimble, eds. *The Future of the Highlands.* London: Routledge and Kegan Paul, 1968, pp. 95–150.

Gillies, William. "Scottish Gaelic—The Present Situation," in G. MacEoin et al., eds. *Proceedings of the Third International Conference on Minority Languages.* Philadelphia: Clevedon, 1987.

Goody, J. *The Domestication of the Savage Mind.* Cambridge: Cambridge University Press, 1977.

Grant, James Shaw. *Discovering Lewis and Harris.* Edinburgh: John Donald, 1998.

Gray, Malcolm. "The Abolition of Runrig in the Highlands of Scotland," *The Economic History Review, New Series, 5, 1* (1952):46–57.

Gunn, Neil Miller. *Whisky and Scotland.* London: Souvenir, 1970 (1935).

Hannerz, U. "Culture between Center and Periphery: Toward a Macro-anthropology," *Ethnos 54* (1989): 200–216.

Heaney, Seamus. "Seamus Heaney Celebrates the Life and Work of Scots Gaelic Poet Sorley MacLean," *The Guardian,* November 30, 2002.

Hendry, Barbara Ann. *Ethnic Identity in Lewis and Harris, Western Isles, Scotland.* M.A. Thesis, Florida State University, 1983.

Herzfeld, Michael. *Anthropology Through the Looking-Glass: Critical Ethnography in the Margins of Europe.* Cambridge: Cambridge University Press, 1987.

———. *Ours Once More: Folklore, Ideology, and the Making of Modern Greece.* Austin: University of Texas Press, 1982.

Hill, Jonathan D. (ed.). *Rethinking History and Myth: Indigenous South American Perspectives on the Past.* Urbana: University of Illinois Press, 1988.

James Hunter. *A Dance Called America: The Scottish Highlands, the United States and Canada.* Edinburgh: Mainstream, 1994.

———. *The Claim of Crofting: The Scottish Highlands and Islands, 1930–1990.* Edinburgh: Mainstream, 1991.

———. *The Making of the Crofting Community.* Edinburgh: John Donald, 1976.

Hunter, Janet. *The Islanders and the Orb: The History of the Harris Tweed Industry, 1835–1995.* Stornoway: Acair, 2001.

Jedrej, M. J., and Mark Nuttall. *White Settlers: The Impact of Rural Repopulation in Scotland.* Nework, NJ: Harwood Academic, 1996.

Kearney, Michael. *Reconceptualizing the Peasantry: Anthropology in Global Perspective.* Boulder, CO: Westview, 1996.

Keating, Michael, and David Bleiman. *Labour and Scottish Nationalism.* London: Macmillan, 1979.

Kohn, Tamara. "Becoming an Islander through Action in the Scottish Hebrides," *Journal of the Royal Anthropological Institute 8* (2002): 143–158.

Leaska, Mitchell A. *Virginia Woolf's Lighthouse: A Study in Critical Method.* New York: Columbia University Press, 1970.

Logan, James. *The Scotish Gael; or, Celtic Manners, as Preserved among the Highlanders.* Boston: Marsh, Capen and Lyon, 1833.

Lubell, Ceil. "High Fashion on the Hebrides," *American Fabrics 58* (1962):91–94.

Macalister, F. *Memoir of the Right Hon. Sir John McNeill.* London: John Murray, 1910.

Macdonald, Fraser. Personal communication, 2003.

_____. "Towards a Spatial Theory of Worship. Some Observations from Presbyterian Scotland," *Social and Cultural Geography 3* (2002): 61–80.

_____. "Scenes of Ecclesiastical Theatre in the Free Church of Scotland, 1981-2000," *Northern Scotland 20* (2000):125–148.

Macdonald, Sharon. *Reimagining Culture: Histories, Identities and the Gaelic Renaissance.* Oxford: Berg, 1997.

MacKinnon, K. *Gaelic in Scotland 1971: Some Sociological and Demographic Considerations of the Census Report for Gaelic.* Hatfield: Hatfield Polytechnic, 1978.

MacLean, Sorley. (Tr. Iain Crichton Smith; Introduction by Donald Meek) *Eimhir.* Stornoway: Acair, 1999.

MacLeod, James Lachlan. "The Second Disruption: the Free Church in Victorian Scotland and the Origins of the Free Presbyterian Church," *Scottish Historical Review Monograph, No. 8* (2000).

MacLeod, Morag. Personal Communication, 1971. See the School of Scottish Studies for an extensive collection of tapes and written materials on numerous aspects of Highland culture.

Marcus, George E., and D. Cushman. "Ethnographies as Texts," *Annual Review of Anthropology 11* (1982):25–69.

Marcus, George E., D. Cushman, and M. M. J. Fischer. *Anthropology as Cultural Critique: An Experimental Moment in the Human Sciences.* Chicago: Chicago University Press, 1986.

McDonald, Maryon. "Celtic Ethnic Kinship and the Problem of Being English," *Current Anthropology 27*, 4 (1986):333–347.

Meek, Donald. "The Language of Heaven? The Highland Churches, Culture Shift and the Erosion of Gaelic Identity in the Twentieth Century," in S. J. Brown and R. Pope, eds. *Religion and National Identity in Wales and Scotland.* Cardiff: University of Wales Press, 2001.

_____. *The Quest for Celtic Christianity.* Edinburgh: Handsel, 2000.

_____. "'The Land Question Answered from the Bible'; The Land Issue and the Development of a Highland Theology of Liberation," *Scottish Geographical Magazine 103* (1987):84–89.

Mitchison, Rosalind. *Life in Scotland.* London: B. T. Batsford, 1978.

Moisley, H. A. "The Highlands and Islands. A Crofting Region?" *Transactions and Papers (Institute of British Geographers), 31* (1962):83–95.

Moisley, H. A., and members of the Geographical Field Group. *Uig, a Hebridean Parish, Parts I and II, Parts III and IV.* Department of Geography, University of Glasgow; Department of Geography, University of Nottingham, 1961.

Moore, S. F. "Explaining the Present: Theoretical Dilemmas in Processual Ethnography," *American Ethnology 14* (1987):727–736.

Murray, W. H. *The Hebrides.* London: Heinemann, 1966.

Nadel-Klein, Jane. "Crossing a Representational Divide: From West to East in Scottish Ethnography" in A. James et al., eds. *After Writing Culture: Epistemology and Praxis in Contemporary Anthropology.* London: Routledge, 1997, pp. 86–102.

Napier, Lord. *Report of the Commissioners of Inquiry into the Condition of the Crofters and Cottars in the Highlands and Islands of Scotland.* HMSO, 1884.

Needler, G. H. *The Lone Shieling: Origin and Authorship of the Blackwood 'Canadian Boat-Song.'* Toronto: University of Toronto Press, 1941.

Nicolaisen, W. F. H. Scottish Place-Names: Their Study and Significance. London: B. T. Batsford, 1986 (1976).

Nicolson, Nigel. *Lord of the Isles: Lord Leverhulme in the Hebrides*. London: Weidenfeld and Nicolson, 1960.

Ong, W. J. *Orality and Literacy: The Technologizing of the Word*. London: Methuen, 1982.

Orr, Willie. *Deer Forests, Landlords and Crofters: The Western Highlands in Victorian and Edwardian Times*. Edinburgh: John Donald, 1982.

Parman, Susan. "The Bogey's Walking Stick," *Spectacle 4* (2001):33–44.

_____. "The Future of European Boundaries: A Case Study," in Thomas M. Wilson and M. Estellie Smith, eds. *Cultural Change and the New Europe: Perspectives on the European Community*. Boulder, CO: Westview, 1993, pp. 189–202.

_____. "*Orduighean*: A Dominant Symbol in the Free Church of the Scottish Highlands," *American Anthropologist 92* (1990): 295–305.

_____. "An Evolutionary Theory of Dreaming and Play," in Edward Norbeck and Claire R. Farrer, eds. *Forms of Play of Native North Americans* (1977 Proceedings of the American Ethnological Society). New York: West, 1979: 17–34.

_____. "General Properties of Naming, and a Specific Case of Nicknaming in the Scottish Outer Hebrides," *Ethnos 41* (1976), 99–115.

_____. "Changing Land Use and Social Organisation in a Lewis Crofting Township," *Scottish Agriculture 51* (1972):330–332.

Peel, J. D. Y. "History, Culture and the Comparative Method: A West African Puzzle," in L. Holy, ed. *Comparative Anthropology*. New York: Basil Blackwell, 1987.

Phillips, Alastair. *My Uncle George: The Respectful Recollections of a Backslider in a Highland Manse*. London: Pan, 1984.

Piggott, Stuart. *Ancient Europe*. Chicago: Aldine, 1965.

_____. *Celts, Saxons and the Early Antiquaries*. Edinburgh: Edinburgh University Press, 1967.

Poliakov, Leon. *The Aryan Myth: A History of Racist and Nationalist Ideas in Europe*. New York: Basic, 1974 (1971).

Price, Richard. *First Time: The Historical Vision of an Afro-American People*. Baltimore: Johns Hopkins University Press, 1983.

Ray, Celeste. *Highland Heritage: Scottish Americans in the American South*. Chapel Hill: University of North Carolina Press, 2001.

Reid, W. Stanford. "John Knox's Theology of Political Government," *Sixteenth Century Journal 19* (1988):529–540.

Richards, E. S. "Structural Change in a Regional Economy: Sutherland and the Industrial Revolution, 1780–1830," *The Economic History Review, New Series 26* (1973):63–76.

Rosaldo, Renato. *Ilongot Headhunting, 1883–1974: A Study in Society and History.* Stanford: Stanford University Press, 1980.

Sahlins, Marshall. *Islands of History.* Chicago: University of Chicago Press, 1985.

Sanjek, Roger (ed.). "The Ethnographic Present 26 (1991):609–628.

_____. *Fieldnotes: The Makings of Anthropology*. Ithaca: Cornell University Press, 1990.

Scottish Executive. *Crofting Reform Proposals for Legislation: Laid before the Scottish Parliament by the Scottish Ministers* (SE/2002/105), July 4, 2002.

Severy, Merle. "The Celts," *National Geographic 151*, 5 (May 1977):581–633.

Smith, Robert J. "Hearing Voices, Joining the Chorus: Appropriating Someone Else's Fieldnotes," in Roger Sanjek, ed. *Fieldnotes: The Makings of Anthropology*. Ithaca: Cornell University Press, 1990.

Stewart, A., and J. Kennedy Cameron. *The Free Church of Scotland: The Crisis of 1900*. Edinburgh: Knox, 1989.

Sturtevant, W. "Anthropology, History, and Ethnohistory," in J. Clifton, ed. *Introduction to Cultural Anthropology*. Boston: Houghton Mifflin, 1968.

Svensson, Tom G. "Review of *Scottish Crofters,* by Susan Parman." *Ethos 56* (1992): 120–121.

Szasz, Thomas. *The Myth of Mental Illness: Foundations of a Theory of Personal Conduct*. New York: Dell, 1961.

Tarasti, Eero. *Myth and Music*. The Hague: Mouton, 1979.

_____. *A Theory of Musical Semiotics.* Bloomington: Indiana University Press, 1994.

Thomson, Derick. "Gaelic in Scotland: Assessment and Prognosis," in E. Haugen et al., eds. *Minority Languages Today.* Edinburgh: Edinburgh University Press, 1980, pp. 10–20.

Trevor-Roper, Hugh. "The Invention of Tradition: The Highland Tradition of Scotland," in Eric Hobsbawn and Terence Ranger, eds. *The Invention of Tradition.* Cambridge: Cambridge University Press, 1983.

Ulin, Robert C. "The Current Tide in American Europeanist Anthropology." *Anthropology Today* 7 (1991).

Wallis, R. "A Theory of Propensity to Schism," in R. Wallis, ed. *Salvation and Protest: Studies of Social and Religious Movements.* London: Pinter, 1979, pp. 174–192.

Whittet, Martin M. "Problems of Psychiatry in the Highlands and Islands," *Scottish Medical Journal 8,* 8 (1963):293–302.

Withers, C. W. J. "The Historical Creation of the Scottish Highlands," in I. Donnachie and C. Whatley, eds. *The Manufacture of Scottish History.* Edinburgh: Polygon.

Wolf, Eric. *Europe and the People without History.* Berkeley: University of California Press, 1982.

Wylie, Reverend James A. *Disruption Worthies: A Memorial of 1843.* Edinburgh: Thomas C. Jack, Grange, 1881.

USEFUL WEB SITES

http://www.Scotland.gov.uk

http://www.w-isles.gov.uk/

http://www.gro-scotland.gov.uk/grosweb/grosweb.nsf/pages/pes2000

http://www.nas.gov.uk

http://www.jiscmail.ac.uk/lists/briathrachas.html

http://www.freechurch.org

Index